9th edition

BasicEnglishReview

Karen Schneiter Williams

San Diego Mesa College
San Diego, California

Contributing Author

Elaine Langlois

Educational Consultant
Cincinnati, Ohio

SOUTH-WESTERN
CENGAGE Learning

Australia • Brazil • Japan • Korea • Mexico • Singapore • Spain • United Kingdom • United States

SOUTH-WESTERN
CENGAGE Learning™

Basic English Review, 9th Edition
Karen Schneiter Williams

Vice President of Editorial, Business:
  Jack W. Calhoun

Vice President/Editor-in-Chief: Karen Schmohe

Vice President/Marketing: Bill Hendee

Acquisitions Editor: Jane Phelan

Senior Developmental Editor: Dr. Inell Bolls

Marketing Specialist: Linda Kuper

Content Project Manager: D. Jean Buttrom

Manager of Technology, Editorial: John Barans

Media Editor: Mike Jackson

Website Project Manager: David Freitag

Manufacturing Coordinator: Kevin Kluck

Production Service: Macmillan Publishing
  Solutions

Senior Art Director: Tippy McIntosh

Cover and Internal Designer: Ke Design,
  Mason, OH

Cover Image: © iStock, Alex Slobodkin

Photography Manager: Mandy Groszko

Photo Researcher: Darren Wright

ExamView® is a registered trademark of eInstruction Corp. Windows is a registered trademark of the Microsoft Corporation used herein under license. Macintosh and Power Macintosh are registered trademarks of Apple Computer, Inc. used herein under license. Microsoft and PowerPoint are registered trademarks of Microsoft Corporation in the United States and/or other countries. The Bureau of Labor Statistics is the source of much of the information in the English on the Job features.

© 2008 Cengage Learning. All Rights Reserved.

Student Edition ISBN 13: 978-0-538-73095-2

Student Edition ISBN 10: 0-538-73095-1

South-Western Cengage Learning
5191 Natorp Boulevard
Mason, OH 45040
USA

Cengage Learning products are represented in Canada by Nelson Education, Ltd.

For your course and learning solutions, visit **school.cengage.com**

Printed in the United States of America
1 2 3 4 5 6 7   13 12 11 10 09

Preface

Basic English Review, ninth edition, introduces English grammar and mechanics in an easy-to-learn format. This short, yet intensive, text-workbook provides practical, varied, and meaningful new content and exercises that will stimulate your interest.

Proven Instructional Design

The ninth edition of *Basic English Review* uses a self-teaching, highly motivational, classroom-tested plan of instruction that will meet a variety of needs and expectations. This one-of-a-kind, user-friendly approach has proven effective for a wide range of students. *Basic English Review* can be used as a text for basic English, basic English review, or developmental courses or as a supplemental text for other courses in which only a limited amount of time can be given to English fundamentals.

Key Features That Ensure Success

This popular text-workbook covers the basics of grammar, punctuation, capitalization, number expression, word choice, spelling, vocabulary, and writing skills with these proven features:

Objectives. Each unit begins with objectives for you to have mastered upon completion of the unit.

Well-Organized Format. Subject matter is organized into small, easily mastered segments. Each segment covers a specific part of the unit.

Extensive Examples. Examples and analyses explain and clarify the concepts and rules presented. Illustrations help define difficult concepts and reinforce learning.

Try It Exercises. These exercises, which occur throughout the units, allow you to check your understanding of the concepts just presented.

Applications. Applications provide extensive, hands-on practice to further reinforce understanding of concepts presented in a unit. Varied content and difficulty in these sentences and paragraphs will challenge and stimulate a wide range of abilities and interests. A Writing Improvement application gives you the opportunity to reinforce and strengthen your writing skills. Each unit includes at least one Unit Review that emphasizes topics from throughout the unit and a Comprehensive Review that adds topics from previous units.

Pretest and Posttest. A unit Pretest allows you to test your knowledge of the concepts to be presented and to identify areas in which to focus your efforts. The Posttest shows you how well you understand and can apply what you have learned.

Appendices. Spelling, Vocabulary Practice, and Proofreaders' Marks appendices serve as additional communication skill builders and as handy references.

Website. The *Basic English Review* website offers chapter review quizzes, Proofreading Challenge activities, flashcards, a glossary, links to useful sites, and other helpful materials.

Additional Features That Enhance Learning

With increasing emphasis on workplace readiness, the ninth edition of *Basic English Review* includes additional features designed to sharpen your critical thinking skills and to show how good communication skills are vital to career success.

Workplace Focus. The new Workplace Focus feature at the beginning of each unit provides information on topics and skills that will contribute to your success in the work environment and in your personal life. They include soft skills, networking, personal financial management, business ethics, teamwork, ergonomics, diversity, and electronic resources.

Rules That Work. This feature offers suggestions, tips, shortcuts, and hints for rules of grammar or mechanics.

Proofreading Tips. Proofreading Tips (a new feature) tell you what to look for when you proofread and how to proofread effectively. Consistency, the spell checker, and numbers are a few of the topics covered.

WRITE Now. New to this edition, the WRITE Now feature in every unit highlights basic writing skills needed for creating effective sentences and paragraphs. Clarity, conciseness, and parallelism are examples of the writing skills presented.

English on the Job. This feature profiles a variety of occupations and fields, with a focus on the communication skills they require. It shows that communicating effectively directly affects an individual's ability to perform his or her job. The occupations and fields are drawn from the following six career clusters: (1) Business Management and Administration, (2) Marketing, (3) Hospitality and Tourism, (4) Law, Public Safety, Corrections, and Security, (5) Health Science, and (6) Information Technology.

Proof It. New to this edition, the Proof It exercise in every unit lets you apply and improve your proofreading skills. You will proofread a variety of business documents, including e-mail, a letter, and an agenda. For some of these documents, you will then prepare clean copies. Your goal will be to produce professional-looking and error-free documents that reflect positively on your capabilities and your employer's reputation.

A Look to the Future

Sincere thanks are extended to the reviewers whose advice and constructive suggestions helped shape this ninth edition of *Basic English Review:*

Harinder Boparai
International Business College
El Paso, TX

Sujata Chohan
Heald College
Milpitas, CA

Diane Franklin
Uintah Basin Applied Technology College
Vernal, UT

Dr. Bruce W. Miles
Metro Business College
Jefferson City, MO

Ricardo Vergara
Laredo Community College
Laredo, TX

I am confident that *Basic English Review,* ninth edition, will contribute significantly to the improvement of your communication skills, which are necessary for career success.

Karen Schneiter Williams

Contents

Unit 11   **Number Expression and Capitalization 259**

Unit 12   **Word Choice 277**

unit 1
The Sentence

Objectives

1. To understand that a sentence expresses a complete thought
2. To recognize the different kinds of sentences
3. To identify the eight parts of speech
4. To recognize how the parts of speech function in sentences
5. To write sentences effectively

Sections

1 The Sentence Defined
2 Kinds of Sentences
3 Parts of Speech

Pretest

Directions Identify the parts of speech represented by the underlined words. Use *n* for noun, *pro* for pronoun, *v* for verb, *adj* for adjective, *adv* for adverb, *prep* for preposition, and *conj* for conjunction.

<u>Enrique</u> <u>and</u> Laura <u>submitted</u> a <u>budget</u> <u>request</u> <u>for</u> 12 defibrillators. <u>They</u> <u>nearly</u> <u>missed</u> the <u>submission</u> deadline.

(underlined word numbers: 1 Enrique, 2 and, 3 submitted, 4 budget, 5 request, 6 for, 7 They, 8 nearly, 9 missed, 10 submission)

1. _____   2. _____   3. _____   4. _____   5. _____

6. _____   7. _____   8. _____   9. _____   10. _____

Directions Indicate the kind of sentence each group of words represents by writing the correct letter in the blank at the right. End punctuation has been omitted.

a. declarative   b. interrogative   c. exclamatory   d. imperative   e. incomplete

1. Jonas at his desk   1. _____

2. Ji Lee was promoted to loan officer last week   2. _____

3. Did Suri organize the training on the new telephone system   3. _____

4. Don't touch that wire   4. _____

5. Please keep the aisles clear   5. _____

WORKPLACE FOCUS

Soft Skills Spell SUCCESS

What is that "something extra" employers look for in an employee? Certainly, a candidate must have the qualifications, skills, and work experience the job requires. But what about so-called soft skills like the ability to write clearly or to get along with others?

Each year, the National Association of Colleges and Employers surveys its employer members to determine what qualities and skills they consider critical for prospective employees. In a recent survey, communication skills (both verbal and oral), a strong work ethic, and teamwork skills topped the list. Other highly rated soft skills were initiative, interpersonal skills (relating well to others), problem-solving and analytical skills, and flexibility. Employers also sought workers who were detail-oriented and good at organizing. All these intangible skills were rated as essential to success in the workplace.

Many people don't have all the soft skills in this list. But with practice, soft skills can be developed and improved. Think about which skills you lack and which you could improve. Look for practical opportunities to exercise those skills.

The Sentence Defined

A **sentence** expresses a complete thought. A **simple sentence** has two important parts, the **subject** (a **noun** or **pronoun**) and the **verb**. The subject is the person, place, or thing spoken of, spoken to, or speaking, and the verb tells what the subject does or is or what happens to it. A group of words is not a complete sentence unless it includes both a subject and a verb.

Below are examples of complete and incomplete sentences with subjects underlined once and verbs underlined twice. Remember that a complete sentence must have both a subject and a verb.

Mr. Navarro spoke to the class about various careers in health care.

    Mr. Navarro—person spoken of—subject

    spoke—tells what Mr. Navarro did—verb

You searched for job openings on Monster.com.

    You—person spoken to—subject

    searched—tells what you did—verb

I at my station in the computer lab.

    I—person speaking—subject

    There is no verb to tell what I did—the sentence is incomplete. A verb such as *worked, sat, read,* or *waited* is needed to complete the sentence: I worked at my station in the computer lab.

The Bureau of Labor Statistics analyzes employment data.

    Bureau of Labor Statistics—thing spoken of—subject

    analyzes—tells what the Bureau of Labor Statistics does—verb

Compound subjects (more than one) usually take plural verbs.

Jake and I design slide shows for all their class presentations.

    Jake and I—persons spoken of—subject

    design—tells what Jake and I do—verb

TRY IT!

Directions Identify the subjects by underlining them once. Identify the verbs by underlining them twice. Check your answers on page 318 or with your instructor before continuing with your assignment.

1. Lindsay scored high on the entrance exam.

2. Lawrence and Ken worked four hours of overtime on Thursday.

3. Dispatchers answer calls for help.

4. Ricky took detailed notes at the accident scene.

5. Carmen questioned the security guard.

6. The investigation involved law enforcement officers from two states.

APPLICATION ❯   **Complete Applications 1–3, pages 5–7, at this time.**

A **declarative** sentence makes a statement. It ends with a period.

> Lola prepared two versions of her resume.
>
> One version emphasized her education.

An **interrogative** sentence asks a question. It ends with a question mark.

> Did you include your part-time job at PetSmart on your resume?
>
> What kind of job interests you?

An **exclamatory** sentence expresses surprise, disbelief, or deep feeling. It ends with an exclamation point.

> That job sounds perfect for me!
>
> You're going to be late!

An **imperative** sentence gives a command or requests someone to do something. It usually ends with a period, but a strong command may end with an exclamation point. The subject *you* is often omitted, but understood.

> Listen to the entire question before answering it. (*you* understood)
>
> Project a professional image during the interview. (*you* understood)
>
> Look at these new career websites. (*you* understood)
>
> Don't press the Delete key! (*you* understood—imperative and exclamatory)

TRY IT!

Directions Classify the sentences by placing a check mark at the right. *D* stands for *declarative, Int* for *interrogative, E* for *exclamatory*, and *Imp* for *imperative*. Check your answers on page 318 or with your instructor before continuing with your assignment.

	D	Int	E	Imp
1. Nervousness during an interview is common.	___	___	___	___
2. What is your greatest strength?	___	___	___	___
3. Be prepared!	___	___	___	___
4. Practice answering possible interview questions.	___	___	___	___
5. Arrive at least 15 minutes early.	___	___	___	___

APPLICATION > **Complete Applications 4–6, pages 8–10, at this time.**

1 | Subject and Verb Recognition

Directions Identify the subjects by underlining them once. Identify the verbs by underlining them twice. Score one point for each correctly identified subject and one point for each correctly identified verb.

Your Score

1. Opportunities in computer forensics continue to grow.　　　　　　　1. _____
2. The field merges elements of law and computer science.　　　　　　2. _____
3. Forensics deals with the recovery and analysis of hidden evidence.　　3. _____
4. Evidence exists in many forms.　　　　　　　　　　　　　　　　4. _____
5. Investigators examine computers for hidden information.　　　　　　5. _____
6. They follow a standard set of procedures.　　　　　　　　　　　　6. _____
7. Many workers learn their skills on the job.　　　　　　　　　　　　7. _____
8. These analysts possess in-depth knowledge of the legal system.　　　　8. _____
9. This career requires technical expertise and attention to detail.　　　　9. _____
10. It also demands investigative, analytical, and communication skills.　　10. _____
11. Salaries range from $65,000 to more than $100,000.　　　　　　　　11. _____

_____

_____

12. America bought Alaska from Russia in 1867.　　　　　　　　　　　12. _____
13. Our government paid $7,200,000 for the land.　　　　　　　　　　13. _____
14. People call Alaska "The Last Frontier."　　　　　　　　　　　　　14. _____
15. A schoolboy designed the state flag.　　　　　　　　　　　　　　15. _____
16. The population exceeds 680,000.　　　　　　　　　　　　　　　　16. _____
17. Alaska entered the Union in 1959.　　　　　　　　　　　　　　　17. _____
18. The gold rush brought thousands of miners and settlers to the state.　18. _____
19. This event changed Alaska forever.　　　　　　　　　　　　　　　19. _____
20. Jack London wrote great stories about Alaska.　　　　　　　　　　20. _____
21. The discovery of oil at Prudhoe Bay led to an oil boom.　　　　　　21. _____
22. The Iditarod pits people and dogs against nature.　　　　　　　　　22. _____
23. The teams race over 1,150 miles of Alaskan terrain.　　　　　　　　23. _____
24. The landmass of Alaska equals one-fifth of the continental United States.　24. _____
25. Sitka National Park contains a large totem pole collection.　　　　　25. _____

Your Total Score _____ /50
If your score was 38 or less, review Section 1, page 3, before continuing.

2 | Subject and Verb Recognition

Directions Identify the subjects by underlining them once. Identify the verbs by underlining them twice. Score one point for each correctly identified subject and one point for each correctly identified verb.

Your Score

1. People write blogs on every imaginable subject.   1. _____

2. Experts count more than 100 million blogs.   2. _____

3. A blog is an online log or journal on a topic or area of interest.   3. _____

4. Comments usually appear in reverse chronological order.   4. _____

5. Many writers express their opinions in blogs.   5. _____

6. Professionals read blogs for current information in their field.   6. _____

7. Companies use blogs for communications with customers.   7. _____

8. Blogs boost consumer awareness of online companies and products.   8. _____

9. They played an important role in the 2004 and 2008 elections.   9. _____

10. Candidates presented issues on their blogs.   10. _____

11. Americans keep blogs for many different reasons.   11. _____

12. Many bloggers focus on their lives and experiences.   12. _____

13. Other topics include politics, entertainment, and sports.   13. _____

14. Efren started a blog for his history class.   14. _____

---

15. Podcasting involves the distribution of digital media files over the Internet.   15. _____

16. The files contain information, entertainment, and news.   16. _____

17. Users replay podcasts at their convenience.   17. _____

18. Podcasts run on almost any media player or computer.   18. _____

19. Subscribers get new episodes of their favorite podcasts automatically.   19. _____

20. Organizations produce podcasts on all kinds of subjects.   20. _____

21. Many large businesses create customer support podcasts.   21. _____

22. Professors deliver lectures as podcasts.   22. _____

23. Museums offer their visitors podcast tours.   23. _____

24. Amazingly, most podcasts are free.   24. _____

25. The popularity of podcasts continues to grow.   25. _____

Your Total Score _____ /50
If your score was 38 or less, review Section 1, page 3, before continuing.

3 | Complete or Incomplete Sentences

Directions Identify the complete sentences by writing *c* in the blank at the right. Identify the incomplete sentences by writing *i* in the blank at the right. In the space below each set, rewrite the incomplete sentences, adding whatever words are necessary to make them complete sentences. Score one point for each complete and incomplete sentence identified and one point for each correctly revised incomplete sentence.

Answers

1. My friends started a computer repair business.   1. _____
2. Matthew gained experience working in their store.   2. _____
3. Buyers and sellers together at the computer swap meet.   3. _____
4. 48-hour turnaround service.   4. _____
5. Their work schedules vary from week to week.   5. _____
6. House calls to fix computers.   6. _____
7. Their parents bought supplies for them.   7. _____

_____

_____

_____

8. Our building has central air-conditioning.   8. _____
9. The hot day and lack of sleep.   9. _____
10. Mrs. Nguyen conducts an orientation for all new employees.   10. _____
11. Many students in their jobs.   11. _____
12. Sharon McNally works in the main office.   12. _____
13. I'm never late for work.   13. _____
14. Always on time.   14. _____
15. At her desk near a telephone.   15. _____
16. Louis and Rudy started their business at home.   16. _____
17. Hires students for his company.   17. _____

_____

_____

_____

_____

_____

Your Total Score _____ /25
If your score was 19 or less, review Section 1, page 3, before continuing.

4 | Kinds of Sentences

Directions Classify the sentences by placing a check mark at the right. *D* stands for *declarative*, *Int* for *interrogative*, *E* for *exclamatory*, and *Imp* for *imperative*. Score one point for each correct answer.

	D	Int	E	Imp
1. Who was the sixth president of the United States?	1. ___	___	___	___
2. Write the name in your notebook.	2. ___	___	___	___
3. What document sets term limits for U.S. presidents?	3. ___	___	___	___
4. Some say Thomas Jefferson was the most accomplished president.	4. ___	___	___	___
5. Jefferson served two terms.	5. ___	___	___	___
6. List his qualifications right now.	6. ___	___	___	___
7. How many presidents have served in the U.S. Senate?	7. ___	___	___	___
8. Tell us about the executive branch of government.	8. ___	___	___	___
9. How much money do presidential candidates raise on the Internet?	9. ___	___	___	___
10. Franklin Roosevelt was elected president four times.	10. ___	___	___	___

11. Ariel got a parking ticket yesterday.	11. ___	___	___	___
12. Tell me where she was parked.	12. ___	___	___	___
13. Are you sure it wasn't for speeding?	13. ___	___	___	___
14. Look how fast that car is going!	14. ___	___	___	___
15. Was the driver using his cell phone?	15. ___	___	___	___
16. The driver barely missed the pedestrian.	16. ___	___	___	___
17. Keep back from his car.	17. ___	___	___	___
18. What a terrible driver he is!	18. ___	___	___	___
19. Watch out for that truck!	19. ___	___	___	___
20. Will she lose her driver's license?	20. ___	___	___	___
21. She had to go to traffic court.	21. ___	___	___	___
22. Liz took her driver's license test.	22. ___	___	___	___
23. Did she pass?	23. ___	___	___	___
24. My driver's license expires in four years.	24. ___	___	___	___
25. Can I renew it by mail?	25. ___	___	___	___

Your Total Score _____ /25

If your score was 19 or less, review Section 2, page 4, before continuing.

5 | Kinds of Sentences

Directions Compose five examples of each kind of sentence (declarative, interrogative, exclamatory, and imperative). The examples should relate to the career field you plan to enter. Score one point for each correct sentence.

Declarative Sentences (Declarative sentences make a statement and end with a period.)

1. _____
2. _____
3. _____
4. _____
5. _____

Interrogative Sentences (Interrogative sentences ask a question and end with a question mark.)

1. _____
2. _____
3. _____
4. _____
5. _____

Exclamatory Sentences (Exclamatory sentences express surprise, disbelief, or deep feeling and end with an exclamation point.)

1. _____
2. _____
3. _____
4. _____
5. _____

Imperative Sentences (Imperative sentences give commands or request someone to do something. They usually end with a period. Strong commands may end with an exclamation point.)

1. _____
2. _____
3. _____
4. _____
5. _____

Your Total Score _____ /20
If your score was 15 or less, review Section 2, page 4, before continuing.

6 | Sentences

A | Directions
Identify the complete sentences by writing *c* in the blank at the right. Identify the incomplete sentences by writing *i* in the blank at the right. Remember that a complete sentence must have a subject and a verb. Score one point for each correct answer.

Answers

1. The doctor's assistants and her friend Pete.   1. _____
2. Be careful around those machines.   2. _____
3. Laura Paules enjoys her temporary nursing position.   3. _____
4. A group of nurses with their supervisors.   4. _____
5. Dr. Willis knows the importance of continuing education.   5. _____
6. Lack of training and experience.   6. _____
7. The chance for more profits and business.   7. _____
8. All our employees receive medical benefits.   8. _____
9. I worked hard to get this job.   9. _____
10. We attempt to please our patients.   10. _____

Your Total Score _____ /10
If your score was 7 or less, review Section 1, page 3, before continuing.

B | Directions
Classify the sentences by writing *d* for *declarative, int* for *interrogative, e* for *exclamatory,* and *imp* for *imperative* in the blank at the right. Score one point for each correct answer.

1. Who was the first person on the moon?   1. _____
2. Neil Armstrong stepped on the moon on July 20, 1969.   2. _____
3. Edwin "Buzz" Aldrin followed shortly after.   3. _____
4. Tell us about that historic event.   4. _____
5. What an unforgettable sight that was!   5. _____
6. How long was the first moon walk?   6. _____
7. It lasted 2 1/2 hours.   7. _____
8. When did assembly of the International Space Station begin? 8. _____
9. Mission specialists walk in space and operate the station's robot arm. 9. _____
10. Did you know that John Glenn flew in space when he was 77? 10. _____
11. Tell us about the first woman to command a space shuttle. 11. _____
12. Thousands of people plan space travel in the next 10 to 20 years. 12. _____
13. That's amazing!   13. _____
14. Visit the Kennedy Space Center in Florida.   14. _____
15. Look at the size of that spacecraft!   15. _____

Your Total Score _____ /15
If your score was 11 or less, review Section 2, page 4, before continuing.

Parts of Speech

Most of the words that are used to make sentences can be sorted into eight classifications called **parts of speech.** Some words can be more than one part of speech depending on their position or use in a sentence. The eight parts of speech are discussed briefly here. They will be treated in greater detail in later units.

Nouns

A **noun** names a person, a place, a thing, a concept, a quality, or an activity. (See pages 31–45 for a detailed treatment of nouns.)

> <u>Shane Deppler</u> plays <u>football</u> in <u>Calgary</u>.
> > <u>Shane Deppler</u>—names a person—noun
> > <u>football</u>—names a thing—noun
> > <u>Calgary</u>—names a place—noun

> <u>Pat Quillin</u> owns a <u>boutique</u> in <u>Atlanta</u>.
> > <u>Pat Quillin</u>—names a person—noun
> > <u>boutique</u>—names a thing—noun
> > <u>Atlanta</u>—names a place—noun

> <u>Creativity</u> and <u>knowledge</u> are powerful <u>tools</u>.
> > <u>Creativity</u>—names a quality—noun
> > <u>knowledge</u>—names a concept—noun
> > <u>tools</u>—names things—noun

> <u>Trail running</u>, <u>ultra marathons</u>, and <u>climbing</u> keep <u>Mike</u> fit.
> > <u>Trail running</u>—names an activity—noun
> > <u>ultra marathons</u>—names activities—noun
> > <u>climbing</u>—names an activity—noun
> > <u>Mike</u>—names a person—noun

NOUNS

Pronouns

A **pronoun** is a word used as a substitute for a noun. (See pages 55–78 for a detailed treatment of pronouns.)

She checked the book out of the school library.

> She—used in place of the name of the individual—pronoun

I created a personal website to use for job searches.

> I—used in place of the name of the individual—pronoun

They suggested I submit a portfolio to prospective employers.

> They—used in place of the names of the individuals—pronoun
> I—used in place of the name of the individual—pronoun

Joseph gave them a recommendation for next year's budget.

> them—used in place of the names of the individuals—pronoun

Verbs

A **verb** tells what the subject does or is or what happens to it. Verbs can make a statement, ask a question, or give a command. (See pages 91–108 for a detailed treatment of verbs.)

Yeongri Kim designed a letterhead for her new business.

> designed—tells what the subject, *Yeongri Kim*, did—verb

Was your service good?

> Was—asks a question about the subject, *service*—verb

Submit your travel expense report by noon today!

> Submit—gives a command to the understood subject, *you* (You submit your travel expense report by noon today!)—verb

TRY IT!

Directions Identify the nouns, verbs, and pronouns. Underline the nouns once, the verbs twice, and the pronouns three times. Check your answers on page 318 or with your instructor before continuing with your assignment.

1. We planned a party for Jennifer.
2. Gillian gave us a cooking lesson.
3. David paired each course with a complementary wine.
4. They decorated the table with confetti and flowers.
5. She and Tom wrapped the leftovers in foil.

APPLICATION   **Complete Applications 7–8, pages 13–14, at this time.**

7 | Nouns, Verbs, and Pronouns

Directions Identify the nouns, verbs, and pronouns. Underline the nouns once, the verbs twice, and the pronouns three times. Score one point for each correct identification.

Your Score

1. Ms. Rivera gave us hints for better communication.   1. _____

2. We discussed with her the importance of first impressions.   2. _____

3. She gave me advice on preemployment tests.   3. _____

4. Jerzee demonstrated icebreakers for conversations.   4. _____

5. I read an article on the value of effective listening.   5. _____

6. He researched the company on the Internet.   6. _____

7. She prepared questions for the interviewer.   7. _____

8. Monica and I sought information on careers.   8. _____

9. She and he bought a book on skills for new employees.   9. _____

10. They sent me a contract for the assignment.   10. _____

11. The article pointed them and me in the right direction.   11. _____

12. She applied for a position at Aetna.   12. _____

13. We purchased a CD about the different occupations.   13. _____

14. Dmitri proofread the resume carefully.   14. _____

15. He checked dates and addresses.   15. _____

16. The shortage of nurses means more opportunities for us.   16. _____

17. I made an appointment for you.   17. _____

18. They conduct interviews of applicants in Room C.   18. _____

19. She identified potential jobs in the list of openings.   19. _____

20. We realize the importance of the benefits.   20. _____

21. Joan and I met the supervisor at the clinic.   21. _____

22. Lance and I answered ads for dieticians.   22. _____

23. He and she trained at a hospital in town.   23. _____

24. They hired Adrian and me as pharmacists.   24. _____

25. Carlota and I talked with counselors about the various professions.   25. _____

Your Total Score _____ /115
If your score was 87 or less, review pages 3 and 11–12 before continuing.

8 | Nouns, Verbs, and Pronouns

Directions Identify the nouns, verbs, and pronouns. Underline the nouns once, the verbs twice, and the pronouns three times. Score one point for each correct identification.

Your Score

1. Connie and I introduced Dr. Singh to the other members.   1. _____

2. She taught us about the founders of the country.   2. _____

3. Scholars consider her an expert on the Revolutionary period.   3. _____

4. Nicki and I showed a film about the distinguished statesmen.   4. _____

5. We heard of the brilliant leaders of the early days.   5. _____

6. He and I learned about Washington, Adams, and Jefferson.   6. _____

7. The dedicated patriots gave us pride in the country.   7. _____

8. African-Americans served on both sides in the war.   8. _____

9. Women also fought for the cause.   9. _____

10. Molly Pitcher brought water to soldiers during a famous battle.   10. _____

11. She manned a cannon under heavy fire.   11. _____

12. The speaker described the heroism of Crispus Attucks.   12. _____

13. Thomas Jefferson drafted the Declaration of Independence.   13. _____

14. John Adams served with him on the committee.   14. _____

15. They worked carefully on the assignment.   15. _____

16. The delegates approved the final draft.   16. _____

17. Historians refer to Jefferson as a scholar.   17. _____

18. He spoke seven languages.   18. _____

19. Jefferson served as governor of Virginia, minister to France, secretary of state, vice president, and president.   19. _____

20. They read letters from Jefferson to other Revolutionary leaders.   20. _____

21. The Declaration contains democratic ideas for them and me.   21. _____

22. John Hancock signed his name in large cursive on the document.   22. _____

23. The founders shaped the nation for future generations.   23. _____

24. Thomas Jefferson and John Adams died on the Fourth of July.   24. _____

25. Both men signed the Declaration 50 years earlier on the same date.   25. _____

Your Total Score _____ /112
If your score was 84 or less, review pages 3 and 11–12 before continuing.

Adjectives

An **adjective** modifies (describe or limits) a noun or pronoun. It answers the question *how many, what kind,* or *which one.* **Articles** (*a, an,* and *the*) are adjectives. They can be **definite** (*the*) or **indefinite** (*a, an*). (See pages 169–174 and 182–183 for a detailed treatment of adjectives.)

Two friends restored a 1957 Thunderbird.

> Two—tells how many friends—adjective
>
> a—indefinite article
>
> 1957—tells what kind of Thunderbird—adjective

The landscape company designed a beautiful garden.

> The—definite article
>
> landscape—tells what kind of company—adjective
>
> a—indefinite article
>
> beautiful—tells what kind of garden—adjective

The winning driver wore a fire-resistant jumpsuit.

> The—definite article
>
> winning—tells which driver—adjective
>
> a—indefinite article
>
> fire-resistant—tells what kind of jumpsuit—adjective

Crowded roadways are an everyday occurrence in California.

> Crowded—tells what kind of roadways—adjective
>
> an—indefinite article
>
> everyday—tells what kind of occurrence—adjective

SMART | CUTE
QUIET | SWEET
CUNNING | FRIENDLY
CURIOUS | FURRY
| HAPPY
| PLAYFUL
| DEVOTED

ADJECTIVES DESCRIBE NOUNS AND PRONOUNS.

Adverbs

An **adverb** modifies (describes) a verb, an adjective, or another adverb. It answers the question *when, where, why, how,* or *to what extent.* Most words ending in *ly* are adverbs. Five common exceptions are *friendly, lively, lonely, lovely,* and *ugly,* which are adjectives. (See pages 177–179 and 183–184 for a detailed treatment of adverbs.)

The traffic light finally turned green.

> finally—modifies the verb *turned* by telling when—adverb

I frequently finish my work before the deadline.

> frequently—modifies the verb *finish* by telling when—adverb

The high winds turned over vehicles on the highway.

> over—modifies the verb *turned* by telling where (in what direction)—adverb

Alex quickly scanned the sports page for game results.

> quickly—modifies the verb *scanned* by telling how—adverb

The <u>very</u> old structure needs a renovation.

> <u>very</u>—modifies the adjective *old* by telling to what extent (how old)—adverb

The engine runs <u>more</u> <u>smoothly</u> <u>now</u>.

> <u>more</u>—modifies the adverb *smoothly* by telling to what extent (how smoothly)—adverb
>
> <u>smoothly</u>—modifies the verb *runs* by telling how—adverb
>
> <u>now</u>—modifies the verb *runs* by telling when—adverb

ADVERBS DESCRIBE VERBS, ADJECTIVES, OR OTHER ADVERBS.

Proofreading is the final check you make on a document, after you have written and revised it, to ensure it is error-free. Keyboarding errors, mistakes in grammar, punctuation, and spelling, incorrect formatting, and computational errors are common kinds of mistakes that people find when proofreading.

- Spell check a document just before you proofread.

- Read the document aloud from beginning to end, focusing on the content. Then read it again, paying particular attention to grammar, punctuation, and spelling.

TRY IT!

Directions Identify the adjectives, verbs, and adverbs. Underline the adjectives once, the verbs twice, and the adverbs three times. Check your answers on page 318 or with your instructor before continuing with your assignment.

1. Many people agreed with the final results of the election.

2. The natural athlete quickly recovered from the knee injury.

3. A knowledgeable manager often makes wise decisions.

4. Suzanne created a visually appealing centerpiece.

5. The captain of the losing team rarely made a right decision.

6. Jake performed poorly on the entrance exam.

7. Garrett nearly missed the last plane to Miami.

8. We played there last summer.

APPLICATION   **Complete Applications 9–10, pages 17–18, at this time.**

9 | Adjectives, Verbs, and Adverbs

A | **Directions** Identify the adjectives, verbs, and adverbs. Underline the adjectives once, the verbs twice, and the adverbs three times. Score one point for each correct identification.

Your Score

1. Joshua discussed strategies for good study skills with two friends.   1. _____

2. Cheryl listened actively to the anatomy lecture.   2. _____

3. The instructor speaks quite softly and quickly.   3. _____

4. Jaye writes down the main points of the lecture.   4. _____

5. Kara wisely prepared for the next algebra test with a classmate.   5. _____

6. Ellyn quickly organized the new sets of grammar handouts.   6. _____

7. Carlos intentionally focused on the important ideas in the English lecture.   7. _____

8. Zadoque methodically constructed a detailed outline for math notes.   8. _____

9. Illyana carefully read the assigned material for biology class.   9. _____

10. Lyudmila periodically reviews class notes.   10. _____

11. Zeke studies at a large desk with a comfortable chair, a bright lamp, and soft music.   11. _____

12. Schools often provide quiet rooms for study in the library.   12. _____

13. Mike sat at the front of the classroom.   13. _____

14. Ms. Ohman purposely arranged the classroom for group participation.   14. _____

15. Jason attends classes regularly with excellent results.   15. _____

B | **Directions** Indicate whether the words are adjectives, verbs, or adverbs by writing *adj, v,* or *adv* in the blank at the right. Score one point for each correct answer.

1. loudly	_____	11. drove	_____
2. quickly	_____	12. colorful	_____
3. always	_____	13. excessively	_____
4. sings	_____	14. smaller	_____
5. selfish	_____	15. often	_____
6. manipulate	_____	16. rough	_____
7. moves	_____	17. sustain	_____
8. helpful	_____	18. excellent	_____
9. never	_____	19. immensely	_____
10. quietly	_____	20. lucky	_____

Your Total Score _____ /90
If your score was 68 or less for A and B, review pages 12 and 15–16 before continuing.

10 | Adjectives, Verbs, and Adverbs

A | **Directions** Identify the adjectives, verbs, and adverbs. Underline the adjectives once, the verbs twice, and the adverbs three times. Score one point for each correct identification.

Your Score

1. The school offered a variety of workshops for interested students. 1. _____

2. Janell developed memory tips for key points. 2. _____

3. Frances spent too much time on the phone. 3. _____

4. Quyenlinh regularly reviewed lab notes before a chemistry lecture. 4. _____

5. Ben generally studies alone. 5. _____

6. Sarann memorized the periodic table of the elements for the midterm exam. 6. _____

7. Students appreciate effectively delivered lectures. 7. _____

8. Smaller classes usually allow more opportunities for questions. 8. _____

9. Good work habits relate closely to success in college. 9. _____

10. Maryam highly recommended the biology teacher. 10. _____

11. Four students quickly formed a study group. 11. _____

12. The group meets regularly at a local bookstore. 12. _____

13. Students frequently take notes in class on a laptop computer. 13. _____

14. We wanted a conscientious notetaker in the group. 14. _____

15. Motivated students often have the very best listening skills. 15. _____

B | **Directions** Indicate whether the words are adjectives, verbs, or adverbs by writing *adj, v,* or *adv* in the blank at the right. Score one point for each correct answer.

1. beautiful _____ 11. carefully _____

2. very _____ 12. orally _____

3. annual _____ 13. scenic _____

4. previous _____ 14. writes _____

5. read _____ 15. jogs _____

6. personal _____ 16. nearly _____

7. harshly _____ 17. down _____

8. large _____ 18. speak _____

9. convenient _____ 19. partially _____

10. seldom _____ 20. really _____

Your Total Score _____ /85
If your score was 64 or less for A and B, review pages 12 and 15–16 before continuing.

Prepositions

A **preposition** shows the relationship of a noun or pronoun to some other part of the sentence. (See pages 197–198 for a detailed treatment of prepositions.)

PREPOSITIONS

They went <u>through</u> the park and <u>into</u> the gazebo <u>near</u> the duck pond.

> <u>through</u>—shows relationship between *park* and *went*—preposition
>
> <u>into</u>—shows relationship between *gazebo* and *went*—preposition
>
> <u>near</u>—shows relationship between *pond* and *gazebo*—preposition

The election <u>in</u> November established the winner <u>by</u> a majority <u>of</u> votes.

> <u>in</u>—shows relationship between *November* and *election*—preposition
>
> <u>by</u>—shows relationship between *majority* and *established*—preposition
>
> <u>of</u>—shows relationship between *votes* and *majority*—preposition

Conjunctions

A **conjunction** joins words, **phrases** (groups of related words that do not contain a subject and a verb in combination), and **clauses** (groups of related words containing a subject and a verb). (See pages 201–202 for a detailed treatment of conjunctions and pages 213–221 for a detailed treatment of phrases and clauses.)

Watermelon <u>and</u> grapefruit are my favorite fruits.

> <u>and</u>—joins the words *Watermelon* and *grapefruit*— conjunction

Did you request a compact rental car <u>or</u> a midsize rental car?

> <u>or</u>—joins the phrases *a compact rental car* and *a midsize rental car*—conjunction

Bill plans to sell his truck <u>and</u> to buy a hybrid.

> <u>and</u>—joins the phrases *to sell his truck* and *to buy a hybrid*—conjunction

<u>When</u> I opened the door, I smelled smoke.

> <u>When</u>—introduces and joins the clause *When I opened the door* with the clause *I smelled smoke*—conjunction

Interjections

An **interjection** is a word or words used to express strong and sudden feeling—surprise, fear, suspense, anger, love, joy, and other emotions. Words such as *wow, ouch, oh,* and *hooray* are interjections. Words such as *help, hurry,* and *stop* (usually verbs) may be used as interjections.

<u>Stop</u>! You're going to hit that car!

> <u>Stop</u>!—expresses sudden feeling—interjection

<u>Wow</u>! Those fireworks were amazing!

> <u>Wow</u>!—expresses sudden feeling—interjection

WRITE NOW!

The Simple Sentence

You have learned that a simple sentence expresses a complete thought and has a subject and a verb.

> Brenda rides the train to work every morning.
> > Brenda—subject
> > rides—verb

A simple sentence may have a compound subject (more than one) or a compound verb or both.

> The plaintiff and his attorney decided to appeal.
> > plaintiff and attorney—compound subject
> > decided—verb

> The witness stuttered and stammered.
> > witness—subject
> > stuttered and stammered—compound verb

> Mrs. Eversman and Mr. Joyner appeared in court and testified for the defense.
> > Mrs. Eversman and Mr. Joyner—compound subject
> > appeared and testified—compound verb

TRY IT!

Directions Identify the prepositions, conjunctions, and interjections. Underline the prepositions once, the conjunctions twice, and the interjections three times. Check your answers on page 318 or with your instructor before continuing with your assignment.

1. Hooray! The Leopards won the championship!

2. Hector and Allen could go skiing at Squaw Valley or at Sugar Bowl.

3. Wait! The mountain roads are covered with ice, and there are wind advisories!

4. When you finish your homework, meet me at the movie theater in the mall.

5. Shh! Listen to the waves lapping on the shore.

APPLICATION ❯ **Complete Applications 11–16, pages 21–24 and 27–28, at this time.**

11 | Prepositions, Conjunctions, and Interjections

Directions Identify the prepositions, conjunctions, and interjections. Underline the prepositions once, the conjunctions twice, and the interjections three times. Score one point for each correct identification.

Your Score

1. When she knew the facts, she was relieved and happy.   1. _____

2. The copier is through the double doors, near the conference room.   2. _____

3. Retirees will be honored for their service at a dinner on Friday, June 25.   3. _____

4. Akato is running the projector for the presentation in Conference Room A.   4. _____

5. My firm is looking for a self-starter with a proven record of success and earnings.   5. _____

6. We need employees with fluency in Spanish and English.   6. _____

7. Mail or fax your resume and salary history to Ace Credit Systems within two days.   7. _____

8. Cole designs marketing pieces for new products.   8. _____

9. Tony must submit all the bids and proposals by noon tomorrow.   9. _____

10. Randy or Keith will file the documents with the court.   10. _____

11. Pat is getting quotes for laptop computers from Fry's, Micro Center, and Best Buy.   11. _____

12. She will talk with you about the pension plan.   12. _____

13. Cheryl manages the office and the website.   13. _____

14. Alan was excited and nervous on his first day of work at Gemini Feature Films.   14. _____

15. Hey! Is that your suitcase?   15. _____

16. Hurry! We'll miss our flight!   16. _____

17. Oh! I left my wallet and keys in my room.   17. _____

18. My supervisor gave us tickets to a Broadway play! Terrific!   18. _____

19. Lin went into her office and closed the door.   19. _____

20. Wow! I am amazed by the work environment at our company!   20. _____

21. Yikes! You lost all your work!   21. _____

22. Congratulations! You're the top salesperson on the West Coast!   22. _____

23. Oops! I dropped the coffee cup, and it broke.   23. _____

24. The sales conference is in Hawaii? Great!   24. _____

25. He heard a soft noise behind him.   25. _____

Your Total Score _____ /55

If your score was 42 or less, review page 19 before continuing.

12 | Unit Review

A | **Directions** Identify the underlined nouns, verbs, adjectives, and prepositions. Write *n* for *noun, v* for *verb, adj* for *adjective,* or *prep* for *preposition* above each underlined word. Score one point for each correct identification.

Your Score

1. Janine combined a sensible diet with moderate workouts and lost 20 pounds.　　　　1. _____

2. Dr. Kim, the orthopedist, recommends 30 minutes of daily physical activity.　　　　2. _____

3. Cardiovascular exercise increases the work of the heart and lungs.　　　　3. _____

4. Many exercise facilities offer the services of a personal trainer.　　　　4. _____

5. Consider the location of a gym or pool carefully.　　　　5. _____

6. Karen, the tall lifeguard, swims every day.　　　　6. _____

7. For Olivia, yoga meets personal needs and fitness goals.　　　　7. _____

8. Three nutritionists wrote an article for the magazine.　　　　8. _____

Your Total Score _____ /69
If your score was 52 or less, review pages 11, 12, 15, and 19 before continuing.

B | **Directions** Identify the underlined pronouns, adverbs, conjunctions, and interjections. Write *pro* for *pronoun, adv* for *adverb, c* for *conjunction,* or *i* for *interjection* above each underlined word. Score one point for each correct identification.

1. Terry told me the name *California* came from a Spanish story.　　　　1. _____

2. We saw simple and very sparsely decorated buildings in the Pueblo style.　　　　2. _____

3. He and I planned the trip carefully.　　　　3. _____

4. Mr. Healy and she usually give us directions.　　　　4. _____

5. We gratefully accepted help from them.　　　　5. _____

6. You got us a helicopter tour of the Grand Canyon? Great!　　　　6. _____

7. They will take four or five of us on the tour.　　　　7. _____

8. She rode down into the canyon on an unbelievably narrow and steep trail.　　　　8. _____

9. That trail takes you directly to the top of the waterfall.　　　　9. _____

10. He stopped frequently for Isabel and me.　　　　10. _____

Your Total Score _____ /32
If your score was 24 or less, review pages 12, 15–16, and 19 before continuing.

13 | Unit Review

A | **Directions** Identify the nouns, verbs, adjectives, and prepositions. Write *n* for *noun, v* for *verb, adj* for *adjective,* or *prep* for *preposition* above the word. Score one point for each correct identification.

Your Score

1. The instructor posts a science fact on the board every day.   1. _____

2. In a lightbulb, electrons flow through the filament and strike atoms.   2. _____

3. Millions of people live near active volcanoes.   3. _____

4. The skeleton of an adult contains 206 bones.   4. _____

5. The first passengers in a hot-air balloon were a duck, a rooster, and a sheep.   5. _____

6. Otto Hahn, a German chemist, discovered nuclear fission in 1938.   6. _____

7. Alex and I took an exciting virtual tour of Mars.   7. _____

8. The longest cells in the human body are the motor neurons.   8. _____

9. An electron microscope uses magnets and a beam of electrons.   9. _____

10. Lake Baikal in southern Siberia in Russia is the deepest lake in the world.   10. _____

Your Total Score _____ /100
If your score was 75 or less for A, review pages 11, 12, 15, and 19 before continuing.

B | **Directions** Identify the pronouns, adverbs, conjunctions, and interjections. Write *pro* for *pronoun, adv* for *adverb, c* for *conjunction,* or *i* for *interjection* above the word. Score one point for each correct identification.

1. Terrific! A prestigious school finally admitted her and me!   1. _____

2. Colleges usually look first at test scores.   2. _____

3. Yes! I received a $5,000 grant and a $2,500 scholarship.   3. _____

4. We already know about the meal plan and the student housing there.   4. _____

5. Oh, no! We missed the application deadline.   5. _____

6. He and I painstakingly completed applications for scholarships and grants.   6. _____

7. She worked diligently in high school for good grades.   7. _____

8. Yesterday, they took us on a tour of the campus and the athletic field.   8. _____

Your Total Score _____ /27
If your score was 21 or less, review pages 12, 15–16, and 19 before continuing.

14 | Unit Review

A | **Directions** Identify the nouns, verbs, adjectives, and prepositions. Write *n* for *noun*, *v* for *verb*, *adj* for *adjective*, or *prep* for *preposition* above the word. Score one point for each correct identification.

Your Score

1. A wise shopper looks for bargains at the supermarket.   1. _____

2. Strict laws protect consumers from unsafe food.   2. _____

3. Steve cooks raw vegetables in a microwave or steamer.   3. _____

4. Susan checks labels for the amount of sugar and fat.   4. _____

5. Some people prefer organic products.   5. _____

6. Quality ingredients usually result in a fine meal.   6. _____

7. Mrs. Radner buys many items in bulk for the discounts.   7. _____

8. We purchased fresh fruit at the market on the corner.   8. _____

Your Total Score _____ /63
If your score was 48 or less, review pages 11, 12, 15, and 19 before continuing.

B | **Directions** Identify the pronouns, adverbs, conjunctions, and interjections. Write *pro* for *pronoun*, *adv* for *adverb*, *c* for *conjunction*, or *i* for *interjection* above the word. Score one point for each correct identification.

1. She and I finally left work and packed quickly for the business seminar.   1. _____

2. Wow! They engaged the audience completely.   2. _____

3. The organizers thoughtfully provided an interpreter for him and me.   3. _____

4. The afternoon presentations ran much more smoothly.   4. _____

5. When Donnel and Jace finished, we applauded enthusiastically.   5. _____

6. The last speaker gave us a useful set of handouts.   6. _____

7. You could attend sessions on time management or goal setting.   7. _____

8. The speakers often paused and patiently answered questions.   8. _____

9. He and Michael spoke particularly well.   9. _____

10. Oops! I foolishly left the handouts on the table.   10. _____

Your Total Score _____ /32
If your score was 24 or less, review pages 12, 15–16, and 19 before continuing.

ENGLISH ON THE JOB /
Retail Sales Worker

Consumers spend millions of dollars every day on merchandise, and they rely on a store's sales force for help. Retail sales workers must have the ability to communicate clearly with customers. They must be able not only to describe the features and benefits of a product but also to demonstrate its use. The primary focus of retail sales workers is to create interest in their products and to influence customers' decisions about purchasing. Knowing how to communicate effectively with customers leads to increased sales and satisfied customers. Retail sales workers with poor communication skills create a negative impression and lose sales. For a retail salesperson, customer service is the key to success.

Retail sales personnel are often asked to receive payment for purchases (cash, checks, debit cards, or credit cards) and to open or close registers. In some instances, they may open or close the retail establishment and set up displays. Performing these and other tasks well may result in promotions and additional responsibilities. Many sales workers gain skills through on-the-job experience.

This occupation offers many opportunities for part-time work; therefore, it is especially appealing to college students, retirees, and anyone looking to supplement his or her income. The U.S. Bureau of Labor Statistics projects that job opportunities in retail sales will continue to grow, due in part to the growing population. Many beginning workers earn minimum wage, but compensation may include commissions in addition to a salary or an hourly wage. Skills developed by retail sales workers can be transferred to many other occupations.

© Blend Images/Jupiter Images

A | **Directions** Identify the subjects by underlining them once. Identify the verbs by underlining them twice. Score one point for each correctly identified subject and one point for each correctly identified verb.

Your Score

1. Maria chose to work in retail because of the constant interaction with people.

1. _____

2. A friendly attitude greatly helps in selling.

2. _____

3. The best salespeople demonstrate enthusiasm for their products.

3. _____

4. A pleasant manner usually contributes to sales.

4. _____

5. A competent salesperson generates goodwill and confidence through verbal and written communication.

5. _____

Your Total Score _____ /10

If your score was 7 or less, review Section 1, page 3, before continuing.

B | **Directions** Identify the nouns, adjectives, and adverbs. Underline the nouns once, the adjectives twice, and the adverbs three times. Score one point for each correct identification

Your Score

1. Diligent and attentive salespeople frequently sell many products.　　　　　　　1. _____

2. Successful workers usually possess several transferable skills.　　　　　　　2. _____

3. Many opportunities exist for skilled temporary employees.　　　　　　　3. _____

4. A capable salesperson often gets promoted quickly.　　　　　　　4. _____

5. Customers speak favorably about the service and recommend the company to friends.　　　　　　　5. _____

Your Total Score _____ /29
If your score was 22 or less, review pages 11 and 15–16 before continuing.

C | **Directions** Identify the prepositions, conjunctions, and interjections. Underline the prepositions once, the conjunctions twice, and the interjections three times. Score one point for each correct identification.

Your Score

1. For retail sales workers, attitude and appearance matter.　　　　　　　1. _____

2. Experienced sales representatives train new employees on the types of products offered.　　　　　　　2. _____

3. Helen or Faye will be our new manager. Fantastic!　　　　　　　3. _____

4. Retail salespeople handle exchanges and returns of merchandise.　　　　　　　4. _____

5. It was good news about the need for temporary help and wages.　　　　　　　5. _____

Your Total Score _____ /11
If your score was 7 or less, review page 19 before continuing.

15 | Writing Improvement

Directions Complete the sentences. The subject is underlined. Review the WRITE Now feature on page 20 if you need help.

Example Retail sales <u>workers</u> *need good communication skills.* _____

1. An unexpected <u>customer</u> _____

2. The unusual sales <u>event</u> _____

3. Wow! The new <u>clerk</u> _____

4. A <u>shipment</u> _____ _____

5. <u>Salesclerks</u> _____ _____ _____ _____ _____

6. In a small store, <u>employees</u> ___ _____

7. A <u>customer</u> _____

8. A positive <u>attitude</u> _____

9. <u>Knowledge</u> of your products _____

10. The <u>supervisor</u> _____

11. The regional <u>manager</u> _ _____

12. This <u>outfit</u> _____

13. <u>Clients</u> _____

14. <u>Clerks</u> at video stores _____

15. Most successful <u>people</u> _____

16. A <u>degree</u> in retail management ___ _____ _____

17. Those <u>shelves</u> _____

18. The <u>manager and</u> her <u>assistant</u> _____

19. After the 15-hour sale, <u>we</u> _____

20. Our <u>sales team</u> _____

APPLICATION **Give your completed application to your instructor for evaluation**

Optional Activity Interview a sales associate at a local retail store. Ask about the training and education required for the job and what the person likes best about it. Write a short summary of what you learn to share with the class.

16 | Comprehensive Review

A | **Directions** Indicate the kind of sentence each group of words represents by writing the correct letter in the blank at the right. End punctuation has been omitted. Score one point for each correct answer.

a. declarative   b. interrogative   c. exclamatory

d. imperative   e. incomplete

1. You will make your group presentation on Thursday   1. _____

2. The trip to Boston   2. _____

3. Did you receive a bonus this quarter   3. _____

4. Send these files to Dr. Chen   4. _____

5. Watch out   5. _____

B | **Directions** Identify the subjects by underlining them once. Identify the verbs by underlining them twice. Score one point for each correctly identified subject and one point for each correctly identified verb.

Your Score

1. Andrea and Logan sold the most long-term health care policies.   1. _____

2. John hired several temporary employees.   2. _____

3. Graciela and I evaluated the performance of Mr. Nguyen.   3. _____

4. Employers expect loyalty from their workers.   4. _____

5. During the telethon, the phones rang constantly.   5. _____

C | **Directions** Study the sentences. Identify which part of speech each word represents. Write the correct letter in the blank at the right. Score one point for each correct answer.

a. noun   b. pronoun   c. verb   d. adjective

e. adverb   f. preposition   g. conjunction   h. interjection

I saw Aaron and Thun quietly enter the lecture hall.

1. I _____   4. and _____   7. enter _____   10. hall _____

2. saw _____   5. Thun _____   8. the _____

3. Aaron _____   6. quietly _____   9. lecture _____

The design project by Sue and Avery won first prize!

1. The _____   4. by _____   7. Avery _____   10. prize _____

2. design _____   5. Sue _____   8. won _____

3. project _____   6. and _____   9. first _____

Paul and I regularly write business proposals for clients.

1. Paul _____   4. regularly _____   7. proposals _____

2. and _____   5. write _____   8. for _____

3. I _____   6. business _____   9. clients _____

Your Total Score _____ /44

PROOF IT!

Directions Proofread the e-mail, circling all errors. Write a correction above each error. Give your completed application to your instructor for evaluation.

```
 ◉ ○ ○                                    ✉ Mail

 New Message   Send   Address   Attach   Options   Spelling   Print   Save   File   Edit   Format   Insert   Tools   View   Help

        To:  "All Employees" <allemp@barnardinc.com>
        Cc:
   Subject:  Company-Sponsored Commuter Service
▶ Attachments:  Commuter Survey.doc (24 KB)
```

The Worker Satisfaction Committee is investigating the feasibility of offering ride-share services form

several location within a one-hour radius of our company. These pickup points would be located in

commuter parking lots at Racine Road in Elmhurst, Highway 36 in Collegeville, Cedar Valley Road in

Offerman, and Nadir Boulevard in Aragon. The morning pickup times would be 5:30, 6:15, 7, and 7:45,

and return trips would leave our sight at 3:15, 4, 4:45, and 5:30. There would be no cost to you? You

would need to check with you department head to see whether the arrival an departure times would work

with your schedule.

At this time, we are asking whether you would be interested in this service. If so, which pickup location

would you prefer? What time best? Please file out the attached form and return it by Friday, April 16.

A | **Directions** Study the sentences. Write the letter for the correct part of speech in the blank at the right.

Jessica and Ramon wanted a house near the lake at a good price. They carefully researched properties to be sold at auction.

1. Jessica   (a) adverb   (b) noun   (c) pronoun   (d) preposition   _____

2. and   (a) conjunction   (b) noun   (c) interjection   (d) adjective   _____

3. a   (a) pronoun   (b) interjection   (c) preposition   (d) adjective   _____

4. house   (a) adjective   (b) adverb   (c) noun   (d) pronoun   _____

5. near   (a) verb   (b) adjective   (c) preposition   (d) adverb   _____

6. good   (a) pronoun   (b) adjective   (c) verb   (d) noun   _____

7. They   (a) preposition   (b) noun   (c) pronoun   (d) interjection   _____

8. carefully   (a) adverb   (b) pronoun   (c) adjective   (d) verb   _____

9. researched   (a) adjective   (b) verb   (c) conjunction   (d) adverb   _____

10. auction   (a) interjection   (b) conjunction   (c) noun   (d) preposition   _____

B | **Directions** Identify the complete sentences by writing *c* in the blank at the right. Identify the incomplete sentences by writing *i* in the blank at the right.

1. Spencer presented the marketing plan for the new PDA.   _____

2. The people at the meeting.   _____

3. Joseph audited the books.   _____

4. Elected as chair of the Training and Development Committee.   _____

5. Paid the overdue account.   _____

C | **Directions** Classify the sentences by placing a check mark at the right. *D* stands for *declarative*, *Int* for *interrogative*, *E* for *exclamatory*, and *Imp* for *imperative*.

	D	Int	E	Imp
1. It is so hot today!	1. ____	____	____	____
2. Where can we find a cool place?	2. ____	____	____	____
3. The mall is air-conditioned.	3. ____	____	____	____
4. Close the windows and curtains in the morning.	4. ____	____	____	____

unit 2
Nouns

Objectives

1. To recognize common, proper, and collective nouns
2. To learn how to form noun plurals and noun possessives
3. To write clear sentences that use nouns appropriately

Sections

Pretest

A | **Directions** Underline each noun. Write *c* for *common* or *p* for *proper* above the noun.

1. After only four lessons at the Good News Cooking School, Mario prepared a

   five-course meal for his family.

2. Chef Renaldo suggested a tossed green salad, baked fish with steamed

   vegetables, and a dessert platter of fresh fruits and cheeses.

3. The class sampled the food they prepared.

B | **Directions** Write the plural form of each noun.

1. reference _____   4. freshman _____   7. solo _____
2. foot _____   5. inch _____   8. business _____
3. leaf _____   6. category _____   9. basket _____

C | **Directions** Rewrite each item using the singular and plural possessive. Make both nouns plural in the plural possessive.

	Singular Possessive	**Plural Possessive**
Example cry of the baby	*baby's cry*	*babies' cries*
1. best season of the team	_____	_____
2. computer of the school	_____	_____
3. homework of the class	_____	_____

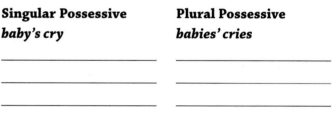

WORKPLACE FOCUS

Emotional Intelligence

Have you developed your emotional intelligence to its fullest? One of the most critical elements for a student's success in school is an understanding of how to learn. The key factors for this understanding include confidence, self-motivation and self-control, the capacity to communicate, and the ability to work well with others. Successful employees exhibit these same skills on an even higher level. Many corporations now include emotional intelligence in training programs to help employees cooperate, motivate, and collaborate more, thereby increasing productivity and profits.

To start boosting your emotional intelligence, evaluate yourself to determine if you are self-motivating, take initiative, set goals and priorities, can recognize other people's feelings (and their nonverbal cues), and work well with others.

If your emotional intelligence is well developed, that will directly impact all your other abilities in a positive way.

Major Classes of Nouns

Common Nouns

Nouns name people, places, things, concepts, qualities, or activities. A **common noun** is a noun that does not refer to a *particular* person, place, thing, concept, quality, or activity.

> <u>Lemons</u>, <u>limes</u>, and <u>oranges</u> are citrus <u>fruits</u>.
>> <u>Lemons</u>, <u>limes</u>, <u>oranges</u>, <u>fruits</u>—general terms not naming anything in particular—common nouns
>
> The <u>managers</u> in our <u>organization</u> value <u>teamwork</u>.
>> <u>managers</u>, <u>organization</u>—general terms not naming anyone or anything in particular—common nouns
>>
>> <u>teamwork</u>—name of a concept—common noun
>
> <u>Reading</u> is a relaxing <u>hobby</u>.
>> <u>Reading</u>—name of an activity—common noun
>>
>> <u>hobby</u>—general term not naming anything in particular—common noun

Proper Nouns

Proper nouns name particular persons, places, things, or activities. Proper nouns should always be capitalized. (See pages 264–266 for a detailed treatment of capitalization.)

PROPER NOUNS

Independence Hall

Liberty Bell

Ben Franklin

> <u>Annalise Norton</u> works in <u>Casper, Wyoming</u>.
>> <u>Annalise Norton</u>—name of a particular person—proper noun
>>
>> <u>Casper, Wyoming</u>—name of a particular place—proper noun
>
> When we were in <u>England</u>, we saw the <u>Crown Jewels</u>.
>> <u>England</u>—name of a particular place—proper noun
>>
>> <u>Crown Jewels</u>—name of particular things—proper noun
>
> The last <u>Monday</u> in <u>May</u> is <u>Memorial Day</u>.
>> <u>Monday</u>, <u>May</u>, <u>Memorial Day</u>—names of particular things—proper nouns
>
> <u>Julio Carceno</u> completed the <u>Boston Marathon</u> in 2 hours and 45 minutes.
>> <u>Julio Carceno</u>—name of a particular person—proper noun
>>
>> <u>Boston Marathon</u>—name of a particular activity—proper noun

Collective Nouns

Collective nouns are names of groups or collections, such as *mob*, *crowd*, *committee*, or *herd*. Collective nouns may be common or proper.

> The <u>crowd</u> cheers for the home <u>team</u>.
>> <u>crowd</u>—name of a group of persons—collective noun
>>
>> <u>team</u>—name of a group of persons—collective noun
>
> The <u>Marshfield City Council</u> faces a budget shortfall this year.
>> <u>Marshfield City Council</u>—name of a group of persons—collective noun

Collective nouns may take either the singular or the plural form of the verb, depending on how they are used in a sentence. If a collective noun refers to a group acting as a whole, a singular verb is used. If a collective noun refers to a group in which the members act individually, a plural verb is used. Collective nouns usually take a singular verb.

COLLECTIVE NOUNS

TEAM

The jury has arrived at a decision.

jury—collective noun. The singular form of the verb is used because the jury, acting as a group, has arrived at a decision.

The jury are in disagreement about an important issue.

jury—collective noun. The plural form of the verb is used because the members of the jury are acting individually (they are disagreeing with one another).

Proofreading TIP

Don't proofread a document immediately after you have finished working on it. Take a break, and then come back to it with fresh eyes.

Frequently Used Collective Nouns

army	class	crowd	jury	number	school
assembly	club	faculty	legislature	office force	staff
audience	committee	family	majority	orchestra	swarm
band	company	flock	mass	panel	team
cast	congregation	gang	mob	platoon	trio
choir	corps	group	nation	police	troop
chorus	crew	herd	navy	public	

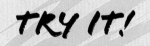

Directions Underline each noun. Check your answers on page 318 or with your instructor before continuing with your assignment.

1. Girl Scout Troop 6134 plans a field trip to a local company.

2. The Girl Scout family extends to 145 countries worldwide.

3. The troop are gathering their belongings and then meeting at the campsite.

How many common nouns are there? Proper nouns? Collective nouns?

Complete Applications 17–18, pages 35–36, at this time.

17 | Noun Identification

Directions Underline each noun. Write *c* for *common* or *p* for *proper* above the noun. Score one point for each correct identification.

Your Score

1. In our honors seminar, we learned interesting facts about leaders of the United States.   1. _____

2. Miss Robb told Joey that the teddy bear was named after Theodore Roosevelt.   2. _____

3. George Washington was elected unanimously twice.   3. _____

4. In 1863, Abraham Lincoln issued the Emancipation Proclamation.   4. _____

5. Andrew Jackson led his army to victory at the Battle of New Orleans.   5. _____

6. "Old Hickory" was the nickname given to him by his soldiers.   6. _____

7. My sister read that James Monroe was the first senator to become president.   7. _____

8. James Buchanan was the only bachelor elected to that office.   8. _____

9. Richard Nixon became the first person to resign from the presidency.   9. _____

10. When Woodrow Wilson suffered a stroke, his wife took over routine duties.   10. _____

11. After his term, William Howard Taft became Chief Justice of the United States.   11. _____

12. Four presidents are memorialized in a sculpture on Mount Rushmore.   12. _____

13. This monument is located in the Black Hills of South Dakota.   13. _____

14. The four men are Washington, Jefferson, Lincoln, and Theodore Roosevelt.   14. _____

15. Their heads were sculpted by Gutzon Borglum over a period of 14 years.   15. _____

16. William Henry Harrison died one month after his inauguration.   16. _____

17. Franklin Delano Roosevelt was elected to four terms.   17. _____

18. Herbert Hoover wrote many books.   18. _____

19. Dwight D. Eisenhower served in both World War I and World War II.   19. _____

20. Ronald Reagan appointed the first woman to the Supreme Court.   20. _____

Your Total Score _____ /64

If your score was 48 or less, review page 33 before continuing.

18 | Noun Identification

A | **Directions** Underline each noun. Write *c* for *common* or *p* for *proper* above the noun. Score one point for each correct identification.

Your Score

1. Electronic and digital technologies are used daily in businesses today.   1. _____

2. One of the first computers, ENIAC, weighed 30 tons and filled a room.   2. _____

3. Search engines provide users with a single place to find useful information.   3. _____

4. David Filo and Jerry Yang started Yahoo! as a way to track sites of interest to them

    on the Internet.   4. _____

5. They pursued their hobby in a trailer on the campus of Stanford University.   5. _____

6. Paul Allen and Bill Gates founded Microsoft.   6. _____

7. Steve Jobs and Steve Wozniak started Apple.   7. _____

8. Today these two companies are industry leaders.   8. _____

9. The Bill and Melinda Gates Foundation donates money to worthy causes.   9. _____

10. Thomas Watson, An Wang, and Ken Olsen are legendary names.   10. _____

Your Total Score _____ /36
If your score was 27 or less, review page 33 before continuing.

B | **Directions** Underline each collective noun. Score one point for each correct identification.

1. Liz Chavez spoke about computers to a large audience.   1. _____

2. The technology user group has arranged for a panel of experts to speak with us.   2. _____

3. A majority of the students use Google for their Web searches.   3. _____

4. The office force has decided to try open-source software.   4. _____

5. Dr. Holt arranged for the faculty to tour Cisco headquarters.   5. _____

6. An ad hoc committee has evaluated the various operating systems.   6. _____

7. The investment club has bought stock in Google, Microsoft, and Yahoo!   7. _____

8. A mass of prospective employees is flooding us with job applications.   8. _____

9. The school is arranging internships for students in Silicon Valley.   9. _____

10. We sent a team of students to the Computer Quiz Bowl.   10. _____

Your Total Score _____ /11
If your score was 7 or less, review pages 33–34 before continuing.

Nouns and the Plural Form

Remember that a noun names a person, a place, a thing, a concept, a quality, or an activity. It is a **singular noun** when it names one person, one place, one thing, one concept, one quality, or one activity. It is a **plural noun** when it names more than one. You must know whether a noun is singular or plural. To form the plural of nouns, remember a few rules.

Simple Plurals

Rule 1: Most nouns become plural by adding the letter *s* to the singular noun.

allowance	allowances	lemon	lemons
building	buildings	list	lists
chair	chairs	river	rivers
desk	desks	trip	trips
lake	lakes		

Rule 2: For nouns ending in *s, x, z, sh,* or *ch,* you must add *es* to form the plural.

address	addresses	hunch	hunches
box	boxes	inch	inches
bush	bushes	tax	taxes
flash	flashes	waltz	waltzes
glass	glasses		

RULES that work   Most personal names are made plural by following Rules 1 and 2.

Mrs. Weiss	the Weisses	Judge Doan	the Doans
Dana Hatch	the Hatches	Emma Bailey	the Baileys

TRY IT!

Directions Write the plural form of each noun. Check your answers on page 318 or with your instructor before continuing with your assignment.

1. wish   _____
2. monitor   _____
3. password   _____
4. fax   _____
5. batch   _____
6. department   _____

Plurals of Words with Special Endings

Rule 3 (Y-Ending Plurals): If a noun ends with a *y* preceded by a consonant, change the *y* to *i* and add *es*. If the final *y* is preceded by a vowel (*a, e, i, o, u*), add *s*.

army	armies	day	days
copy	copies	ray	rays
legacy	legacies	valley	valleys

Rule 4 (*O*-Ending Plurals): For nouns ending with an *o* preceded by a consonant, the plural is formed in different ways. For some, add *s*; for others, add *es*. For a few, either *s* or *es* is acceptable. Musical terms ending in *o* preceded by a consonant are made plural by adding *s*. Consult a dictionary if you are not sure.

echo	echoes	solo	solos
hero	heroes	tomato	tomatoes
memo	memos	veto	vetoes
photo	photos	zero	zeros or zeroes
piano	pianos		

If a noun ends with an *o* preceded by a vowel (*a, e, i, o, u*), add *s* to form the plural.

patio	patios	studio	studios
radio	radios	taboo	taboos
stereo	stereos	video	videos

Rule 5 (*F*- or *Fe*-Ending Plurals): To form the plural of most nouns ending in *f* or *fe*, change the *f* or *fe* to *v* and add *es*. For some nouns, either *s* or *es* is acceptable. Consult a dictionary if you are not sure.

knife	knives	wife	wives
life	lives	wolf	wolves
shelf	shelves	yourself	yourselves
thief	thieves		

Note these common exceptions to the above rule: *belief, beliefs; brief, briefs; chef, chefs; chief, chiefs; proof, proofs; roof, roofs; safe, safes; sheriff, sheriffs;* and *staff, staffs.*

TRY IT!

Directions Write the plural form of each noun. Check your answers on page 318 or with your instructor before continuing with your assignment.

1. hero _____
2. shelf _____
3. holiday _____
4. proof _____
5. photo _____

6. veto _____
7. self _____
8. entry _____
9. territory _____

APPLICATION   **Complete Application 19, page 41, at this time.**

Words with Irregular Plurals

The following words are among those that have no set rules for forming the plural. Some do not change at all from the singular to the plural. Many nouns with a foreign origin use their foreign plural; others have been given an additional English plural. Study these words carefully, for they are often used incorrectly.

analysis	analyses	man	men
appendix	appendixes or appendices	moose	moose
child	children	mouse	mice
deer	deer	ox	oxen
diagnosis	diagnoses	salmon	salmon
fish	fish or fishes (if different kinds of fish)	sheep	sheep
foot	feet	tooth	teeth
goose	geese	trout	trout
index	indexes or indices		

Nouns Always in Plural Form

Some nouns are always written in the plural form. The following are among the more commonly used ones:

athletics	goods	proceeds	species
clothes	pants	riches	statistics
earnings	pliers	scissors	thanks
economics	politics	series	

Some of these nouns, like *clothes*, are plural in meaning and take a plural verb. Others, like *statistics*, may take a singular or a plural verb, depending on how they are used.

Several nouns have a plural form but a singular meaning. These nouns require a singular verb.

civics	genetics	mathematics	mumps	news

TRY IT!

Directions Write the plural form of each noun. Check your answers on page 318 or with your instructor before continuing with your assignment.

1. earnings _____
2. foot _____
3. man _____

4. child _____
5. goods _____

Compound Nouns

Compound nouns consist of two or more words. Some are written as one word, some are hyphenated, and some consist of separate words.

If a compound noun is written as one word without a hyphen, the last element is made plural.

businessman	businessmen
letterhead	letterheads
stepchild	stepchildren

If a compound noun consists of separate or hyphenated words and includes a noun, make the main or base part plural.

brother-in-law	brothers-in-law	post office	post offices
cross-examination	cross-examinations	runner-up	runners-up
editor in chief	editors in chief	style sheet	style sheets
hard copy	hard copies	website	websites
mayor-elect	mayors-elect		

If no part of a hyphenated compound noun is itself a noun, the last element is made plural.

follow-up	follow-ups
trade-in	trade-ins

Other Rules

Figures and alphabetic letters are made plural by adding *s*. Isolated words are made plural by adding *s* or *es*. For some words, both plural forms are acceptable.

1990	1990s	and	ands
7	7s	no	nos or noes
B	Bs		

Isolated lowercase letters and the capital letters *A*, *I*, *M*, and *U* require *'s* for clarity.

a	a's
A	A's

Abbreviations are usually made plural by adding *s* to the singular form.

IOU	IOUs	amt.	amts.
Ph.D.	Ph.D.s	dept.	depts.

TRY IT!

Directions Write the plural form of each noun. Check your answers on page 318 or with your instructor before continuing with your assignment.

1. CEO _____
2. board of directors _____
3. acct. _____
4. run-through _____
5. 1980 _____
6. clipboard _____

APPLICATION ▶ **Complete Applications 20–21, pages 42–43, at this time.**

19 | Simple Plurals and Nouns Ending in *Y, O, F,* or *FE*

Directions Write the plural form of each noun. Score one point for each correct answer.

1. document _____

2. fly _____

3. salary _____

4. experience _____

5. agency _____

6. recess _____

7. player _____

8. key _____

9. spoonful _____

10. tie _____

11. quantity _____

12. solo _____

13. lady _____

14. duplex _____

15. Westwood _____

16. echo _____

17. cable _____

18. security _____

19. committee _____

20. brief _____

21. wish _____

22. half _____

23. party _____

24. church _____

25. city _____

26. dress _____

27. berry _____

28. computer _____

29. query _____

30. question _____

31. patio _____

32. Sanchez _____

33. bunch _____

34. studio _____

35. loaf _____

36. activity _____

37. incident _____

38. piano _____

39. wolf _____

40. testimony _____

41. community _____

42. address _____

43. class _____

44. veto _____

45. watch _____

46. boundary _____

47. hero _____

48. branch _____

49. allergy _____

50. holiday _____

Your Total Score _____ /50

If your score was 38 or less, review pages 37–38 before continuing.

20 | The Difficult Noun Plurals

Directions Write the plural form of each noun. Score one point for each correct answer.

1. life	_____	26. handkerchief	_____
2. goose	_____	27. foot	_____
3. scissors	_____	28. glassful	_____
4. chief of staff	_____	29. Alvarado	_____
5. M.B.A.	_____	30. birdhouse	_____
6. man	_____	31. sheep	_____
7. stereo	_____	32. thief	_____
8. pants	_____	33. if	_____
9. 1500	_____	34. mouse	_____
10. bookshelf	_____	35. duo	_____
11. mother-in-law	_____	36. appendix	_____
12. portfolio	_____	37. riches	_____
13. leaf	_____	38. write-off	_____
14. ox	_____	39. radio	_____
15. chief	_____	40. board of directors	_____
16. know-it-all	_____	41. index	_____
17. politics	_____	42. batch	_____
18. series	_____	43. athletics	_____
19. woman	_____	44. analysis	_____
20. tooth	_____	45. sheriff	_____
21. child	_____	46. leave of absence	_____
22. deer	_____	47. knife	_____
23. CPA	_____	48. McKay	_____
24. species	_____	49. fish	_____
25. zero	_____	50. potato	_____

Your Total Score _____ /50

If your score was 38 or less, review pages 38–40 before continuing.

21 | Noun Plurals

Directions Write the plural form of each noun. Score one point for each correct answer.

1. no-show _____
2. by-product _____
3. cupful _____
4. DVD _____
5. front-runner _____
6. toothbrush _____
7. tablespoonful _____
8. foreman _____
9. M.D. _____
10. cameo _____
11. A _____
12. photo _____
13. speech _____
14. statistics _____
15. civics _____
16. ratio _____
17. URL _____
18. currency _____
19. belief _____
20. sheep _____
21. memo _____
22. lottery _____
23. trout _____
24. fox _____
25. wharf _____

26. tomato _____
27. self _____
28. elf _____
29. moose _____
30. news _____
31. port of entry _____
32. measles _____
33. bench _____
34. briefcase _____
35. waltz _____
36. boss _____
37. thanks _____
38. wife _____
39. salmon _____
40. economics _____
41. delay _____
42. attorney _____
43. stress _____
44. 2 _____
45. calf _____
46. trolley _____
47. editor in chief _____
48. diagnosis _____
49. play-off _____
50. RN _____

Your Total Score _____ /50

If your score was 38 or less, review Section 5, pages 37–40, before continuing.

Nouns and the Possessive Form

Nouns used in the possessive form show ownership or possession. The apostrophe (') is used to show the possessive form. Guides for forming possessives follow. (For use of the apostrophe in a contraction, see page 247.)

Singular Possessive

To show the possessive form of most singular nouns, merely place the apostrophe (') after the last letter of the word and add *s*.

> The executive's briefcase was very expensive.
>
> > executive's—singular noun. The apostrophe after *executive* and before *s* tells whose briefcase it was (briefcase of the executive).
>
> Jason's aunt bought a GPS system.
>
> > Jason's—singular noun. The apostrophe after *Jason* and before *s* tells whose aunt it is (aunt of Jason).

For nouns ending in an *s*, *x*, or *z* sound, if adding an apostrophe plus *s* makes the word hard to pronounce, add just an apostrophe.

> Thomas's interests include acting, karate, and crew.
>
> > Thomas's—An apostrophe plus *s* is used because the word is not hard to pronounce.

Plural Possessive

To show the possessive form of a plural noun ending in *s*, place the apostrophe (') after the *s*.

> All the supervisors' electronic files were corrupted by a virus.
>
> > supervisors'—plural noun. The apostrophe is placed after the *s* to indicate plural possession (files of the supervisors).
>
> The nurses' strike started two weeks ago.
>
> > nurses'—plural noun. The apostrophe is placed after the *s* to indicate plural possession (strike of the nurses).

To show the possessive form of a plural noun not ending in *s*, add the apostrophe (') and the *s*.

> The children's preschool closed early on Tuesday.
>
> > children's—plural noun. The apostrophe is placed before the *s* because the plural noun does not end in *s* (preschool of the children).
>
> The geese's feathers made a trail from the nest to the pond.
>
> > geese's—plural noun. The apostrophe is placed before the *s* because the plural noun does not end in *s* (feathers of the geese).
>
> The women's dressing room at the health club was recently remodeled.
>
> > women's—plural noun. The apostrophe is placed before the *s* because the plural noun does not end in *s* (room of the women).

The plural possessive may be followed by a singular noun.

> The students' reception is scheduled for the last week of the term.
>
> > students'—plural noun. The apostrophe is placed after the *s* to indicate plural possession with a singular noun (reception of the students).

TRY IT!

A | **Directions** Rewrite each item using the singular and plural possessive. Make both nouns plural in the plural possessive. Check your answers on page 318 or with your instructor before continuing with your assignment.

	Singular Possessive	Plural Possessive
Example tire of the car	*car's tire*	*cars' tires*
1. classroom of the instructor	_____	_____
2. movie of the week	_____	_____
3. action of the nanny	_____	_____

B | **Directions** Find the noun in each sentence that requires an apostrophe ('). Write the correct possessive form of the noun with the apostrophe in the correct place. Check your answers on page 319 or with your instructor before continuing with your assignment.

1. My drivers license will expire next month.   _____

2. Sales representatives bonuses are distributed once a year.   _____

3. Some applicants rely heavily on former employers references.   _____

APPLICATION ➤ **Complete Applications 22–27, pages 46–49 and 51–52, at this time.**

WRITE NOW!

Clarity

The most important rule for effective writing is to write with clarity—to make your writing so clear that the reader will understand exactly what you want him or her to know. Here are some guidelines for achieving clarity:

- Use words that are understandable, appropriate, precise, and positive. Don't use technical terms unless the receiver of the message is familiar with the terminology.

- Present only one main thought in each sentence. If you have two thoughts to convey, write two sentences.

- Use the active voice and action verbs most of the time. (See pages 131–132 for a detailed treatment of the active voice.)

- Keep related words together; for example, be sure adjectives and adverbs are close to the words they modify.

- Write grammatically correct sentences.

Name _____   Date _____   Score _____

22 | Singular and Plural Possessives

Directions Rewrite each item using the singular and plural possessive. Make both nouns plural in the plural possessive. Score one point for each correct answer.

Examples	Singular Possessive	Plural Possessive
a. page of the book	a. *book's page*	a. *books' pages*
b. candy of the child	b. *child's candy*	b. *children's candies*
c. pencil of the secretary	c. *secretary's pencil*	c. *secretaries' pencils*
d. foot of the duck	d. *duck's foot*	d. *ducks' feet*
1. lunch of the worker	1. _____	1. _____
2. wish of the hero	2. _____	2. _____
3. file of the clerk	3. _____	3. _____
4. computer of the receptionist	4. _____	4. _____
5. toy of the baby	5. _____	5. _____
6. fee of the doctor	6. _____	6. _____
7. eye of the mouse	7. _____	7. _____
8. debt of the consumer	8. _____	8. _____
9. life of the leader	9. _____	9. _____
10. plane of the pilot	10. _____	10. _____
11. cry of the wolf	11. _____	11. _____
12. reply of the executive	12. _____	12. _____
13. den of the fox	13. _____	13. _____
14. shoe of the runner	14. _____	14. _____
15. melody of the band	15. _____	15. _____
16. liner of the shelf	16. _____	16. _____
17. sculpture of the artist	17. _____	17. _____
18. bus of the community	18. _____	18. _____
19. class of the toddler	19. _____	19. _____
20. duty of the family	20. _____	20. _____
21. echo of the valley	21. _____	21. _____
22. piano of the museum	22. _____	22. _____
23. job of the man	23. _____	23. _____
24. responsibility of the attorney	24. _____	24. _____
25. office of the programmer	25. _____	25. _____

Your Total Score _____ /50

If your score was 38 or less, review Sections 5 and 6, pages 37–40 and 44–45, before continuing.

23 | Singular and Plural Possessives

Directions Find the noun in each sentence that requires an apostrophe ('). Write the correct possessive form of the noun with the apostrophe in the correct place. Score one point for each correct answer.

Examples

Answers

a. The speakers remarks showed her to be well informed.

a. **_speaker's_** _____

b. This customers receipt was misplaced.

b. **_customer's_** _____

c. Mr. Feeneys computer developed electrical problems.

c. **_Feeney's_** _____

1. That reports conclusions call for immediate action.

1. _____

2. Linhs application was submitted after the deadline.

2. _____

3. One of Jeans aunts is the comptroller of the company.

3. _____

4. Ms. Changs duties were varied and interesting.

4. _____

5. Larrys colleagues helped him with his year-end report.

5. _____

6. Levi Kamarski voiced shareholders concerns at the annual meeting.

6. _____

7. All managers certification test results exceeded the national average.

7. _____

8. The secretaries receipts for office supplies were filed.

8. _____

9. We shouldn't change our strategy because of one elections results.

9. _____

10. Two of the pumps were in Freds shop for repairs.

10. _____

11. Lees sister was hired by Mr. Daniels.

11. _____

12. The security guards name is David Emry.

12. _____

13. This employees skills are exceptionally good.

13. _____

14. Our clients names and addresses are in this database.

14. _____

15. Both companies electric bills were lower this month.

15. _____

16. The supervisors offices are near the conference room.

16. _____

17. Most of that students papers were in order.

17. _____

18. Much of our recruiters success depends on their location.

18. _____

19. After ten years at Niko Manufacturing, you are eligible for three weeks vacation.

19. _____

20. All of Mrs. Grants marketing campaigns are successful.

20. _____

21. The Smiths catering business is doing well.

21. _____

22. The womens stores were located in four area cities.

22. _____

23. This calculator is my co-workers; he lent it to me for the day.

23. _____

24. Three vendors deliveries arrived at the stores two days late.

24. _____

25. Next years budget has been approved.

25. _____

Your Total Score _____ /25

If your score was 19 or less, review Section 6, pages 44–45, before continuing.

24 | Singular and Plural Possessives

A | **Directions** Rewrite each item using the singular and plural possessive. Make both nouns plural in the plural possessive. Score one point for each correct answer.

Examples	Singular Possessive	Plural Possessive
a. assistant of the boss	a. *boss's assistant*	a. *bosses' assistants*
b. dream of the grandfather	b. *grandfather's dream*	b. *grandfathers' dreams*
1. decision of the court	1. _____	1. _____
2. mandate of the committee	2. _____	2. _____
3. life of the product	3. _____	3. _____
4. partner of West	4. _____	4. _____
5. reporter of the newspaper	5. _____	5. _____
6. assignment of the crew	6. _____	6. _____
7. routine of the aide	7. _____	7. _____
8. phone of the girl	8. _____	8. _____
9. address of the author	9. _____	9. _____
10. salary of the CEO	10. _____	10. _____

Your Total Score _____ /20

If your score was 15 or less, review Sections 5 and 6, pages 37–40 and 44–45, before continuing.

B | **Directions** Find the noun in each sentence that requires an apostrophe ('). Write the correct possessive form of the noun with the apostrophe in the correct place. Score one point for each correct answer.

Examples   Answers

a. Getting a financial planners advice might be useful.   a. *planner's* _____

b. Joan borrowed Annies manuals on office procedures.   b. *Annie's* _____

1. Several investors questions were answered.   1. _____

2. My departments supervisor will meet the new president soon.   2. _____

3. Erics brothers kept changing jobs.   3. _____

4. Cherylls interview took an hour.   4. _____

5. Mr. Chases priority is to expand our manufacturing facility.   5. _____

6. You have to consider an options opportunity cost.   6. _____

7. The supervisor tried not to hurt Elsas feelings.   7. _____

8. Both members expense accounts were always on time.   8. _____

9. Todays business environment is very competitive.   9. _____

10. Miss Fosters paintings were displayed in the outer offices.   10. _____

Your Total Score _____ /10

If your score was 7 or less, review Section 6, pages 44–45, before continuing.

25 | Unit Review

A | **Directions** Match each definition in Column A with the item it describes in Column B. Write the identifying letter from Column A in the blank at the right. Score one point for each correct answer.

Column A	Column B	Answers
a. does not refer to a particular person, place, thing, concept, quality, or activity	1. singular noun	1. _____
b. made up of two or more words	2. possessive noun	2. _____
c. names more than one person, place, thing, concept, quality, or activity	3. compound noun	3. _____
d. shows ownership	4. apostrophe	4. _____
e. names a group or collection	5. plural noun	5. _____
f. used to show a word is possessive	6. common noun	6. _____
g. names one person, place, thing, concept quality, or activity	7. collective noun	7. _____
h. names a particular person, place, thing, or activity	8. proper noun	8. _____

Your Total Score _____ /8

B | **Directions** Find the noun in each sentence that requires an apostrophe ('). In the blank at the right, write the correct possessive form of the noun with the apostrophe in the correct place. Score one point for each correct answer.

Example

Mr. Wilsons firms often need many accountants. *Wilson's* _____

1. Mr. Latimers letter needed to be keyed. 1. _____
2. This portfolios contents include charts and graphs. 2. _____
3. Ms. Morenos inquiry resulted in an investigation. 3. _____
4. The auditors message says he'll be in next week. 4. _____
5. The graphic designers website showcases her talents. 5. _____
6. Halifaxs executives signed a contract with the government. 6. _____
7. Mr. Taylors e-mail was sent to all employees. 7. _____
8. Tess transcribed both officers reports. 8. _____
9. Kate worked for Burger Kings marketing division. 9. _____
10. One of Mr. Quintanas sons interns in our payroll department. 10. _____
11. The agencys proposal has many attractive features. 11. _____
12. That consultants specialty is conflict resolution. 12. _____

Your Total Score _____ /12

ENGLISH ON THE JOB /
Travel Agent

© Digital Vision/Getty Images

A travel agent helps clients to access and compare information so they can make the best possible travel plans. Travel agents offer advice on destinations and arrange transportation, lodging, car rentals, cruises, and tours. The biggest competition travel agents face is from travel and airline websites. However, many travelers prefer to use travel agents for convenience or for their expertise, particularly when planning complex or multiple-destination travel.

Travel agents spend the majority of their time meeting with clients, using the telephone or computer to research travel itineraries, and completing paperwork. Strong communication, interpersonal, and computer skills are essential for working in this field. It is also important to be well organized, accurate, detail-oriented, and courteous.

The nature of the work offers flexibility in terms of career choices. Computer and telecommunications technology makes it possible for an individual to be self-employed and to work at home. Some agents may choose to have an office presence to attract walk-in business, while others may opt to work for someone else.

Opportunities are strongest for travel agents who specialize in a specific destination or region, a particular demographic group, or luxury travel. The demand for services fluctuates depending on the economic and political climates. The soft skills and computer skills developed by travel agents can be applied in many other occupations.

Directions Underline each noun. Write *c* for *common* or *p* for *proper* above the noun. Score one point for each correct identification.

Your Score

1. Mrs. Johannes presented a video tour of her recent trip to Belize to a group from

   John Adams Senior Center in Rochester.   1. _____

2. The audience asked many questions about the weather, the sights, and the cost.   2. _____

3. The staff of Destinations Travel Agency moderated a panel to answer questions

   about the services a travel agency provides.   3. _____

Your Total Score _____ /18
If your score was 13 or less, review page 33 before continuing.

26 | Writing Improvement

A | **Directions** The following sentences lack clarity. Revise them to reflect the guidelines for clarity in writing presented in the WRITE Now feature on page 45.

Example Kerry just spent $100. (Does the sentence mean that Kerry spent $100 recently, or does it mean that he spent a reasonable amount?) *Kerry spent just $100.*

1. Xanni told Nancy she'd forgotten her cell phone. _____ _____ _____

   _____

2. We ate the cookies that Bill made in the car. _____ _____

   _____

3. Vinh got five As. _____ _____

4. Lot C is for our employee's use. _____

5. Keep going on this street for a while, and when you see a grocery store, turn right. (Make the directions

   more specific.) _____ _____ _____ _____ _____

   _____

   _____

B | **Directions** Add a second sentence to each sentence below. Your second sentence should relate to the first. Be sure your sentences are clear.

Example Her father's new car is a hybrid. *It gets great mileage.*

1. Meagen's music was very loud. _____

   _____

2. The group has approved the motion. _____

   _____

3. Meeting and travel costs are spiraling out of control. _____ _____ __ __

   _____

4. Tiffany's personality makes her stand out in the crowd. _____ _____

   _____

5. Sam showed me how to transfer money online from my savings account to my checking account. _____

   _____

APPLICATION **Give your completed application to your instructor for evaluation.**

Name _____ Date _____ Score _____

27 | Comprehensive Review

A | **Directions** Underline each noun. Write *c* for *common* or *p* for *proper* above the noun. Score one point for each correct identification.

Your Score

1. The Walt Disney Company employs a large number of graphic artists and animators. 1. _____

2. Adrianna designs pins for Walt Disney World Resort in Orlando. 2. _____

3. Her cousin and boyfriend visited Universal Studios, SeaWorld Orlando,

   and the Kennedy Space Center on their vacation last September. 3. _____

4. Creativity and vision are two qualities that successful animators possess. 4. _____

5. Did Junko include projects that showcase her art background and multimedia

   skills in the portfolio for her interview? 5. _____

Your Total Score _____ /25
If your score was 19 or less, review page 33 before continuing.

B | **Directions** Underline the collective nouns once and the verbs twice. Score one point for each correct identification.

1. The committee check their calendars for available meeting dates. 1. _____
2. The jury asked the judge for more time. 2. _____
3. The nation depends heavily on foreign oil. 3. _____
4. Only 55 percent of the faculty completed the survey. 4. _____
5. The U.S. Navy hosts the joint exercises every year. 5. _____

Your Total Score _____ /10
If your score was 7 or less, review pages 3, 12, and 33–34 before continuing.

C | **Directions** Rewrite each item using the singular and plural possessive. Make both nouns plural in the plural possessive. Score one point for each correct answer.

	Singular Possessive	**Plural Possessive**
Examples location of the seminar	*seminar's location*	*seminars' locations*
1. studio of the artist	1. _____	1. _____
2. analysis of the boss	2. _____	2. _____
3. entry of the dictionary	3. _____	3. _____
4. proof of the photographer	4. _____	4. _____
5. clothes of the businesswoman	5. _____	5. _____

Your Total Score _____ /10
If your score was 7 or less, review Sections 5 and 6, pages 37–40 and 44–45, before continuing.

PROOF IT!

Directions Proofread the memo, circling all errors. Write a correction above each error. Make sure the memo follows the guidelines for clarity in the WRITE Now feature on page 45. Give your completed application to your instructor for evaluation.

TO: Real Estate Department

FROM: Chris McKay, Director of Acquisitions

DATE: April 26, 2010

SUBJECT: Acquisition of Commercial Propertys

We are looking for ways to built our asset base and to increase our return on investment. In the companies strategic plan, which was released last week, our Board of Directors indicated that aquiring commercial real estate will help us reach these goals.

Over the next few months, we would like you department to locate suitable commercial propertys for purchase and possible development in the areas of San Francisco, California; Seattle, Washington; Austin, Texas; Charlotte, North Carolina; and Boston, Massachusetts. Currently, property values in these areas are depressed, and our investments would earn a good rate of return in the long run.

Once you have identified a property, prepare a feasability study that include return on investment calculations. Senior managment will then evaluate the proposal and make their decision based on the information provided.

Posttest

A | **Directions** Underline each noun. Write *c* for *common* or *p* for *proper* above the noun.

1. Only ten minutes into the interview, Leigh Ann had formed an opinion about the

   contributions Issac could make to the company.

2. The panel was looking for someone with at least five years of experience in banking.

3. The staff had prepared questions and hypothetical situations earlier.

4. Alberto copied the materials for each interviewer.

5. The directors like to have teams interview applicants.

6. Elena Vasquez was hired as the new manager of our branch.

B | **Directions** Write the plural form of each noun.

1. tax _____   4. appendix _____   7. veto _____

2. child _____   5. branch _____   8. IOU _____

3. statistics _____   6. history _____   9. shelf _____

C | **Directions** Rewrite each item using the singular and plural possessive. Make both nouns plural in the plural possessive.

	Singular Possessive	**Plural Possessive**
Examples suit of the man	*man's suit*	*men's suits*
1. ring of the woman		
2. overpass of the highway		
3. contribution of the employee		
4. heading of the newspaper		
5. idea of the genius		

unit 3
Pronouns

Objectives

1. To understand the function of a pronoun in a sentence
2. To recognize the different types of pronouns
3. To write clear and concise sentences and paragraphs using pronouns correctly

Sections

Pretest

Directions If the underlined pronoun or pronouns are correct, write *C* in the blank at the right. If they are incorrect, write the correct pronoun.

1. The agreement was reviewed by Mr. Morales and <u>I</u> yesterday.

1. _____

2. <u>Us</u> employees will receive a bonus in December.

2. _____

3. One of the women left <u>her</u> coat at the banquet.

3. _____

4. It was <u>me</u> who placed the order for new office furniture.

4. _____

5. <u>Both</u> of the bids provides for days lost due to bad weather.

5. _____

6. The person to <u>whom</u> the speaker referred was Mr. Stanton.

6. _____

7. <u>Whose</u> proposal was adopted?

7. _____

8. Compuland is having <u>it's</u> largest year-end sale ever.

8. _____

9. The team was recognized for <u>their</u> contribution.

9. _____

10. Every attendee found <u>his</u> or <u>her</u> chair.

10. _____

WORKPLACE FOCUS

Teamwork

Teamwork skills are essential in any job or career. The underlying concept of a team is that people working together toward a common goal can achieve more than an individual can by working alone. Teams bring a greater pool of knowledge, experiences, abilities, and perspectives to any task or problem. No individual can know everything and have all the answers, but sharing information can lead to better decisions and a commitment to the solution.

Teamwork has many benefits for organizations, such as improved quality of products and services and improved productivity. Teams are flexible; they can be quickly assembled, organized, refocused, and dispersed once a task has been completed. Cross-functional teams made up of members representing the various areas of an organization are one of the most common types of teams in business today.

Employees also benefit from being part of a team. There is, for example, the emotional bond and sense of belonging and contributing that team members feel.

Effective teams (1) recognize that each member has something to contribute to the team effort, (2) formulate team objectives carefully and take them seriously, and (3) support one another and the common goal of the group. There is no limit to the potential of a good team. Remember, *T.E.A.M.—together, everyone achieves more.*

Section 7 **Personal Pronouns**

Personal pronouns are used in place of the person or persons speaking (*I, me, we, us*), in place of the person or persons spoken to (*you*), and in place of the person, persons, thing, or things spoken of (*he, him, she, her, it, its, they, them*). Personal pronouns replace nouns.

Personal Pronouns

	Singular	**Plural**
1st person	I, me, my, mine	we, us, our, ours
2nd person	you, your, yours	you, your, yours
3rd person	he, him, his, she, her, hers, it, its	they, them, their, theirs

Person speaking: <u>I</u> bought a new computer.

Person spoken to: <u>You</u> negotiated an excellent price.

Person spoken of: <u>He</u> installed security software on the new computer.

Pronoun Agreement in Person, Number, and Gender

The **antecedent** is the word or words to which the pronoun refers. A pronoun must agree with its antecedent in person (first, second, or third), number (singular or plural), and gender (masculine, feminine, or neuter). **Agreement** means that the words match in form. If the antecedent is singular, a singular form of the pronoun is used. If the antecedent is plural, a plural form of the pronoun is used.

Raul finished <u>his</u> paper over the weekend.

> <u>his</u>—singular pronoun—agrees in person, number, and gender with the antecedent *Raul*

Audra distributes <u>her</u> survey at shopping malls.

> <u>her</u>—singular pronoun—agrees in person, number, and gender with the antecedent *Audra*

Calvin and Nasreen key <u>their</u> papers in the computer lab.

> <u>their</u>—plural pronoun—agrees in person and number with the antecedent *Calvin and Nasreen*

The students arrived early for <u>their</u> group presentation.

> <u>their</u>—plural pronoun—agrees in person and number with the antecedent *students*

Avoid using *his* or *her* to refer to persons when the antecedent does not indicate gender. You can instead change the wording from singular to plural, eliminate the pronoun, or use *his or her*. You can also alternate use of the masculine and feminine pronouns.

Avoid	A good doctor listens to his patients.
Use	Good doctors listen to their patients.
	A good doctor listens to patients.
	A good doctor listens to his or her patients.

Case Forms of Personal Pronouns

The three case forms of personal pronouns are nominative, objective, and possessive.

The nominative case pronouns (*I, you, he, she, it, we, they*) are used as subjects or as predicate pronouns.

The objective case pronouns (*me, you, him, her, it, us, them*) are used as objects of verbs, indirect objects, or objects of prepositions.

The possessive case pronouns (*my, mine, your, yours, his, her, hers, its, our, ours, their, theirs*) are used to show ownership.

Nominative Case

Pronouns (and nouns) used as subjects are in the nominative case. The subject noun is the person, place, or thing spoken of. The subject pronoun, however, may be the person, place, or thing spoken of or the person spoken to or speaking.

Nominative Case Pronouns (Subject Pronouns)

	Singular	**Plural**
First person	I	we
Second person	you	you
Third person	he, she, it	they

I create websites for my clients.

> I—person speaking—subject—nominative case

You learned how to operate the new system.

> You—person spoken to—subject—nominative case

She taught Jon how to bookmark frequently visited websites.

> She—person spoken of—subject—nominative case

Personal pronouns may be used in compound subjects. Use the plural form of the verb with most compound subjects. (See page 102 for a discussion of the plural form with compound subjects.)

He and his cousin buy computer magazines.

> He—singular pronoun. Since it is used with the word *cousin* as part of the compound subject, a plural verb is required.

When a pronoun (or noun) is used after a verb and refers to the same person or thing as the subject of the verb, it is called a predicate pronoun (or noun). A predicate pronoun (or noun) appears in the predicate—the part of the sentence that comprises everything that is said about the subject, including the verb and any related words. A predicate pronoun means the same thing as the subject to which it refers and is in the nominative case.

Predicate pronouns follow a form of the verb *be*. Forms of *be* are called linking verbs because they link a subject with a predicate noun, pronoun, or adjective. (See pages 93–94 for a discussion of the use of linking verbs with predicate nouns, pronouns, and adjectives.)

Linking Verbs Used with Predicate Pronouns

be	am	is	are
was	were	has been	have been
had been	shall be	will be	shall have been
will have been			

It was he who designed the brochure.

> he—predicate pronoun—nominative case—follows the linking verb *was* and refers to the subject *It*

The most popular speaker is <u>she</u>.

> she—predicate pronoun—nominative case—follows the linking verb *is* and refers to the subject *speaker*

The new officers will be Shelly and <u>I</u>.

> I—predicate pronoun—nominative case—follows the linking verb *will be* and refers, with the predicate noun *Shelly*, to the subject *officers*

TRY IT!

Directions Underline the nominative case pronoun in each sentence. Check your answers on page 319 or with your instructor before continuing with your assignment.

1. They made appointments to get physicals.
2. Erik and he are the night-duty nurses.
3. The most experienced cardiologist is she.
4. Daniel and I are completing our internship rotation.
5. It took only ten minutes for the ambulance to arrive.

Write a sentence using the pronoun *they* and a second sentence using the pronoun *I*.

A. _____

B. _____

APPLICATION **Complete Application 28, page 64, at this time.**

Objective Case

Pronouns (and nouns) are in the objective case if they are used as direct objects, objects of prepositions, or indirect objects.

Objective Case Pronouns

	Singular	Plural
First person	me	us
Second person	you	you
Third person	him, her, it	them

A **direct object** receives the action of the verb. It answers the question *what* or *whom*.

Did you ask <u>her</u> for a copy of the advertisement?

> her—direct object—objective case—receives the action of the verb *ask* and answers the question *whom*—ask whom?

A recruiter told <u>us</u> about the requirements for the job.

> us—direct object—objective case—receives the action of the verb *told* and answers the question *whom*—told whom?

The accountant puts <u>it</u> in the spreadsheet.

> it—direct object—objective case—receives the action of the verb *puts* and answers the question *what*—puts what?

RULES that work

When a personal pronoun modifies a noun, how can you tell whether to use the nominative (*we athletes*) or objective (*us athletes*) case? Mentally omit the noun.

- **She gave (<u>us</u> or <u>we</u>?) employees the afternoon off.**
  (Mentally omit *employees*. The sentence becomes *She gave us the afternoon off*. <u>us</u>—objective case)

- **(<u>We</u> or Us?) students receive movie passes.**
  Mentally omit *students*. The sentence becomes *We receive movie passes*. <u>We</u>—nominative case)

A pronoun (or noun) that follows a preposition is the object of the preposition. This pronoun (or noun) must be in the objective case. (See page 198 for a list of prepositions.)

The instructor goes with <u>him</u> to the lab.

<u>him</u>—object of the preposition *with*—objective case

The project was divided among <u>them</u>.

<u>them</u>—object of the preposition *among*—objective case

A manager talked to <u>me</u> for an hour about the new project.

<u>me</u>—object of the preposition *to*—objective case

An indirect object indirectly receives the action of the verb. It answers the question *to whom, for whom, to what,* or *for what* something is done.

His brother gave <u>him</u> a new MP3 player.

<u>him</u>—indirect object—objective case—answers the question *to whom*—gave a player to whom? (The preposition *to* is omitted.)

Ms. Lee sends <u>me</u> e-mail every day.

<u>me</u>—indirect object—objective case—answers the question *to whom*—sends e-mail to whom? (The preposition *to* is omitted.)

The company buys <u>them</u> airline tickets.

<u>them</u>—indirect object—objective case—answers the question *for whom*—bought airline tickets for whom? (The preposition *for* is omitted.)

In both the nominative and the objective case, pairs of pronouns can be used in teams. The following is a list of common pairs of pronouns:

Nominative	Objective
he and she	him and her
he and we	him and us
she and I	her and me
she and they	her and them
we and they	us and them
they and I	them and me

A pronoun (or noun) that follows *than* or *as* can be in the nominative or the objective case, depending on its use. When part of a clause has been left out but is understood, the clause must be completed mentally in order to determine the correct use of the pronoun (or noun).

She studies as hard as I (study).

She likes him as well as (she likes) me.

She speaks faster than I (speak).

He talks to them more than I (talk to them).

He talks to them more than (he talks to) me.

✓ RULES that work

To choose the correct pronoun in a compound object, mentally omit the part of the compound object that does not contain the pronoun.

- **The taxi driver took Caryn and (me or I?) home.**
  (Mentally omit *Caryn and*. The sentence now becomes *The taxi driver took me home.* me— objective case)

- **Mr. Lin sits with Quinn and (me or I?).**
  (Mentally omit *Quinn and*. The sentence now becomes *Mr. Lin sat with me.* me—objective case)

TRY IT!

Directions Underline the objective case pronoun in each sentence. In the blank at the right, write *DO* if the pronoun is a direct object, *IO* if it is an indirect object, or *OP* if it is the object of a preposition. Check your answers on page 319 or with your instructor before continuing with your assignment.

1. Gavin questioned her about the new prescription.   1. _____

2. Medical files are confidential; do not share them with others.   2. _____

3. The doctor gave us instructions for postoperative care.   3. _____

4. You should check on him hourly after the surgery.   4. _____

5. Dr. Fraser e-mailed his post-op notes to us.   5. _____

6. Aldo showed Morgan and me four versions of the new uniform.   6. _____

Write three sentences using the pronoun *them* as a direct object, the object of a preposition, and an indirect object.

A. _____

B. _____

C. _____

APPLICATION **Complete Application 29, page 65, at this time.**

Possessive Case

Pronouns (and nouns) showing ownership are in the possessive case. Do not use an apostrophe with possessive case personal pronouns. *Its* (no apostrophe) is the possessive form of the personal pronoun *it*. Possessive pronouns are often used as adjectives and when so used are called possessive adjectives. (See page 172 for a discussion of possessive adjectives.)

Possessive Case Pronouns

	Singular	Plural
First person	my, mine	our, ours
Second person	your, yours	your, yours
Third person	his, her, hers, its	their, theirs

Mine is the report with graphs in color.

> Mine—possessive pronoun—shows ownership

Yours is the longest report.

> Yours—possessive pronoun—shows ownership

The company opened its fifth store.

> its—possessive pronoun used as an adjective—tells whose store

The shareholders vote for their new board of directors.

> their—personal pronoun—possessive case—tells whose board of directors

Her father owns a medical supply company.

> Her—possessive pronoun used as an adjective—tells whose father

Verb forms ending in *ing* and used as nouns are called verbal nouns or gerunds. Pronouns modifying verbal nouns are in the possessive case (*my, his, her, its, our, their, your*).

Her talking about the merger violated the confidentiality agreement.

> Her—possessive pronoun—modifies the verbal noun *talking*

His dealing with the situation so promptly pleased me.

> His—possessive pronoun—modifies the verbal noun *dealing*

Their wanting an exclusive listing for the property is a problem.

> Their—possessive pronoun—modifies the verbal noun *wanting*

proofreading **TIP**

The spell checker (which includes a grammar and style checker) can be a very useful tool. Follow these tips for effective spell checking:

- Read each item the spell checker presents to you. Do not just click through the items.

- Be aware that the spell checker will not recognize words that are not in its dictionary, like proper names; words that are spelled correctly but used incorrectly, like *to* instead of *too*; and certain keyboarding errors, such as *ice* when you meant to key *nice*.

- Be aware that the grammar and style checker does not detect all grammar and style errors, and occasionally, the changes it suggests are incorrect.

WRITE NOW!

Conciseness

Effective writing is concise. It uses only those words that are needed to convey the message and no more. Concise messages are stronger than wordy messages. In addition, being concise shows respect for the reader's time. Conciseness does not mean using only short sentences, however. You should use both shorter and longer sentences to add interest to your writing. The following tips will help you write concise messages:

- Repeat a word only if necessary for clarity or emphasis.
- Omit redundant words (words that say the same thing).
- Delete important-sounding phrases that add nothing to the meaning.
- Use the active voice when appropriate. (For a discussion of the active voice, see pages 131–132.)
- Condense your writing. (Instead of *He is a man who enjoys golf*, try *He enjoys golf*.)

TRY IT!

Directions Replace the word or words in parentheses with the correct possessive case pronoun. Check your answers on page 319 or with your instructor before continuing with your assignment.

Example   (Your and my) son is in the recovery room.   _____*Our*_____

1. (Jane's) explanation for treating a burn is very clear.   1. _____

2. Patients need to have (patients') questions answered before going into surgery.   2. _____

3. (Belonging to you) cardiac care team is the best in the hospital.   3. _____

4. Dr. Sofia Smith is often praised for (Dr. Sofia Smith's) bedside manner.   4. _____

5. (Don's) walking up and down hills aggravated the injury.   5. _____

6. (Abigail's) are the only patient charts missing.   6. _____

Write a sentence using the possessive case of the pronoun *it* and a second sentence using the possessive pronoun *our*.

A. _____

B. _____

APPLICATION > **Complete Applications 30–33, pages 66–69, at this time.**

28 | Nominative Case Pronouns

A | **Directions** Underline the nominative case pronoun in each sentence. In the blank at the right, write *S* if the pronoun is a subject or *PP* if it is a predicate pronoun. Score one point for each correct pronoun and one point for each correct identification.

Answers

1. She researched the job outlook for police officers.

1. _____

2. The most experienced officer is he.

2. _____

3. Arturo and you will demonstrate the proper technique for sit-ups.

3. _____

4. He is the first person in his family to attend college.

4. _____

5. The person selected to speak at the graduation ceremony was she.

5. _____

B | **Directions** If the underlined pronoun is correct, write *C* in the blank at the right. If it is incorrect, write the correct pronoun. Score one point for each correct answer.

1. You and <u>me</u> will attend the police academy together.

1. _____

2. Shizuyo and <u>him</u> are studying for the test on arrest procedures.

2. _____

3. <u>It</u> took more time to complete than anticipated.

3. _____

4. The fastest runners are Kevin and <u>me</u>.

4. _____

5. It wasn't <u>him</u> who won the mile run.

5. _____

6. Alex and <u>she</u> practice reciting the Miranda rights.

6. _____

7. It was <u>him</u> who scored the highest on the fitness exam.

7. _____

8. Scott and <u>her</u> are the strongest and most agile cadets.

8. _____

9. John and <u>them</u> set the pace for the 15-mile endurance run.

9. _____

10. It must have been <u>she</u> who ordered the bottles of water.

10. _____

11. Was that <u>her</u> who went for a run before breakfast?

11. _____

12. The captain and <u>she</u> are measuring the cadets for their uniforms.

12. _____

13. I think it was <u>her</u> who gave the demonstration on subduing a suspect.

13. _____

14. Could the law instructors be <u>them</u>?

14. _____

15. If you were <u>he</u>, would you attend the academy in Denver or the one in Colorado Springs?

15. _____

Your Total Score _____/25

If your score was 19 or less for A and B, review "Nominative Case," pages 58–59, before continuing.

29 | Objective Case Pronouns

A | **Directions** Underline the objective case pronoun in each sentence. In the blank at the right, write *DO* if the pronoun is a direct object, *IO* if it is an indirect object, or *OP* if it is the object of a preposition. Score one point for each correct pronoun and one point for each correct identification.

Answers

1. She sent them an updated schedule for the business ethics seminar.   1. _____

2. They wrote me a short introduction for the keynote speaker.   2. _____

3. The intellectual property lawyer went with him to court.   3. _____

4. If a document is confidential, do not share it with anyone.   4. _____

5. Sok talked to me about posting our mission statement.   5. _____

6. Did you tell him about the stock option plan available to employees?   6. _____

7. Stories on unethical corporate behavior in the paper each day shock me.   7. _____

8. Both of us spoke about what constitutes a conflict of interest.   8. _____

9. Dr. Thornton assigned Michelle and me a case study on Moxton Inc.   9. _____

10. Mai explained for us the difference between *immoral* and *unethical*.   10. _____

B | **Directions** If the underlined pronoun is correct, write *C* in the blank at the right. If it is incorrect, write the correct pronoun. Score one point for each correct answer.

1. Mr. Colt and <u>she</u> often speak about healthful living.   1. _____

2. They provided <u>he</u> and Miguel with a good work environment.   2. _____

3. We learned about a number of stress reducers from <u>them</u>.   3. _____

4. Hard work helps <u>you</u> get ahead on the job.   4. _____

5. Overexercising is a problem for <u>her</u> and other beginners.   5. _____

6. Alyssa and <u>me</u> told the new assistant about the company's wellness program.   6. _____

7. <u>Her</u> and Mr. Guerrero gave Frank several hints on exercise.   7. _____

8. Kaylee makes <u>us</u> healthy lunches.   8. _____

9. Ms. Wu and <u>we</u> trainers focus on nutrition as well as exercise.   9. _____

10. The personal trainers created a health program for you and <u>I</u>.   10. _____

11. We exercise daily with <u>them</u> and a trainer.   11. _____

12. The trainer will start you and <u>me</u> on the weight machine.   12. _____

Your Total Score _____ /32

If your score was 24 or less for A and B, review "Objective Case," pages 58–61, before continuing.

30 | Possessive Case Pronouns

A | Directions Underline the correct possessive case pronoun in parentheses. Score one point for each correct answer.

Your Score

1. Can you see the long-term effects of (him, his) spending?   1. _____
2. Identity theft and (its, it's) far-reaching impact can change lives.   2. _____
3. (Us, Our) adding a financial literacy course was a good idea.   3. _____
4. My credit card has a lower interest rate than (yours, your's).   4. _____
5. Nicole does not know the interest rate on (hers, her's).   5. _____

B | Directions Replace the word or words in parentheses with the correct possessive case pronoun. Score one point for each correct answer.

Example

Answers

Connor pays (Connor's) credit card bill in full each month.   ___*his*___

1. Teachers report that many of (belonging to them) students are financially illiterate.   1. _____
2. (Belonging to you) children can start (belonging to them) financial education early by earning an allowance.   2. _____ _____
3. Vanessa gives (Vanessa's) daughter an allowance each week for doing assigned chores.   3. _____
4. Ed teaches (Ed's) son Rick the difference between wants and needs.   4. _____
5. Phillip wrote down (Phillip's) expenditures for two weeks.   5. _____
6. Phillip could see where (Phillip's) money was being spent.   6. _____
7. He now has a better understanding of (the money's) value.   7. _____
8. Samantha designed a realistic monthly budget for (Samantha's) son.   8. _____
9. Allyson revises (Allyson's) short-term financial goals every year.   9. _____
10. Dominic and Lana showed (Dominic and Lana's) children how $5 a month can increase over time.   10. _____
11. How parents manage (belonging to them) money can be an example.   11. _____
12. Mr. Jefferson taught (Mr. Jefferson's) class how to comparison shop.   12. _____
13. Marilee puts half of (Marilee's) earnings into a savings account.   13. _____
14. She could see (the savings account's) growth after only a few months.   14. _____
15. What are (belonging to you) long-term financial goals?   15. _____
16. How much is in (your and my) emergency cash reserve?   16. _____
17. (Claire's) college offers a course in personal finance.   17. _____
18. Many young adults do not think about planning for (belonging to them) retirement.   18. _____
19. Mike did not pay off (Mike's) credit card balance last month.   19. _____
20. A credit card's minimum payment rises as (the card's) interest rate does.   20. _____

Your Total Score _____ /26

If your score was 20 or less for A and B, review "Possessive Case," pages 62–63, before continuing.

31 | Pronoun Practice for Person, Number, Gender, and Case

Directions Underline the correct pronoun or pronouns in parentheses. Score one point for each correct answer.

Your Score

1. Ms. Eagan and (I, me) received updated job descriptions.   1. _____

2. Colleen Hayes from the Bureau of Labor Statistics gave (her, their) report.   2. _____

3. Was he concerned about (you, your) losing the job?   3. _____

4. Could the new owners be Jackson and (he, him)?   4. _____

5. For outstanding work, they and (we, us) were given a raise.   5. _____

6. How can it be (he, him) who won the trip?   6. _____

7. We kept the report in our desk without (them, their) knowing it.   7. _____

8. We have our copy; send (theirs, their's) to the business address.   8. _____

9. Kim Tran and (she, her) will identify prospective committee members.   9. _____

10. Ms. Ortiz helped her and (I, me) prepare the presentation.   10. _____

11. The assistant and (they, them) often work late into the evening.   11. _____

12. Patti tries harder than (she, her).   12. _____

13. Special insurance rates were offered to (we, us) hospital employees.   13. _____

14. Mr. and Ms. Ashe celebrated (his or her, their) twenty-fifth wedding anniversary. 14. _____

15. After outlining the plan, Lucy described (its, it's) benefits.   15. _____

16. The work was divided between Betty and (I, me).   16. _____

17. Contracts were sent to Elizabeth Flatley and (she, her).   17. _____

18. Carla and Danielle enjoy (her, their) work.   18. _____

19. Roberto and Todd received (his, their) bonuses.   19. _____

20. No one understands the current situation better than (I, me).   20. _____

21. The two accountants are Joe and (he, him).   21. _____

22. (Him, His) wanting to work there was understandable.   22. _____

23. Mr. D'Agostini sent Lois and (I, me) a fax.   23. _____

24. Madison is often mistaken for (she, her).   24. _____

25. Michael heard about (me, my) starting a new at-home business.   25. _____

Your Total Score _____ /25

If your score was 19 or less, review "Case Forms of Personal Pronouns," pages 57–63, before continuing.

32 | Pronoun Practice for Person, Number, and Case

Directions Underline the correct pronoun or pronouns in parentheses. Score one point for each correct answer.

Your Score

1. Ted and (she, her) bought a new laptop computer with their income tax refund.   1. _____

2. At the meeting, Jim sat between Celina and (I, me).   2. _____

3. A wise investor understands (his or her, their) investments.   3. _____

4. (Him, His) speaking about the profit-sharing program was a good idea.   4. _____

5. Because (we, us) investors didn't know, she told us about hard money.   5. _____

6. The investment manager told him and (they, them) about money markets.   6. _____

7. The right to manufacture this new product is (ours, our's).   7. _____

8. Arun showed Jia and (I, me) how to choose a password.   8. _____

9. (Its, It's) purpose is to help us work more efficiently.   9. _____

10. (Me, My) allowing extra time to complete the project was wise.   10. _____

11. It must have been (she, her) who planned the workshops.   11. _____

12. The difference between a financial analyst and a financial specialist was explained to her and (I, me).   12. _____

13. We were worried about (you, your) leaving the meeting early.   13. _____

14. The branch office provides a work space for you and (he, him).   14. _____

15. We and (they, them) know that it takes 150 hours of training to receive a Class A license.   15. _____

16. Mr. Ochi, a stockbroker, knows more about the stock market than (I, me).   16. _____

17. Is the new district manager Shelley or (he, him)?   17. _____

18. The profits are all (theirs, their's).   18. _____

19. Alice gave Mr. Vega and (I, me) ideas for the fund-raiser.   19. _____

20. (We, Us) project administrators know that most of the work is done by the programmers.   20. _____

21. The most promising candidate is (she, her).   21. _____

22. Taurean handed Brian and (I, me) agendas.   22. _____

23. (She, Her) and (I, me) proposed an orientation program for new hires.   23. _____

24. Ms. Jaden and Mrs. Ross donated (her, their) frequent flyer miles.   24. _____

25. Three employees took (his or her, their) vacations in June.   25. _____

Your Total Score _____ /26

If your score was 20 or less, review "Case Forms of Personal Pronouns," pages 57–63, before continuing.

33 | Pronoun Practice for Person, Number, and Case

Directions Underline the correct personal pronoun in parentheses. Score one point for each correct answer.

Your Score

1. They told (we, us) the National Park Service was created by an act of Congress. 1. _____

2. Did Annika and (she, her) buy an annual pass for the national park system? 2. _____

3. My brothers and (I, me) attended a reenactment of the Battle of Gettysburg. 3. _____

4. Hank and (he, him) videotaped the battle for their fathers. 4. _____

5. (Me, My) filming the battle from behind the line of fire provided an interesting perspective. 5. _____

6. It must be (she, her) who will transfer the video to a DVD. 6. _____

7. She told Jun and (I, me) about the bears she saw at Katmai National Park and Preserve. 7. _____

8. Tammy and (I, me) were fascinated to discover that a saguaro cactus can store up to 200 gallons of water. 8. _____

9. Many of (we, us) students learned a lot about Carlsbad Cavern. 9. _____

10. Carol, Dennis, and (I, me) were amazed that the temperature in Crystal Cave is a constant 48 degrees. 10. _____

11. Did Karina and (they, them) get a chance to hike? 11. _____

12. Protecting the natural beauty of the Everglades is important to Sergio and (I, me). 12. _____

13. (Them, Their) reading about the park made our visit more enjoyable. 13. _____

14. Ms. Fogarty showed a film with commentary by Min and (she, her). 14. _____

15. They and (he, him) were amazed by the diversity of animal and plant life in the desert. 15. _____

16. Did Mr. Salcedo and (they, them) show you the new trails? 16. _____

17. What do you think of (me, my) driving through the desert? 17. _____

18. That evening, Mike Harada read a poem to (we, us) campers. 18. _____

19. The person who has visited the most national parks is (he, him). 19. _____

20. Carl goes camping more than (I, me). 20. _____

21. (Them, Their) training for rigorous hikes prepared them for the Royal Arch trail in the Grand Canyon. 21. _____

22. The beauty and size of the Grand Canyon humbled and amazed Curt and (she, her). 22. _____

23. Eduardo and (they, them) told us the South Rim is open 365 days a year. 23. _____

24. Tanya recommended that you and (I, me) take photographs either early or late in the day for the best light. 24. _____

25. Kyle, Christine, and (we, us) are planning a trip to Flagstaff, Arizona. 25. _____

Your Total Score _____ /25

If your score was 19 or less, review "Case Forms of Personal Pronouns," pages 57–63, before continuing.

Indefinite Pronouns

Identification of Indefinite Pronouns

An **indefinite pronoun** is a pronoun that does not define or stand for a particular person, place, thing, concept, quality, or activity. Many indefinite pronouns express some idea of quantity. These are common indefinite pronouns:

all	each	many	other
another	either	none	several
both	everyone	one	some

Everyone will attend the job fair.

> Everyone—indefinite pronoun used as the subject of the verb *will attend*—refers to no particular person

Many train for a specific job, but few are chosen for that job.

> Many—indefinite pronoun used as the subject of the verb *train*—refers to no particular persons
>
> few—indefinite pronoun used as the subject of the verb *are chosen*—refers to no particular persons

They appointed someone with limited banking experience.

> someone—indefinite pronoun used as the direct object of the verb *appointed*—refers to no particular person

Indefinite pronouns are often used as adjectives (when they are followed by a noun).

> Several girls took CPR training, and all girls received certificates.
>
> > Several—indefinite pronoun used as an adjective—modifies the noun *girls*
> >
> > all—indefinite pronoun used as an adjective—modifies the noun *girls*

> Each project manager has a good salary.
>
> > Each—indefinite pronoun used as an adjective—modifies the noun *project manager*

Singular and Plural Indefinite Pronouns

Some indefinite pronouns are always singular, some are always plural, and some may be singular or plural. The following indefinite pronouns are always singular:

another	either	neither	other
anybody	everybody	no one	somebody
anyone	everyone	nobody	someone
anything	everything	nothing	something
each	much	one	

Something is wrong with the copier.

> Something—singular indefinite pronoun—takes a singular verb

The following indefinite pronouns are always plural:

both	few	many	others	several

Both are representing our region at the sales conference.

> Both—plural indefinite pronoun—takes a plural verb

Be careful of these indefinite pronouns. They can be singular or plural, depending on the context.

all	any	more	most	none	some

The directors will speak at the meeting. <u>Most</u> have computer presentations.

> <u>Most</u>—indefinite pronoun—refers to *directors*. *Directors* is plural, so *Most* is plural and takes a plural verb.

<u>Most</u> of the ice has melted.

> <u>Most</u>—indefinite pronoun—refers to *ice*. *Ice* is singular, so *Most* is singular and takes a singular verb.

(See pages 105–106 for a discussion of verb agreement with indefinite pronouns.)

Indefinite Pronouns as Antecedents

Pronouns must agree in number with their antecedents. (Remember that the antecedent is the word or words to which the pronoun refers.) When an indefinite pronoun serves as an antecedent, the personal pronoun must agree in number with the indefinite pronoun.

<u>Each</u> is in <u>its</u> own package.

> <u>its</u>—singular personal pronoun—refers to the singular antecedent *Each*

<u>One</u> of the men has <u>his</u> own company credit card.

> <u>his</u>—singular personal pronoun—refers to the singular antecedent *One*

<u>Several</u> bring <u>their</u> laptops to lectures.

> <u>their</u>—plural personal pronoun—refers to the plural antecedent *Several*

<u>None</u> of the customers received <u>their</u> rebate checks.

> <u>their</u>—plural personal pronoun—refers to the antecedent *None*, an indefinite pronoun that may be singular or plural. *None* refers to *customers*, which is plural, so *None* is plural.

TRY IT!

Directions Underline the indefinite pronoun in each sentence. In the blank at the right, write *S* if it is used as a subject, *O* if it is used as an object, or *A* if it is used as an adjective. Check your answers on page 319 or with your instructor before continuing with your assignment.

1. Both of us turned in our reports before the deadline.   1. _____
2. Several internship opportunities are posted in the placement office.   2. _____
3. Many marketing managers are required to attend product shows.   3. _____
4. None of them attended the trade show held over the holidays.   4. _____
5. The team leader asks everyone to contribute ideas.   5. _____

APPLICATION ▶ **Complete Applications 34–36, pages 72–74, at this time.**

34 | Indefinite Pronoun Identification

Directions Underline the indefinite pronoun in each sentence. In the blank at the right, write *S* if it is used as a subject, *O* if it is used as an object, or *A* if it is used as an adjective. Score one point for each correct answer.

Answers

1. The supervisor distributed the packets to all of them.   1. _____

2. Nobody caught the error in the amount of the insurance premium.   2. _____

3. None of the bids are satisfactory.   3. _____

4. Brad suggested one solution to the problem.   4. _____

5. Cynthia sent everybody a benefits election form.   5. _____

6. Any employee can choose the reduced workload option.   6. _____

7. Each of the options has advantages and disadvantages.   7. _____

8. No one notified us about the buyout option.   8. _____

9. Is anybody considering retirement?   9. _____

10. Either plan is acceptable to me.   10. _____

11. The new proposal generated much discussion.   11. _____

_____

12. Some people experience a serious mood change when the seasons change; this is known
    as seasonal affective disorder (SAD).   12. _____

13. For most sufferers, symptoms appear in the late fall or early winter.   13. _____

14. For others, the onset is in late spring or early summer.   14. _____

15. Anyone in the southern or northern hemisphere can experience SAD.   15. _____

16. Many physicians agree that the most common symptom is depression.   16. _____

17. Light therapy may benefit someone with SAD.   17. _____

18. Both of the women were diagnosed with SAD in November.   18. _____

19. Neither experienced any side effects from light therapy.   19. _____

20. Nothing has been discovered to prevent the onset of SAD.   20. _____

21. A few of the symptoms are fatigue, anxiety, and weight gain.   21. _____

22. More women than men suffer from SAD.   22. _____

23. Several students decided to do their research project on SAD.   23. _____

24. They surveyed everyone in the senior class.   24. _____

25. We added another question to the survey before administering it.   25. _____

Your Total Score _____ /25

If your score was 19 or less, review Section 8, pages 70–71, before continuing.

35 | Indefinite Pronoun Agreement

Directions Underline the correct pronoun or pronouns in parentheses. Score one point for each correct answer.

Your Score

1. If someone fails to make (his or her, their) payments, finance charges will accrue. 1. _____

2. Several were relieved at the end of (his or her, their) tests. 2. _____

3. Each of the classes has (its, their) own representatives. 3. _____

4. Something is broken on this computer, and (it, they) can't be fixed. 4. _____

5. Both of the operating systems have (its, their) advantages. 5. _____

6. Neither of the women brought (her, their) resume. 6. _____

7. Most of the night shift workers documented (his or her, their) fatigue. 7. _____

8. Many use (his or her, their) credit cards to pay student loans. 8. _____

9. All of the employees in the company will remember (his or her, their) first day. 9. _____

10. Before somebody applies for a job, (he or she, they) should learn about the company. 10. _____

11. One of the girls made (her, their) best presentation ever. 11. _____

12. If either of the companies chooses to terminate the contract, (it, they) should notify the other company within ten days. 12. _____

13. More of the customers exceeded (his or her, their) credit limit. 13. _____

14. Everybody should pay (his or her, their) credit card bill in full to avoid interest charges. 14. _____

15. Much is left to be done, but (it, they) can wait until tomorrow. 15. _____

16. Anyone can request (his or her, their) credit report online. 16. _____

17. None of the cardholders realized how high (his or her, their) interest rates were. 17. _____

18. No one knew (he or she, they) could ask for a reduced interest rate. 18. _____

19. The others bring (his or her, their) lunches to conferences. 19. _____

20. You can order anything, and (it, they) will be delivered on time. 20. _____

21. Some of the speakers left (his or her, their) coats in the meeting room. 21. _____

22. Anybody can manage (his or her, their) credit cards wisely. 22. _____

23. Few of the attendees have voiced (his or her, their) opinion of Daryl's speech. 23. _____

24. Everyone should cut up (his or her, their) expired credit cards. 24. _____

25. Any of the managers can use (his or her, their) corporate credit card. 25. _____

Your Total Score _____ /25

If your score was 19 or less, review Section 8, pages 70–71, before continuing.

36 | Indefinite Pronouns

Directions Underline the correct pronoun in parentheses. Score one point for each correct response.

Your Score

1. Both of the applicants brought (his or her, their) portfolios. 1. _____

2. Some completed (his or her, their) application forms ahead of time. 2. _____

3. A few forgot to turn off (his or her, their) cell phones. 3. _____

4. Everyone understood how to list (his or her, their) references properly. 4. _____

5. Neither of the women was disappointed when (she, they) did not get the job. 5. _____

6. Did any of the men say when (he, they) could start? 6. _____

7. If someone is late for an interview, (he or she, they) may be unprofessional on the job. 7. _____

8. Some of the employers screen (his or her, their) potential employees carefully. 8. _____

9. Most of the applicants realize (he or she, they) should be punctual. 9. _____

10. Either of these women would be an asset if we hired (her, them). 10. _____

11. If you forget anything the day of the interview, be prepared to do without (it, them). 11. _____

12. Each of the boys carefully proofread (his, their) resume. 12. _____

13. Get out everything you need the night before, and put (it, them) in one place. 13. _____

14. Before anybody goes on an interview, (he or she, they) should practice. 14. _____

15. A few videotaped (his or her, their) mock interviews. 15. _____

16. Somebody who wants to work for us should make sure (his or her, their) resume is neat and error-free. 16. _____

17. None of the companies had a wellness program for (its, their) employees. 17. _____

18. One of the men had (his, their) own computer business. 18. _____

19. If you think of something you want to ask, write (it, them) down. 19. _____

20. Others publish (his or her, their) resume on a website. 20. _____

21. Many know that (he or she, they) will be happier in the right job. 21. _____

22. Anyone can visit the Career Center for help with (his or her, their) job search. 22. _____

23. More of our graduates said (he or she, they) used networking to get a job. 23. _____

24. All of the applicants did (his or her, their) best in the interviews. 24. _____

25. Several were eager for (his or her, their) appointments. 25. _____

Your Total Score _____ /25

If your score was 19 or less, review Section 8, pages 70–71, before continuing.

Section 9 · Relative, Interrogative, and Demonstrative Pronouns

Relative Pronouns

Relative pronouns relate or refer to nouns or other pronouns in a sentence. The nouns or pronouns referred to are antecedents. A relative pronoun begins a **dependent clause**, a clause that has a subject and a verb but cannot stand on its own (it does not express a complete thought).

Relative Pronouns

who	whom	whose
which	that	what

compounds such as *whoever*

Who, whom, and their compounds refer to persons. *Who* or *whoever* is used as the subject of a verb or as a predicate pronoun and is in the nominative case. *Whom* or *whomever* is used as the object of a verb or the object of a preposition and is in the objective case. *Whose* is used to show possession. (See pages 76–78 for more information on *who* and *whom* and their compounds.)

My cousin, <u>who</u> lives in Akron, is visiting me next weekend.

> <u>who</u>—subject of the verb *lives*—refers to *cousin* (person)

She is a woman <u>whom</u> many young female athletes admire.

> <u>whom</u>—object of the verb *admire*—refers to *woman* (person)

Which and *whichever* refer to things. *Whose, what*, and *whatever* refer to persons or things. *That* refers to things and people. Use *that* when a clause is necessary to the meaning of a sentence. Use *which* when the clause could be left out without changing the meaning. Clauses beginning with *which* are set off by commas. Clauses beginning with *that* are not.

The park, <u>which</u> is large, is beautifully landscaped.

> <u>which</u>—subject of the verb *is*—refers to *park* (thing)

The turtle <u>that</u> lives in our backyard is named Myrtle.

> <u>that</u>—subject of the verb *lives*—refers to *turtle* (thing)

She met Pari Yarkovian, <u>whose</u> team won the Academic Super Bowl.

> <u>whose</u>—possessive pronoun modifying *team*—refers to *Pari Yarkovian* (person)

Proofreading *Tip*

To proofread a document you have written on the computer:

1. Spell check the document.

2. Read the document on screen. Proofread a paragraph or block of information at a time to be sure the text makes sense. Make any needed corrections.

3. Print the document and proofread it again. Correct any errors.

TRY IT!

Directions Underline the relative pronoun in each sentence. Check your answers on page 319 or with your instructor before continuing with your assignment.

1. Juliette interviewed with Alex Jacobs, whose company recently announced major expansion plans.

2. He has certain personality traits that I value highly.

3. Tiberius Negelusco is the financial planner whom I recommend.

4. The college president, who recently wrote his memoirs, is a former NFL referee.

5. The shelter offers help to whoever needs it.

6. This is what I mean.

Interrogative Pronouns

The **interrogative pronouns** are used in asking questions. They are *who* (nominative, referring to persons), *whom* (objective, referring to persons), *which* (referring to persons or things and telling one object from another), *what* (referring to things), *whose* (referring to persons), and compounds such as *whoever*. The interrogative pronouns *whose*, *which*, and *what* may be used as adjectives.

Who read the employment contract before signing it?

> Who—asks a question—refers to persons—subject of the verb *read*

Whom did you tell about the new rewards program?

> Whom—asks a question—refers to persons—object of the verb *tell* (*You did tell whom about the new rewards program?*)

Which has better fuel efficiency: a Toyota Prius or a Honda Civic?

> Which—asks a question—refers to things and tells one object from another

What are the advantages of a 529 plan?

> What—asks a question—refers to things

A traveler left her cell phone on the counter. Whose is it?

> Whose—asks a question—refers to persons

Whatever is the matter?

> Whatever—asks a question—refers to things

Who and *Whom*

Perhaps the two pronouns that cause the most confusion are *who* and *whom*. Although the pronoun *who* is used most frequently in daily conversation, it is worthwhile knowing when it should be used and when it is better to use *whom*. Most of the difficulty lies in sentences of inverted order like this one:

Who do they think will be elected?

If you rearrange the sentence as a statement, it is easier to see that *who* is correct. (Substitution of *he* or *she* is a handy check here.)

They do think *he* or *she* will be elected.

TRY IT!

Directions Underline the correct pronoun in parentheses. Check your answers on page 319 or with your instructor before continuing with your assignment.

1. (Which, Whose) turn is it to buy bagels and juice for the meeting?

2. (What, Which) report is due on Monday?

3. (Who, Whom) should I talk to regarding a temporary job?

4. (Who, Whom) will be our new team leader?

5. (What, Which) is easier to work: a smartphone or a PDA?

6. (What, Which) are some guidelines for giving a good presentation?

Remember that *who* is used as the subject of a verb or as a predicate pronoun and is in the nominative case. *Whom* is used as the object of a verb or the object of a preposition and is in the objective case. Look at the dependent clause in this sentence:

The president, whom he respected, lost the election.

Again, change the order of the clause to see whether *whom* is correct.

he respected *whom*

Whom is the object of the verb *respected* and is therefore correct. (Substitution of *him* is a handy check here.)

Who watched the webcast yesterday?
> Who—subject of the verb *watched*—nominative case

The person who communicates effectively on the job is usually successful.
> who—subject of the verb *communicates*—nominative case

It was who I thought it was.
> who—predicate pronoun—nominative case

Who shall I say is representing us at the job fair?
> Who—subject of the verb *is representing*—nominative case

To whom did you submit your conference expenses?
> whom—object of the preposition *To*—objective case

For whom was the appointment made?
> whom—object of the preposition *For*—objective case

The job was given to Demetri, whom you recommended.
> whom—object of the verb *recommended*—objective case

Keifer Goree, whom you met this morning, is a well-known expert on business ethics.
> whom—object of the verb *met*—objective case

A common mistake is made with *who, whom, whoever,* and *whomever* in noun clauses (see page 221). When you use a noun clause as the object of a verb or preposition, remember that *who, whom, whoever,* or *whomever* is not the object of the main clause but is either the subject or the object of the noun clause.

Who do you believe had the winning time?

> Who had the winning time—dependent clause used as the object of the verb *do believe. Who* is the subject of the clause *who had the winning time.*

Let me explain whom I would choose.

> whom I would choose—dependent clause used as the object of the verb *explain. Whom* is the object of the verb *would choose* in the clause *whom I would choose.*

The trainee will be selected by whoever is in charge.

> whoever—nominative case—subject of the noun clause *whoever is in charge.*
>
> (The entire clause *whoever is in charge* is the object of the preposition *by.*)

She will send the official transcript to whomever you select.

> whomever—objective case—object of the verb *select* in the noun clause *whomever you select.* (The entire clause *whomever you select* is the object of the preposition *to.*)

Demonstrative Pronouns

Demonstrative pronouns are used to point out, to designate, or to demonstrate the particular antecedent to which they refer. The singular demonstrative pronouns are *this* and *that.* The plural demonstrative pronouns are *these* and *those.* When demonstrative pronouns are used as adjectives, they are called **demonstrative adjectives**.

This is my favorite painting.

> This—demonstrative pronoun—designates a painting

Is that one of the sculptures that are for sale?

> that—demonstrative pronoun—designates a sculpture

Those paintings will sell for top dollar.

> Those—demonstrative adjective—tells which paintings

TRY IT!

Directions Underline the correct pronoun in parentheses. Check your answers on page 319 or with your instructor before continuing with your assignment.

1. He is an artist (who, whom) we believe represents our gallery well.

2. You will never guess (who, whom) we saw at the gallery opening.

3. The painting will be sold to (whoever, whomever) submits the highest bid.

4. The art director position will be filled by (whoever, whomever) the owner hires.

Complete Applications 37–43, pages 79–83 and 85–86, at this time.

37 | Relative and Interrogative Pronouns

A | **Directions** In the blank in the sentence, write the correct relative pronoun: *who, whom, whose, which, that,* or *what*. Score one point for each correct answer.

Your Score

1. Jason, _____ teaches financial literacy, involves parents in the course.

1. _____

2. The course _____ he teaches includes a stock market simulation.

2. _____

3. The class heard Warren Buffett, _____ financial acumen is highly regarded.

3. _____

4. He is a man _____ investors look to for advice.

4. _____

5. Berkshire Hathaway, _____ has a highly diversified portfolio, continues to increase in value.

5. _____

6. Buffett, _____ is known as the Oracle of Omaha, is famous for his frugal ways.

6. _____

7. The Class B stock _____ I bought has one-thirtieth the value of Class A stock.

7. _____

8. He is an investor _____ his staff and other investors respect.

8. _____

9. Buffett met Bill Gates, _____ foundation will be the major beneficiary of Buffett's philanthropy, in 1991.

9. _____

10. Financial markets, _____ can be volatile, are affected by the world and national economies.

10. _____

Your Total Score _____ /10
If your score was 7 or less, review "Relative Pronouns," page 75, before continuing.

B | **Directions** In the blank at the left, write the correct interrogative pronoun: *who, whom, which, what,* or *whose*. Score one point for each correct answer.

1. _____ do you hope to learn in class?

1. _____

2. _____ would you choose to work with on a group project?

2. _____

3. _____ interviewed you at the company's human resources department?

3. _____

4. _____ teacher do you like the most?

4. _____

5. _____ did you want to meet?

5. _____

6. _____ should I do to learn the new phone system?

6. _____

7. _____ idea was it to apply in the first place?

7. _____

8. _____ do you think left the note on your car?

8. _____

9. _____ did they finally select for the job?

9. _____

10. _____ position paper was the most compelling?

10. _____

Your Total Score _____ /10
If your score was 7 or less, review "Interrogative Pronouns," page 76, before continuing.

38 | *Who–Whom* Practice

Directions Underline the correct pronoun in parentheses. Score one point for each correct answer.

Your Score

1. Many people (who, whom) attended the Occupational Forum learned about career pathways.   1. _____

2. Lynn Vo, (who, whom) you met yesterday, schedules our training workshops.   2. _____

3. From (who, whom) did you get the most help?   3. _____

4. Mr. Yamashiro, (who, whom), I believe, is an expert, thinks the company will begin hiring soon.   4. _____

5. I don't know another technician (who, whom) is so knowledgeable.   5. _____

6. (Who, Whom) do you contact to schedule training?   6. _____

7. Technological instruction will be available for (whoever, whomever) they select.   7. _____

8. We don't know anyone else (who, whom) can talk so knowledgeably about health services.   8. _____

9. Ngoc, (who, whom) respects and values her co-workers, is well liked by all.   9. _____

10. For (who, whom) was this training designed?   10. _____

11. Guess (who, whom) we saw today?   11. _____

12. Miss Soto answers questions from (whoever, whomever) is interested in temporary work.   12. _____

13. Kyle, (who, whom) we heard was hired, has experience in international sales.   13. _____

14. People (who, whom) bring different perspectives to the workplace enrich it.   14. _____

15. Katrina will work with Gary or with (whoever, whomever) the department head assigns.   15. _____

16. The personnel manager told us there were jobs for (whoever, whomever) is trained.   16. _____

17. (Who, Whom) are you looking for now?   17. _____

18. It was she (who, whom), I believe, sent the letter.   18. _____

19. (Who, Whom) do you see for guidance counseling?   19. _____

20. None of us know (who, whom) she is bringing to the lecture.   20. _____

21. To (who, whom) do we need to report our findings?   21. _____

22. Peter, (who, whom) conducts our diversity training, has his own consulting firm.   22. _____

23. She is the person to (who, whom) I sent my reservation.   23. _____

24. Efren Garcia, for (who, whom) I work, sees diversity as a strength in the workplace.   24. _____

25. A successful workplace has employees (who, whom) share common goals.   25. _____

Your Total Score _____ /25

If your score was 19 or less, review "*Who* and *Whom*," pages 76–78, before continuing.

39 | Unit Review

Directions Underline the correct pronoun in parentheses. Score one point for each correct answer.

Your Score

1. Javier and (I, me) visited the culinary school in Göteborg.   1. _____

2. (Me, My) reading about the job outlook for chefs helped me make a decision.   2. _____

3. The school's culinary competition was won by (she, her) and (I, me).   3. _____

4. Most of the schools require (its, their) students to train in the workplace.   4. _____

5. The Health Occupations Program invited Hope and (I, me) to their workshop.   5. _____

6. Anthony DiSalvo and (we, us) applicants learned about other allied health programs.   6. _____

7. Sid, Donna, and (they, them) were very interested in the presentations.   7. _____

8. (What, Which) program offers the best training?   8. _____

9. From (who, whom) did they hear about the paralegal program?   9. _____

10. We were surprised at (them, their) recommending that course of study.   10. _____

11. (Who, Whom) did you tell about the seminar?   11. _____

12. They gave Minta and (he, him) a list of good schools.   12. _____

_____

_____

13. One of the girls forgot (her, their) passport.   13. _____

14. Many of the students listened to (his or her, their) MP3 players on the plane.   14. _____

15. The most experienced traveler in our group was (he, him).   15. _____

16. I use a credit card to shop overseas, (which, that) gets me a better exchange rate.   16. _____

17. One of (its, it's) benefits is purchase protection against faulty goods.   17. _____

18. The best tour guide, (who, whom) you met, is Franz Schaber.   18. _____

19. Andy sat between Rainor and (I, me) on the tour.   19. _____

20. Several of the tourists used (his or her, their) debit cards for local currency.   20. _____

21. Everybody should take copies of (his or her, their) prescriptions on trips.   21. _____

22. (Who, Whom) do you think left that suitcase?   22. _____

23. You and (she, her) have stamps from eight countries in your passports.   23. _____

24. Wilma is more knowledgeable about foreign currency than (I, me).   24. _____

25. The city (which, that) she liked the most was London.   25. _____

Your Total Score _____ /26

40 | Unit Review

Directions Underline the correct pronoun or pronouns in parentheses. Score one point for each correct answer.

Your Score

1. Everyone (who, whom) I spoke with encouraged me to consider a career in health care.   1. _____

2. The hospital, (which, that) will open in four months, is hiring nurses for all shifts.   2. _____

3. All of the students completed (his or her, their) prerequisites before being admitted
   to the program.   3. _____

4. Neither of the women considered changing (her, their) major.   4. _____

5 Dan and (he, him) participated in a job shadowing program.   5. _____

6. It was (she, her) who set up the patients' appointments.   6. _____

7. (What, Which) patient should I attend to first?   7. _____

8. Each student will learn how to record (his or her, their) blood pressure.   8. _____

9. Give the dietary guidelines to (whoever, whomever) asks for them.   9. _____

10. Felix put the chart back in (its, it's) proper place.   10. _____

11. Everyone has a right to see (his or her, their) medical records.   11. _____

12. He showed Jesse and (I, me) how to enter patient data.   12. _____

13. Her positive attitude made (we, us) job seekers optimistic.   13. _____

14. Sheila is better qualified for the job than (he, him).   14. _____

15. Is there a good relationship between the supervisor and (he, him)?   15. _____

16. They hand out (them, those) materials to everyone.   16. _____

17. Their friends had interviews set up for Alonso, Selma, and (she, her).   17. _____

18. Four other students and (I, me) registered for the medical assisting program.   18. _____

19. She gave Carlotta and (he, him) some forms to complete.   19. _____

20. (Me, My) telling them what references to use helped.   20. _____

21. We set up many mock interviews with (they, them) and us.   21. _____

22. We were appreciative of (them, their) sharing their expertise.   22. _____

23. It was a difficult choice for him to make about Jack and (we, us).   23. _____

24. Dr. Shaw and her assistant are experts in (her, their) field.   24. _____

25. Their information was well received by Gloria and (we, us) applicants.   25. _____

Your Total Score _____ /25

41 | Unit Review

Directions Underline the correct pronoun or pronouns in parentheses. Score one point for each correct answer.

Your Score

1. (Who, Whom) should I contact for information on Native American history?   1. _____

2. (Him, His) referring us to Google was a good suggestion.   2. _____

3. She is the historian (who, whom) I think will win the Pulitzer Prize.   3. _____

4. (We, Us) students read that Christopher Columbus called the natives of San Salvador Indios.   4. _____

5. Columbus and his men thought (he, they) had reached India.   5. _____

6. He told Cory and (I, me) that Native Americans make up less than 1 percent of the U.S. population, yet they represent a multitude of languages.   6. _____

7. A librarian found some interesting articles for them and (I, me).   7. _____

8. The topic (which, that) Nathan chose was Yupik culture.   8. _____

9. Deanna and (I, me) visited the Navajo Nation, which is in the Southwest.   9. _____

10. It was from Ms. Flores and (they, them) that we learned about the sweat lodge ceremony.   10. _____

11. The highlight of the visit was (you, your) performing three traditional dances.   11. _____

12. Could it have been (he, him) who led the Hopi in the Pueblo Revolt?   12. _____

13. (What, Which) Native American chief was the leader of the Shawnee: Crazy Horse or Tecumseh?   13. _____

14. The true story of Little Big Horn was related to Marlan and (she, her).   14. _____

15. Some tribes have gambling; (it, they) can generate income for tribal members.   15. _____

16. Lindsay is more interested in Native American culture than (he, him).   16. _____

17. It was (they, them) who told us why the Navajo were considered nomads.   17. _____

18. The two brothers visited (his, their) great-uncle, who is a chief.   18. _____

19. Miss Harris will present a book on Native American history to (whoever, whomever) receives the highest score.   19. _____

20. Jeff gave Ron and (she, her) his report on tribal gaming contracts.   20. _____

21. Jay, Jed, and (we, us) saw beautiful beadwork done by Lakota women.   21. _____

22. Whitney knows more about her Native American heritage than (she, her).   22. _____

23. Morgan and (her, she) are one-fourth blood Cherokee, so (she, they) can apply for a Native American scholarship.   23. _____

24. Several of the students asked how (he or she, they) could trace their ancestry and join a tribe.   24. _____

25. The Navajo reservation is the largest in the United States; (its, it's) territory extends to more than 16,000,000 acres.   25. _____

Your Total Score _____ /26

ENGLISH ON THE JOB /
Police Officer

© liquidlibrary/Jupiter Images

Law enforcement officers are public employees whose responsibilities include protecting the lives and property of citizens. There are law enforcement officers on the local, state, and national levels; their duties are determined by the size and type of organization. In all instances, they are expected to exercise their authority to protect citizens when necessary, whether they are on duty or off duty.

Police officers make up the largest group of law enforcement officers. They respond to calls for service, maintain regular patrols, and complete paperwork. As part of their patrol responsibilities, they look constantly for suspicious circumstances and hazards that may present a danger to the community. A police officer may identify, pursue, and arrest suspected criminals; resolve problems and build relationships within the community; and enforce traffic laws. Police officers may also be assigned jail-related duty or may work in the court system. In large police departments, officers may specialize in a particular field.

The work of a police officer can be dangerous and stressful. Police officers confront suspected criminals and threatening situations and witness death and suffering. Officers usually work shifts of 40 hours a week, but overtime is common because protection must be provided at all times.

Prospective police officers must have at least a high school diploma, and some departments may require college course work. Other criteria may include performance on psychological evaluations, physical examinations, and written examinations, as well as previous education and experience. After interviews and preemployment testing, police recruits attend an academy for instruction in constitutional law, civil rights, state laws, and local ordinances. They also receive training and supervised experience in patrol, traffic control, use of firearms, self-defense, first aid, and emergency response.

Personal characteristics required in this career include honesty, integrity, a sense of responsibility, and sound judgment.

Directions Underline the correct pronoun in parentheses. Score one point for each correct answer.

Your Score

1. Derek and (she, her) applied for a position with the Poway Police Department.

1. _____

2. Jose and (I, me) asked to shadow Sergeant Reynolds for a day.

2. _____

3. Just between you and (I, me), do you think our report is well written?

3. _____

4. One of those women says Mark is (her, their) Neighborhood Watch contact.

4. _____

5. (Who, Whom) prepares the work schedules for shifts?

5. _____

6. Please read each suspect (his or her, their) Miranda rights.

6. _____

7. You will receive the procedures for writing an incident report from (whoever, whomever) is on duty when you start your shift.

7. _____

8. Each of the police officers has (his or her, their) specialty area.

8. _____

9. (She, Her) having a minor in psychology is very useful in this profession.

9. _____

10. Conor, (who, whom) I remember from when I was growing up, is a great mentor to me.

10. _____

Your Total Score _____ /10

42 | Writing Improvement

Directions Select three topics. Write four to six sentences for each topic. Put your sentences in a logical sequence, and make them clear and concise. Develop sentences that are amusing, serious, or informational. Review the WRITE Now feature on page 63 if you need help with conciseness. Use at least one pronoun in every sentence.

1. My most interesting experience this past year

2. The best meal I ever ate

3. What I want most in life

4. My first date

5. My favorite vacation

6. A thank-you note for a nice gift

7. How I prepare for my future

8. My first day of college

9. A friendly neighbor

10. My favorite movie scene

11. How I relax

12. The best summer I ever had

(First topic selected) _____

_____

_____

_____

_____

_____

(Second topic selected) _____

_____

_____

_____

_____

_____

(Third topic selected). _____

_____

_____

_____

_____

_____

APPLICATION ▶ **Give your completed application to your instructor for evaluation.**

43 | Comprehensive Review

A | **Directions** Match each item in Column A with the item it describes in Column B. Write the identifying letter from Column A in the blank at the right. Score one point for each correct answer.

Column A	**Column B**	Answers
a. possessive-case pronouns	1. Coe College, Tim Cole, Microsoft Corporation	1. _____
b. common nouns	2. I, we, you	2. _____
c. proper nouns	3. child's, Kathy's	3. _____
d. demonstrative pronouns	4. which, who, whom, whose	4. _____
e. plural nouns	5. all, each, few, many	5. _____
f. collective nouns	6. this, that, these, those	6. _____
g. relative pronouns	7. businesses, gates, mice, Smiths	7. _____
h. indefinite pronouns	8. car, computer	8. _____
i. possessive forms of nouns	9. committee, family, Congress	9. _____
j. nominative case pronouns	10. my, his, our, their	10. _____

Your Total Score _____ /10

B | **Directions** Read the story. Then go back and substitute the correct personal pronoun above the underlined word or words. Refer to the lists of pronouns in Section 7, pages 57–59 and 62, if necessary. Make sure the pronouns agree with their antecedents. A pronoun may be used more than once. Score one point for each correct answer.

           They   **it**   **us**

Example Mr. and Mrs. French sold the picture to my friend and me.

My parents took my brothers, my sister, and me to Glacier National Park last summer.

Father and Mother made reservations for our family at the Fish Creek campsite. Once our family

arrived there, Caleb, Alyssa, and I set up my parents', my brothers', my sister's, and my tents with help

from Mother. Father and Jeremy went to gather some kindling. Mother and I went to the camp store.

When Mother and I returned, Caleb excitedly told Mother and me that Caleb had seen a mountain lion.

The next day, our family met Ralph, my parents', my brothers', my sister's, and my rafting guide,

at the Flathead River landing. The guide showed our family how to paddle and told our family what to

do if our family fell overboard. As our family paddled, the guide identified points of interest and talked

about the wildlife in the area. Alyssa and Jeremy took pictures of the white water as the family entered

the white water. This was a vacation our family will never forget.

Your Total Score _____ /19

If your score was 14 or less for B, review Section 7, pages 57–63, before continuing.

PROOF IT!

Directions Proofread the e-mail, circling all errors. Then key it, making all necessary corrections. Proofread your work (remember to spell check it) and make any corrections that are needed. Turn in both this page and your finished document to your instructor.

| New Message | Send | Address | Attach | Options | Spelling | Print | Save | File | Edit | Format | Insert | Tools | View | Help |

Mail

To: "All Employees" <employees@bkcellars.com>
Cc:
Subject: All-Company Picnic
▶ Attachments:

This past year has brought many challenges to our company, but BK Cellars has done it's job well and has turned a challenging year into a profitable one. Now, everyone in our family of employees can enjoy the results of their hard work.

We have a reservation at the Picnic Grove at Kings Island on Saturday, August 7, for our company picnic, and we cordially invite you and your family members to join us. You and them will receive complimentary tickets for admission to the park and all rides, shows, and attractions. Contact Sandra Laser, our coordinator for this event, and let them know how many tickets you will need. Ticket requests must be mad no later than August 2. Food and drinks will be provided and will be served between 11 and 2.

You have the heartfelt thanks of the Board of Directors and I for contributing to another successful year at BK Cellars.

Posttest

Directions If the underlined pronoun is correct, write *C* in the blank at the right. If it is incorrect, write the correct pronoun.

1. <u>Who</u> should we recommend?

1. _____

2. Everyone on the team has <u>their</u> tasks to complete.

2. _____

3. Ms. Lambert gave a copy of the presentation to Mr. Hoang and <u>I</u>.

3. _____

4. There are no employees who work as hard as Sebastian and <u>him</u>.

4. _____

5. Tuan asked Francis and <u>me</u> for advice.

5. _____

6. The questionnaires were addressed to <u>we</u> accountants.

6. _____

7. Pao said it was <u>they</u> who picked up the package from the front desk.

7. _____

8. Each of the temporary workers has <u>their</u> assignment.

8. _____

9. Claude and Simon had difficulty confirming <u>their</u> seat assignments for the trip.

9. _____

10. Raj is anxious to see <u>your</u> new computer system.

10. _____

unit 4
Verbs

Objectives

1. To recognize and use verbs correctly when making statements, asking questions, or giving commands
2. To identify principal helping verbs and linking verbs
3. To use a verb so that it agrees with the subject of the sentence
4. To consider unity, organization, and length when writing paragraphs

Sections

Pretest

A | Directions
Underline each verb. In the blank at the right, write *S* if the verb makes a statement, *Q* if it asks a question, or *C* if it gives a command.

1. Drive me to the supermarket.   1. _____

2. Fredrico passed his driver's exam on the first try.   2. _____

3. My driver's license expires in four years.   3. _____

4. Who parked the car next to a fire hydrant?   4. _____

5. Siobahn answered all of the questions correctly.   5. _____

B | Directions
Identify the helping verbs by underlining them once. Identify the main verbs by underlining them twice.

1. Mr. Abajian and Mrs. Fox have served as advisors for our business club.

2. Our state competition will be held in Lincoln next month.

3. I could participate in the extemporaneous speaking competition.

4. Our chapter has qualified nine students for the state-level competition.

5. The school may contribute money toward our travel expenses for the trip.

C | Directions
Underline the correct verb form in parentheses. Make the verb agree in person and number with the subject.

1. Our school (was, were) designated as an evacuation center during the wildfires.

2. If he (was, were) in charge of the evacuation, everyone would know exactly what to do.

3. The path of a wildfire (is, are) often unpredictable.

4. Ailene (is, are) a volunteer at the evacuation center.

5. Each of the communities (has, have) an evacuation plan.

WORKPLACE FOCUS

Electronic Resources

Today, many people do both their personal and their professional writing on the computer. While composing, writers may need to refer to several resources. An advantage of using electronic reference tools is being able to look up a reference immediately without leaving the computer.

Among the resources writers frequently use are a dictionary, a thesaurus, a reference manual, the spell checker (which includes a grammar and style checker) in word processing software, and the Internet. Electronic resources can be accessed quickly and easily on a CD-ROM or in application software. Dictionaries, thesauruses, and spell checkers are the electronic resources used most often. The Internet, however, provides the quickest and easiest access to the largest pool of resources. It can be used to research a particular topic or to verify facts or figures.

Functions/Uses of Verbs

A **verb** tells what the subject does or is or what happens to it. A verb can make a statement, ask a question, or give a command.

The verb is one of the two required parts of every sentence. The other required part is the subject. All sentences must have a subject and a verb. When you use verbs properly, your speech and writing skills will improve. The proper use of verbs requires great care. Watch your use of verbs, and you will be amazed at how much more your sentences will communicate.

Verbs Make Statements

Kari <u>lost</u> her calculator.

> <u>lost</u>—a verb. It tells what the subject *Kari* did. It makes a statement.

Ms. Waters <u>rides</u> in the MS 150 bike ride.

> <u>rides</u>—a verb. It tells what the subject *Ms. Waters* does. It makes a statement.

Verbs Ask Questions

Who <u>scheduled</u> the conference room?

> <u>scheduled</u>—a verb. It asks a question about the subject *Who*.

<u>Is</u> Mariel absent today?

> <u>Is</u>—a verb. It asks a question about the subject *Mariel*.

Verbs Give Commands

<u>Check</u> your calendar now.

> <u>Check</u>—a verb. It gives a command to the subject *you* (understood).

<u>Recharge</u> your cell phone tonight, Deenah.

> <u>Recharge</u>—a verb. It gives a command to the subject *you* (understood).

TRY IT!

Directions Underline each verb. In the blank at the right, write *S* if the verb makes a statement, *Q* if it asks a question, or *C* if it gives a command. Check your answers on page 319 or with your instructor before continuing with your assignment.

1. Ming gives tours of the school to new students.   1. _____
2. Jillian welcomes them to the campus during freshman orientation.   2. _____
3. Volunteer as a student ambassador.   3. _____
4. Who received a scholarship?   4. _____
5. Luis attended an orientation session yesterday.   5. _____

APPLICATION **Complete Application 44, page 95, at this time.**

Uses of Helping Verbs

Helping verbs are well-named because they help the main verbs tell what the subjects are doing by asking a question, giving a command, or making a statement. (Helping verbs are also known as auxiliary verbs.) Remember them as words that help connect the subject and the main verb.

Principal Helping Verbs

is	be	am	are
was	were	have	has
had	may	must	ought
can	might	could	would
should	shall	will	do
does	did		

Juan <u>will</u> finalize his term paper tonight.

> <u>will</u>—helping verb. It helps the main verb *finalize* tell about the subject *Juan*.

Rob <u>has</u> written the introduction for his speech.

> <u>has</u>—helping verb. It helps the main verb *written* tell about the subject *Rob*.

The president of the Chamber of Commerce <u>will</u> speak to our economics class.

> <u>will</u>—helping verb. It helps the main verb *speak* tell about the subject *president*.

Students <u>may</u> volunteer to be peer tutors.

> <u>may</u>—helping verb. It helps the main verb *volunteer* tell about the subject *Students*.

Some adults <u>must</u> attend traffic school if they receive too many tickets.

> <u>must</u>—helping verb. It helps the main verb *attend* tell about the subject *adults*.

We <u>should</u> use the Internet to conduct the research for our history project.

> <u>should</u>—helping verb. It helps the main verb *use* tell about the subject *We*.

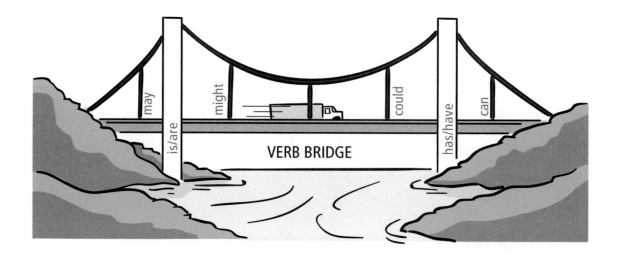

Verb Separations

The helping verb may be separated from the main verb by another word (or words), often a modifier (a word, phrase, or clause that describes, limits, or qualifies another word or group of words). You can find the main verb because it still tells what the subject is doing or what is being done to the subject.

In video stores, customer records <u>are</u> usually <u>stored</u> in a computer database.

> <u>are</u> usually <u>stored</u>—verb separation. The helping verb *are* and the main verb *stored* are separated by the modifier *usually*.

In what ways <u>have</u> computers <u>changed</u> how medical centers operate?

> <u>have</u> computers <u>changed</u>—verb separation. The helping verb *have* and the main verb *changed* are separated by the subject *computers*.

Computers <u>have</u> definitely <u>influenced</u> how police departments operate.

> <u>have</u> definitely <u>influenced</u>—verb separation. The helping verb *have* and the main verb *influenced* are separated by the modifier *definitely*.

TRY IT!

Directions Identify the helping verbs by underlining them once. Identify the main verbs by underlining them twice. Check your answers on page 319 or with your instructor before continuing with your assignment.

1. C. S. Lewis was born in Belfast, Ireland.
2. Many authors, including J. K. Rowling, have been inspired by his writing.
3. Did Lewis and President John F. Kennedy die on the same day?
4. Lewis and his literary friends were known as the Inklings.
5. The "Chronicles of Narnia" series is considered a classic of children's literature.
6. The books are read for their adventure and creativeness.
7. Which Narnia movie has grossed nearly $750 million?
8. Ethan's group should give their oral report on the Space Trilogy.
9. Would you explain allegory to us?
10. Which Narnia movie do you like the best?
11. We must rent *Shadowlands*, a movie about Lewis's life.

APPLICATION > **Complete Application 45, page 96, at this time.**

Use of Linking Verbs with Predicate Nouns, Pronouns, and Adjectives

When a form of the verb *be* (*be, am, is, are, was, were, has been, have been, had been, shall be, will be, shall have been, will have been*) is used alone, the word used to complete the meaning of the verb is called a predicate noun, a predicate pronoun, or a predicate adjective. These forms of the verb *be* are called linking verbs because they link the subject of the sentence with a predicate noun, pronoun, or adjective.

The predicate noun or pronoun refers to the subject of the sentence and is called the predicate nominative. The adjective after the linking verb describes the subject and is called the predicate adjective. Phrases or clauses can sometimes be predicate nominatives or predicate adjectives.

Two other linking verbs are forms of the verbs *become* and *seem*. *Appear, taste, smell, feel, sound,* and *look* are sometimes linking verbs. (See pages 58–59 for a review of the nominative case and linking verbs.)

Predicate Nouns

Clint Eastwood is a famous <u>actor</u>.

> <u>actor</u>—a noun. It is a predicate noun because it completes the meaning of the linking verb *is* and refers to the subject *Clint Eastwood*.

Mr. Eastwood has been a movie <u>director</u> also.

> <u>director</u>—a noun. It is a predicate noun because it completes the meaning of the linking verb *has been* and refers to the subject *Mr. Eastwood*.

Predicate Pronouns

It was <u>he</u> who won the 2005 Oscar® for best director for *Million Dollar Baby*.

> <u>he</u>—a pronoun. It is a predicate pronoun because it completes the meaning of the linking verb *was* and refers to the subject *It*.

The person who wrote that song was <u>he</u>.

> <u>he</u>—a pronoun. It is a predicate pronoun because it completes the meaning of the linking verb *was* and refers to the subject *person*.

Predicate Adjectives

Golfers in his tournament are <u>competitive</u>.

> <u>competitive</u>—an adjective. It is a predicate adjective because it completes the meaning of the linking verb *are* and describes the subject *Golfers*.

His directing is critically <u>acclaimed</u>

> <u>acclaimed</u>—a participle acting as an adjective. It is a predicate adjective because it completes the meaning of the linking verb *is* and describes the subject *directing*. (A **participle** is a verb form usually ending in *ing, ed, t,* or *en*, used as an adjective or combined with a helping verb to form different tenses.)

TRY IT!

Directions Underline the predicate noun, predicate pronoun, or predicate adjective in each sentence. In the blank at the right, write *PN* for *predicate noun*, *PP* for *predicate pronoun*, or *PA* for *predicate adjective*. Check your answers on page 319 or with your instructor before continuing with your assignment.

1. His voice sounds raspy.   1._____

2. Mr. Eastwood is an accomplished jazz pianist.   2._____

3. Was it he who received an honorary doctorate
   from the Berklee College of Music in 2007?   3._____

APPLICATION ➤ Complete Applications 46–47, pages 97–98, at this time.

44 | Find the Verb

Directions Underline each verb. In the blank at the right, write *S* if the verb makes a statement, *Q* if it asks a question, or *C* if it gives a command. Score one point for each correct verb and one point for each correct sentence type identified.

Answers

1. A vacation to Washington, D.C., affords an educational experience for many families.   1. _____

2. The architecture in Washington varies greatly.   2. _____

3. The cherry trees around the Tidal Basin usually bloom from late March to mid-April.   3. _____

4. Which national monument in our nation's capital draws the most visitors each year?   4. _____

5. The National Archives displays documents from our history.   5. _____

6. At Arlington National Cemetery, visitors view the Eternal Flame at the burial site of President John F. Kennedy.   6. _____

7. The guard changes at the Tomb of the Unknowns at Arlington National Cemetery every half hour from April 1 through September 30.   7. _____

8. The President lives in the White House at 1600 Pennsylvania Avenue.   8. _____

9. Visitors to the White House pass through security checks.   9. _____

10. The White House Rose Garden offers a fragrant welcome to visitors.   10. _____

11. Which agency provides security for the president?   11. _____

12. The National Museum of Natural History contains a collection of precious gemstones, including the Hope Diamond.   12. _____

13. How many persons ride the Metro into Washington every day?   13. _____

14. The displays at the United States Holocaust Memorial Museum stimulate a wide range of emotions.   14. _____

15. Get tickets to the Friday night Evening Parade at the Marine Barracks.   15. _____

16. Foreign governments locate their embassies in Washington.   16. _____

17. Streets in Washington radiate from the center of the city like spokes on a bicycle wheel.   17. _____

18. On the Fourth of July, fireworks light up the sky over our nation's capital.   18. _____

19. The Wright 1903 Flyer hangs in the National Air and Space Museum.   19. _____

20. The International Spy Museum educates the public about all aspects of espionage.   20. _____

21. The Bureau of Engraving and Printing prints paper currency and other security documents such as military identification cards.   21. _____

22. Two senators represent each state in the United States Senate.   22. _____

23. Visit the Washington National Cathedral in Georgetown.   23. _____

24. Students enjoy the gargoyle tours at the Washington National Cathedral.   24. _____

25. Visitors hike and bike along the C&O Canal.   25. _____

Your Total Score _____ /51

If your score was 39 or less, review Section 10, page 91, before continuing.

45 | Helping Verbs

Directions Identify the helping verbs by underlining them once. Identify the main verbs by underlining them twice. Score one point for each correct identification.

Your Score

1. Baldur may choose the topic of cloning for his biology research paper.   1. _____

2. The paper should explore both the science and the controversy.   2. _____

3. Baldur has read several articles about cloning and genetic engineering.   3. _____

4. Would you help him with his research?   4. _____

5. Cloning and genetic engineering do not mean the same thing.   5. _____

6. Genetic engineering is manipulating genetic material for a particular trait.   6. _____

7. Cloning is creating an exact copy of a cell, gene, plant, or animal.   7. _____

8. For centuries, farmers have saved the best seeds from the current crop for the next year.   8. _____

9. How do they choose the best seeds?   9. _____

10. They must identify very hardy, productive, or flavorful plants.   10. _____

11. Though similar, genetic engineering does differ from this process.   11. _____

12. With genetic engineering, scientists can introduce genetic material from different types of plants and animals—a concern for many people.   12. _____

13. A clone will have exactly the same DNA as its "parent."   13. _____

14. Clones do not necessarily look identical.   14. _____

15. An example of natural cloning can be found in identical twins.   15. _____

16. The social implications of cloning were explored in the novel *Brave New World*.   16. _____

17. Cloning experiments are continually being conducted by scientists.   17. _____

18. Dolly the sheep was created by cloning.   18. _____

19. Some cloned animals have died prematurely.   19. _____

20. Stem cells are harvested through cloning.   20. _____

21. The cells are then used to research and treat diseases.   21. _____

22. This type of cloning is opposed less often.   22. _____

23. Cloning extinct species was dramatized in the movie *Jurassic Park*.   23. _____

24. Cloning could be used for the reestablishment of endangered animal populations.   24. _____

25. Genetic material from hundreds of species is housed at the Frozen Zoo® in San Diego.   25. _____

Your Total Score _____ /53
If your score was 40 or less, review pages 92–93 before continuing.

46 | Linking Verbs and Predicate Nouns, Pronouns, and Adjectives

A | **Directions** Underline the predicate noun, predicate pronoun, or predicate adjective in each sentence. In the blank at the right, write *PN* for *predicate noun*, *PP* for *predicate pronoun*, or *PA* for *predicate adjective*. Score one point for each correct word and one point for each correct identification.

Answers

1. Nelson Mandela was an anti-apartheid activist.   1. _____

2. It was he who was imprisoned for 27 years.   2. _____

3. He will always be a symbol of self-sacrificing leadership for many South Africans. 3. _____

4. Nelson Mandela was prominent in the African National Congress.   4. _____

5. Was it he who received the 1993 Nobel Peace Prize?   5. _____

6. His commanding presence and air of authority seem so natural.   6. _____

7. His speech after Chris Hani's assassination in 1993 was presidential in tone.   7. _____

8. It must have been he who wrote *Long Walk to Freedom*.   8. _____

9. His speeches are always passionate.   9. _____

10. He became the first democratically elected president of South Africa.   10. _____

B | **Directions** Underline the linking verbs once. Underline the predicate nouns, predicate pronouns, and predicate adjectives twice. In the blank at the right, write *PN* for *predicate noun*, *PP* for *predicate pronoun*, or *PA* for *predicate adjective*. Score one point for each correctly underlined linking verb, predicate noun, predicate pronoun, and predicate adjective and one point for each correct identification.

1. Kai's acting looks effortless.   1. _____

2. Jeremiah has been a director for several years.   2. _____

3. Was it she who starred in last year's production of *Who's Afraid of Virginia Woolf?* 3. _____

4. The set design seems so real.   4. _____

5. The director of the repertory company in Salem was he.   5. _____

6. The period costumes in the play looked quite authentic.   6. _____

7. The Festival's music director is Helene Bagge.   7. _____

8. The voice coach for Emma was she.   8. _____

9. The staging for this play appears complicated.   9. _____

10. The season's final production was *Othello*.   10. _____

Your Total Score _____ /51

If your score was 40 or less for A and B, review pages 93–94 before continuing.

47 | Extra Practice on Verbs

A | **Directions** Identify the helping verbs by underlining them once. Identify the main verbs by underlining them twice. Score one point for each correct identification.

Your Score

1. Have you visited Ashland, Oregon?   1. _____

2. Lynne is going to the Oregon Shakespeare Festival in June.   2. _____

3. Shall we order tickets for *Romeo and Juliet, A Midsummer Night's Dream,* and *Richard II*?   3. _____

4. Would Nhon and Anh like a ride to Ashland?   4. _____

5. You may stay with my sister during the festival.   5. _____

6. We will also attend plays at the Oregon Cabaret Theatre.   6. _____

7. He can help with ticket or souvenir sales.   7. _____

8. The festival should offer residents half-price tickets in the spring and fall.   8. _____

9. Do Brittani and her family really like the classic plays by Shakespeare?   9. _____

10. You must arrive at the theater by 7:30.   10. _____

Your Total Score _____ /20
If your score was 15 or less, review pages 92–93 before continuing.

B | **Directions** Underline the linking verbs once. Underline the predicate nouns, predicate pronouns, and predicate adjectives twice. In the blank at the right, write *PN* for *predicate noun*, *PP* for *predicate pronoun*, or *PA* for *predicate adjective*. Score one point for each correctly underlined linking verb, predicate noun, predicate pronoun, and predicate adjective and one point for each correct identification.

Answers

1. The theater looks full.   1. _____

2. The Ulalena program is magnificent.   2. _____

3. Will you become a season ticket holder to the IMAX theater in Lahaina?   3. _____

4. Be an usher for the season.   4. _____

5. The buffet dinner before the performance tasted delicious.   5. _____

6. Is he the best singer in the show?   6. _____

7. At the current price, the show has been a great value.   7. _____

8. The cast appears very talented.   8. _____

9. Was it he who played the Hawaiian slack guitar?   9. _____

10. It was she who narrated the story of Hawaii's history.   10. _____

Your Total Score _____ /32
If your score was 24 or less, review pages 93–94 before continuing.

Verb Agreement with Subject

A verb should agree with its subject in person and number. A singular (one) subject takes a singular form of a verb. A plural (more than one) subject takes a plural form of a verb. An exception is the pronoun *you*, which takes the plural form of the verb in both singular and plural.

My brother <u>writes</u> short stories and poetry.

<u>writes</u>—singular form of the verb agrees with the singular subject *brother*. A singular subject takes a singular verb.

Noelle <u>manages</u> a convenience store.

<u>manages</u>—singular form of the verb agrees with the singular subject *Noelle*. A singular subject takes a singular verb.

My friends <u>volunteer</u> at the senior citizens' center.

<u>volunteer</u>—plural form of the verb agrees with the plural subject *friends*. A plural subject takes a plural verb.

You <u>are</u> a member of the jazz band.

<u>are</u>—plural form of the verb. The subject *You* always takes the plural form of the verb.

Singular subjects usually do not end in *s* or *es*, but they often take a verb that does end with *s* or *es*. Many plural subjects end in *s* or *es*; the verbs that go with a plural subject usually do not end in *s* or *es*.

<u>He</u> <u>runs</u> two miles every morning.

<u>He</u>—singular subject—does not end in *s*

<u>runs</u>—singular form of the verb—ends in *s*

My <u>cousins</u> <u>organize</u> a scavenger hunt for every family reunion.

<u>cousins</u>—plural subject—ends in *s*

<u>organize</u>—plural form of the verb—does not end in *s*

AGREEMENT OF SUBJECT AND VERB

<u>SHE IS</u> THE FIRST-PLACE WINNER.

<u>THEY ARE</u> THE SECOND-
AND THIRD-PLACE WINNERS.

Forms of the Verb *Be*

Am, *is*, and *was* are singular forms of the verb *be* and require singular subjects. *Are* and *were* are plural forms and require plural subjects. Study the verb forms of *be* so they will become a strong part of your speech and writing. These verb forms are so common that by learning them thoroughly, you can improve your language skills greatly.

She <u>was</u> a recipient of the Kirkwood Foundation scholarship.

> <u>was</u>—singular form of the verb agrees in number with the singular subject *She*

Sophia <u>was</u> our tour guide in Italy.

> <u>was</u>—singular form of the verb agrees in number with the singular subject *Sophia*

He <u>is</u> a colleague of mine.

> <u>is</u>—singular form of the verb agrees in number with the singular subject *He*

I <u>am</u> studying international business at the University of Southern California.

> <u>am</u>—singular form of the helping verb agrees in number with the singular subject *I*

Nick <u>is</u> working his way through college.

> <u>is</u>—singular form of the helping verb agrees in number with the singular subject *Nick*

Two persons in our class <u>are</u> international students.

> <u>are</u>—plural form of the verb agrees in number with the plural subject *persons*

They <u>are</u> both from Japan.

> <u>are</u>—plural form of the verb agrees in number with the plural subject *They*

We <u>were</u> at the airport early.

> <u>were</u>—plural form of the verb agrees in number with the plural subject *We*

My parents <u>were</u> there to meet us.

> <u>were</u>—plural form of the verb agrees in number with the plural subject *parents*

The airline attendants <u>are</u> very helpful.

> <u>are</u>—plural form of the verb agrees in number with the plural subject *attendants*

Contrary-to-Fact Conditions

When stating a condition contrary to fact, use *were* with all subjects, singular or plural. Such a condition does not presently exist; the speaker imagines it or wishes it to be true. The words *if* or *as if* frequently begin these clauses.

He acts as if he <u>were</u> in charge of the entire company.

> <u>were</u>—plural form of the verb is used with a singular subject when stating a condition contrary to fact

If I <u>were</u> the winner, I would take a trip around the world.

> <u>were</u>—plural form of the verb is used with a singular subject when stating a condition contrary to fact

If we <u>were</u> on vacation, we would sleep in every day.

> <u>were</u>—plural form of the verb is used with a plural subject when stating a condition contrary to fact

TRY IT!

Directions Underline the correct verb form in parentheses. Check your answers on page 319 or with your instructor before continuing with your assignment.

1. Shawn (is, are) a restaurant critic in Miami.
2. You (is, are) welcome to join us at our table.
3. If she (was, were) booking a tour of Tuscany, I would go with her.
4. He (is, are) working on his online course while on vacation.
5. Albert (was, were) a server in the resort restaurant.
6. They (is, are) anxious to see the canals of Venice.

proofreading TIP

Knowing how to proofread and correct copy is an important skill for writers. There will be times when you will have a hard copy and will want to mark directly on it what changes need to be made to correct errors or to make it look more professional.

Proofreaders' marks are standardized symbols that you can use to mark changes and errors on a hard copy. Anyone who has a document marked with standardized proofreaders' marks can then make the necessary changes to the document. A list of common proofreaders' marks appears in Appendix C on page 317.

Forms of the Verb *Have*

I **HAVE** A BASEBALL GLOVE.

HE **HAS** A TENNIS RACKET.

THEY **HAD** FOOTBALLS YESTERDAY.

The second-most-used verb is *have*. To express something that is happening at the present time, use *have* with all singular and plural subjects. The exceptions are singular nouns and third-person singular pronouns (*he, she, it*), which require the use of *has*.

To express something that happened in the past, use *had* with all subjects, both singular and plural.

Some students <u>have</u> difficulty understanding instructors with a heavy foreign accent.

> have—plural form of the verb agrees with the plural subject *students*

Mikal <u>has</u> a foreign language minor.

> has—singular form of the verb agrees with the subject *Mikal*—singular noun

He <u>has</u> Spanish tapes to listen to at home.

> has—singular form of the verb agrees with the subject *He*—third-person singular pronoun

Instructors <u>have</u> an important job.

> have—plural form of the verb agrees with the plural subject *Instructors*

They <u>had</u> an orientation session the first day of the semester.

> had—verb expressing past time used with all subjects, singular or plural

Plural Form with Compound Subjects

A **compound subject** (two or more nouns or pronouns joined by a conjunction) generally takes the plural form of the verb when the nouns or pronouns are joined by *and*.

> Lake Como and Lake Maggiore <u>are</u> two popular resorts in Italy.
>> <u>are</u>—plural form of the verb agrees with the compound subject *Lake Como and Lake Maggiore*

> Leather goods, wine, and handblown glass <u>were</u> available in Milan.
>> <u>were</u>—plural form of the verb agrees with the compound subject *Leather goods, wine, and handblown glass*

Intervening Words, Phrases, and Clauses

Sometimes the subject is separated from the verb, often by a phrase serving as a **modifier**. (Remember that modifiers are words, phrases, or clauses that describe, limit, or qualify another word or group of words.) Look for the subject of the sentence and make the verb agree with it. Do not make the mistake of making the verb agree with the modifier. (Refer to pages 105–106 for one exception.)

> Ruth, not Dave and Dominick, <u>is</u> planning the trip to Mexico.
>> <u>is</u>—singular form of the helping verb agrees with the singular subject *Ruth*

> The suitcase with the two red stickers <u>is</u> mine.
>> <u>is</u>—singular form of the verb agrees with the singular subject *suitcase*

> Ian, as well as his brother, <u>is</u> looking forward to this trip.
>> <u>is</u>—singular form of the helping verb agrees with the singular subject *Ian*

> The tour guides at the museum <u>were</u> extremely helpful.
>> <u>were</u>—plural form of the verb agrees with the plural subject *guides*

> Reserved tickets for this evening's concert <u>are</u> available at the will-call window.
>> <u>are</u>—plural form of the verb agrees with the plural subject *tickets*

TRY IT!

Directions Underline the correct verb form in parentheses. Check your answers on page 319 or with your instructor before continuing with your assignment.

1. Shea (has, have) enrolled in two online classes.

2. Jonah and Carly (is, are) taking an ethics course.

3. The shows at the amusement park (has, have) long lines.

4. Tests, assignments, and a presentation (was, were) included in my grade for the course.

5. Teaching assistants (has, have) submitted final grades.

APPLICATION ▶ **Complete Applications 48–49, pages 103–104, at this time.**

48 | Verb and Subject Agreement

Directions Underline the correct verb form in parentheses. Make the verb agree in person and number with the subject. Score one point for each correct verb.

Your Score

1. Our country (is, are) constantly doing business with many foreign countries.

1. _____

2. If Rosemary (was, were) conducting the training on cultural awareness in business, I would definitely attend.

2. _____

3. Canada, Mexico, and Japan (is, are) three major trading partners of the United States.

3. _____

4. Business (is, are) conducted differently in each of those countries.

4. _____

5. The nonverbal messages of a culture (is, are) well worth learning.

5. _____

6. Americans (has, have) some common stereotypes about other cultures.

6. _____

7. All people of the same nationality do not (has, have) the same attitudes or characteristics.

7. _____

8. Yury (is, are) showing interest in his client by maintaining eye contact.

8. _____

9. Facial expressions (is, are) a form of nonverbal communication.

9. _____

10. Lakshmi's smile (is, are) sending a positive message to the person with whom she (is, are) communicating.

10. _____

11. Steven and Edward (is, are) allowing a comfortable distance of two to three feet when greeting a new customer.

11. _____

12. In Paco's culture, it (is, are) appropriate to stand very close to someone you (is, are) meeting for the first time.

12. _____

13. The handshake (is, are) recognized as a universal greeting in business settings.

13. _____

14. By leaning toward Jesus, Angelica (has, have) indicated she (is, are) interested in the conversation.

14. _____

15. You (has, have) dual citizenship.

15. _____

16. Tammi and Chase (was, were) nervously pacing before the interview.

16. _____

17. If he (was, were) not presenting, the meeting would not be as informative.

17. _____

18. Katelyn, as well as Thomas, (was, were) representing the company at the job fair.

18. _____

19. Do not use first names until you (is, are) invited to do so.

19. _____

20. Celia and Beth (has, have) a problem getting to appointments and meetings on time.

20. _____

Your Total Score _____ /23
If your score was 17 or less, review pages 99–102 before continuing.

49 | Verb and Subject Agreement

Directions Underline the correct verb form in parentheses. Make the verb agree in person and number with the subject. Score one point for each correct verb.

Your Score

1. Individuals everywhere (has, have) different perspectives and values based on their own life experiences.

1. _____

2. China (is, are) a powerful influence in the world of international business.

2. _____

3. Cam and Jackie (has, have) asked for some guidelines for doing business with persons in China.

3. _____

4. Hien, Kim, and Yung (is, are) learning Mandarin Chinese.

4. _____

5. Elliot (has, have) told me most businesspeople in China speak English.

5. _____

6. All managers who travel to China (was, were) instructed not to point when speaking.

6. _____

7. Discussing business at meals (is, are) not appropriate.

7. _____

8. Common greetings in China (is, are) nods and slight bows, but with Westerners, people often shake hands.

8. _____

9. Stephen (has, have) always arrived early for meetings with his Chinese colleagues.

9. _____

10. Punctuality (is, are) viewed as a virtue.

10. _____

11. Gender bias (is, are) nonexistent in business in China.

11. _____

12. American gestures (has, have) no meaning there.

12. _____

13. We (has, have) brought several copies of the documents that will be signed.

13. _____

14. Ronald and Cal (has, have) scheduled appointments for their China trip.

14. _____

15. In China, it (is, are) highly inappropriate for a man to touch a woman in public.

15. _____

16. Appropriate business attire for women (is, are) very conservative.

16. _____

17. Introductions (is, are) formal, and formal titles (is, are) used.

17. _____

18. Part of building a business relationship in China (is, are) gift giving.

18. _____

19. A gift (is, are) offered using both hands and must be gift-wrapped.

19. _____

20. Gifts may be refused three times before they (is, are) accepted.

20. _____

21. Visitors' efforts to speak Chinese when in China (is, are) appreciated.

21. _____

22. Certain topics (is, are) not appropriate for visitors to discuss.

22. _____

23. Business cards (is, are) given and received with two hands.

23. _____

24. If I (was, were) to do business in China, I would have one side of my business card translated into Chinese.

24. _____

25. Respect for the elderly (is, are) an unwritten, universal law in all countries.

25. _____

Your Total Score _____ /26

If your score was 19 or less, review pages 99–102 before continuing.

Verb Agreement with Indefinite Pronouns

Whenever you use an indefinite pronoun as the subject of a sentence, the verb must agree in number with the subject. (Refer to pages 70–71 for a review of indefinite pronouns.)

The following indefinite pronouns are singular and are used with singular verbs:

another	each	everyone	neither	nothing	somebody
anybody	either	everything	no one	one	someone
anyone	everybody	much	nobody	other	something

> Everyone <u>is</u> taking a surfing lesson.
>> <u>is</u>—singular form of the helping verb agrees in number with the singular subject *Everyone*

> No one in these classes <u>has</u> surfed before.
>> <u>has</u>—singular form of the helping verb agrees in number with the singular subject *No one* (not with *classes*)

The following indefinite pronouns are plural and are used with plural verbs:

both	few	many	others	several

> Many of the surfboards <u>were</u> made especially for beginners.
>> <u>were</u>—plural form of the helping verb agrees in number with the plural subject *Many* (not with *surfboards*)

> Several <u>are</u> more than ten feet long.
>> <u>are</u>—plural form of the verb agrees in number with the plural subject *Several*

The following indefinite pronouns are sometimes singular and sometimes plural, depending on the context. When the pronoun is singular, it is used with a singular verb. When it is plural, it is used with a plural verb.

INDEFINITE PRONOUNS

EACH NEITHER ANYBODY SOMEBODY

FEW MANY OTHERS SEVERAL

all	any	more	most	none	some

> Some of the surfing instructors <u>are</u> also lifeguards.
>> <u>are</u>—The indefinite pronoun *Some* refers to *instructors*. *Instructors* is plural, so *Some* is plural and takes a plural verb.

> All of the beach in Hanalei <u>is</u> closed until the bacterial level in the water falls.
>> <u>is</u>—The indefinite pronoun *All* refers to *beach*. *Beach* is singular, so *All* is singular and takes a singular verb.

RULES that work

If the subject of a sentence is one of the indefinite pronouns that may take a singular or plural verb, how can you decide which to use?

When indicating *how much*, use a singular verb.

Some of the sand on the beaches <u>was</u> black.

(<u>was</u>—singular form of the verb because you are indicating *how much. How much sand? Some.*)

When indicating *how many*, use a plural verb.

None of the instructors <u>were</u> Native Hawaiian.

(<u>were</u>—plural form of the verb because you are indicating *how many. How many instructors? None.*)

TRY IT!

Directions Underline the correct verb form in parentheses. Check your answers on page 319 or with your instructor before continuing with your assignment.

1. None of those authors (has, have) had a best seller.

2. Many (is, are) graduates of English or writing programs.

3. Neither of his books (was, were) well-received by the literary critics.

4. Both (is, are) political thrillers.

5. One of my friends (is, are) sure that it is a nonfiction book.

Verb Agreement with *There*

There is an **expletive** (meaning "to fill out") that introduces a sentence. The verb agrees with the subject that follows the verb when *there* is used to start the sentence. Ignore the word *there* when looking for the subject. It is never used as the subject of a sentence.

There <u>is</u> a new restaurant on the beach at the Ko Olina Resort and Marina.

> <u>is</u>—singular form of the verb agrees in number with the singular subject *restaurant*

There <u>are</u> lines of people waiting to order Hawaiian shaved ice.

> <u>are</u>—plural form of the verb agrees in number with the plural subject *lines*

Look! <u>There</u> is the ski slope!

Verb Agreement with *Or*

When *or* is used to combine two or more subjects, a singular verb is used if the subject nearest the verb is singular.

> The hula dancers, the surfing champions, or the mayor <u>was</u> to lead the parade.
>> <u>was</u>—singular form of the verb agrees in number with the nearest subject *mayor*

When *or* is used to combine two or more subjects, a plural verb is used if the subject nearest the verb is plural. Placing the plural noun closer to the subject usually makes the sentence sound better.

> Pasta or pizzas <u>are</u> available here.
>> <u>are</u>—plural form of the verb agrees in number with the nearer subject *pizzas*

The rule for verb agreement with *or* applies to the correlative conjunctions *either–or, neither–nor, whether–or,* and *not only–but (also)* as well. The verb agrees with the closer subject.

> Neither Danny nor they <u>were</u> at the big game.
>> (<u>were</u>—agrees with the closer subject, *they*—plural)

Verb Agreement with Collective Nouns

A collective noun that refers to a group acting as a whole requires a singular verb. A collective noun that refers to a group in which the members act individually requires a plural verb. In most sentences, the collective noun is a unit requiring a singular verb. (See pages 33–34 for a review of collective nouns.)

> The awards committee <u>is</u> meeting at two o'clock on Tuesday.
>> <u>is</u>—singular form of the helping verb. The collective noun *committee* is thought of as one.

> The faculty <u>are</u> wearing their academic robes.
>> <u>are</u>—plural form of the helping verb. The collective noun *faculty* is thought of as individuals acting independently.

> The panel <u>is</u> composed of students from each major.
>> <u>is</u>—singular form of the helping verb. The collective noun *panel* is thought of as one.

> The staff <u>were</u> arguing about the setup of the registration area.
>> <u>were</u>—plural form of the helping verb. The collective noun *staff* is thought of as individuals acting independently.

> The company <u>is</u> adjusting to the current economic conditions.
>> <u>is</u>—singular form of the helping verb. The collective noun *company* is thought of as one.

> The crowd <u>was</u> growing restless.
>> <u>was</u>—singular form of the helping verb. The collective noun *crowd* is thought of as one.

RULES that work   *The number* always uses a singular verb. *A number* always uses a plural verb.

The number of graduates in business <u>is</u> increasing.

    (<u>is</u>—singular form of the helping verb—used with *the number*)

A number of excuses <u>were</u> given as to why the project was late.

    (<u>were</u>—plural form of the helping verb—used with *a number*)

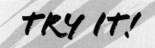

Directions Underline the correct verb form in parentheses. Check your answers on page 319 or with your instructor before continuing with your assignment.

1. His newest novel or his short stories (has, have) been adapted for television.
2. Nelson DeMille or Vince Flynn (is, are) speaking in the lecture series.
3. The class (has, have) a favorite book by Charles Dickens.
4. There (is, are) a good chance John Grisham's most recent book will be made into a movie.
5. The band (is, are) traveling in three vans.

APPLICATION   **Complete Applications 50–54, pages 109–111 and 113–114, at this time.**

WRITE NOW!

The Paragraph

A **paragraph** is made up of one or more sentences that express a single point or relate to a central theme. Its main function is to make reading and understanding information easier by grouping related sentences together. The construction of paragraphs is just as important as that of sentences.

Before starting to write, identify the points you want to make, and put them in the order most likely to achieve your purpose. All the sentences in a paragraph should relate to one topic or point and should be arranged logically.

The length of a paragraph depends on its content. Most average five to seven lines.

50 | Verb Agreement with Indefinite Pronouns, *There*, and *Or*

Directions Underline the correct verb form in parentheses. Make the verb agree in person and number with the subject. Score one point for each correct verb.

Your Score

1. Many of my colleagues (is, are) not practicing proper cell phone etiquette.   1. _____

2. There (is, are) a few simple rules that everyone should follow.   2. _____

3. One of them (is, are) to put your cell phone on vibrate during meetings.   3. _____

4. Jokey voice-mail greetings or cutesy ringtones (is, are) inappropriate in business settings.   4. _____

5. Except for an emergency, there (is, are) no good reason for taking a cell-phone call in the middle of a meeting.   5. _____

6. Both of those managers (has, have) given too much information when on a cell phone with others in close proximity.   6. _____

7. Neither Leticia nor Sophie (is, are) discussing anything private because other people are near.   7. _____

8. There (is, are) a misconception that it is necessary to talk loudly into a cell phone.   8. _____

9. There (is, are) features for adjusting volume; therefore, it is not necessary to speak loudly.   9. _____

10. Everybody in our department (has, have) a company-issued cell phone.   10. _____

---

11. There (is, are) at least fifty applicants for each position.   11. _____

12. (Was, Were) any of our college recruiters asked to prepare a list of questions that would be used in all interviews for a particular position?   12. _____

13. Some of the questions (is, are) designed to gather more information about the personal characteristics of the interviewee.   13. _____

14. All of the application packets (was, were) screened by a committee.   14. _____

15. A number of the applicants for the sales manager position (has, have) no work experience in a similar position.   15. _____

16. Each of the candidates (was, were) granted a one-hour interview.   16. _____

17. Coffee or water (is, are) placed on the table for the interviewee.   17. _____

18. Someone on the interviewing committee (is, are) keeping track of the time for each interview.   18. _____

19. An online portfolio or hard copies of documents (is, are) acceptable.   19. _____

20. There (was, were) a misunderstanding about the time set aside to complete the evaluation forms.   20. _____

Your Total Score _____ /20

If your score was 15 or less, review pages 105–107 before continuing.

51 | Verb Agreement with Collective Nouns

Directions Underline the correct verb form in parentheses. Make the verb agree in person and number with the subject. Score one point for each correct verb.

Your Score

1. The nation (has, have) been shocked by incidents of violence in schools.

1. _____

2. The majority of students (is, are) taking threats made on their schools seriously.

2. _____

3. The crowd (was, were) waiting for the assembly to start.

3. _____

4. The panel at the assembly (was, were) composed of students, parents, faculty, and law enforcement officials.

4. _____

5. A committee (was, were) formed to investigate ways of identifying students who are having problems.

5. _____

6. The counseling staff (has, have) scheduled anger management workshops.

6. _____

7. A team of investigators (has, have) been assembled.

7. _____

8. A number of phone calls (was, were) identified as prank calls.

8. _____

9. The police (has, have) increased their presence on school campuses.

9. _____

10. A group of students (was, were) huddled together consoling one another after the tragedy.

10. _____

_____

_____

11. The officiating crew for the Super Bowl (has, have) been announced.

11. _____

12. Our investment club (is, are) purchasing technology stocks.

12. _____

13. The corps (was, were) stationed at strategic points to prevent looting after the floods.

13. _____

14. A mob (is, are) gathering in front of the courthouse.

14. _____

15. The public (is, are) disillusioned by the negative ads run during political campaigns.

15. _____

16. Sami's family (has, have) agreed to serve meals to the volunteers who are filling sandbags.

16. _____

17. His platoon (was, were) assigned to help in the aftermath of the tornados.

17. _____

18. The herd (is, are) stampeding in every direction.

18. _____

19. The faculty (has, have) published 290 books.

19. _____

20. The number of accidents caused by teenage drivers (is, are) alarming.

20. _____

Your Total Score _____ /20

If your score was 15 or less, review "Verb Agreement with Collective Nouns," page 107, before continuing.

Name _____ Date _____ Score _____

52 | Unit Review

Directions Underline the correct verb form in parentheses. Make the verb agree in person and number with the subject. Score one point for each correct verb.

Your Score

1. The recruiters at the job fair (was, were) very helpful. 1. _____

2. Most of the employers (has, have) expressed a need for employees with strong communication skills. 2. _____

3. Two important work characteristics (is, are) dependability and flexibility. 3. _____

4. Few of the candidates (has, have) asked about the company's benefits package. 4. _____

5. Kaye, not Keoni and Glenn, (is, are) scheduling yearly employee evaluations. 5. _____

6. The committee for quality improvement (has, have) seven members. 6. _____

7. If she (was, were) moderating that panel discussion, I would not participate. 7. _____

8. Binders, programs, and handouts (is, are) packed to send to the conference hotel. 8. _____

9. All of our employees (is, are) expected to be team players. 9. _____

10. Geoffrey (is, are) writing the construction progress reports. 10. _____

11. She (was, were) our contact at the conference hotel. 11. _____

12. Neither Jill nor Brendon (has, have) strong organizational skills. 12. _____

13. Yuri and Norman (is, are) training on the new accounting software today. 13. _____

14. The company (is, are) picking up all travel costs for the conference. 14. _____

15. They (was, were) out with the flu. 15. _____

16. Keiki and her department (has, have) made the room assignments for sessions. 16. _____

17. The staff (has, have) a sincere interest in advocating for clients. 17. _____

18. Each of the new employees (was, were) assigned a mentor. 18. _____

19. There (is, are) an office procedures manual. 19. _____

20. Cruz (was, were) promoted after only six months. 20. _____

21. Eileen or the officers (has, have) arranged for the rental of laptop computers. 21. _____

22. Not only Senobar but also Wylie (is, are) enjoying the business seminar. 22. _____

23. Sang (has, have) the post office hold his mail when he (is, are) on a business trip. 23. _____

24. A number of banquet attendees (was, were) posing for a group photo. 24. _____

25. There (is, are) several computer sessions available on Friday afternoon. 25. _____

Your Total Score _____ /26

Customer service representatives are found in many types of businesses. They are sometimes the only contact customers have with a business or an organization; therefore, they are the company. Retail, hotel, medical, utilities, technology, consumer product, and travel businesses are just some of the types of businesses that employ customer service representatives.

Customer service representatives are responsible for answering inquiries, servicing existing accounts, and selling new products or services. They communicate with customers by telephone, e-mail, fax, or regular mail or in person. When they are dealing with customers on the telephone, a clear speaking voice and a professional manner are necessary.

Most customer service representatives also need computer and data entry skills. Accessing a computer database for information on a customer, a product, or a list of frequently asked questions (with responses) is often a major component of a customer service call. Organizational, problem solving, and prioritizing abilities are essential.

This occupation is well suited to flexible work schedules because many customer service centers are staffed 24 hours a day, seven days a week. It also offers work opportunities for part-time employees and seasonal work in certain industries.

Directions Underline the correct verb form in parentheses. Make the verb agree in person and number with the subject. Score one point for each correct verb.

Your Score

1. Janelle (has, have) been spending most of her time on the phone.   1. _____

2. Some very unusual problems and requests (is, are) handled by our customer service representatives.   2. _____

3. Stephan and the quality control managers (is, are) evaluating recordings of customer service calls.   3. _____

4. Customer service representatives (has, have) a list of questions to ask callers to gather necessary background information.   4. _____

5. The details of each call (is, are) recorded carefully to ensure accuracy.   5. _____

6. A solution (is, are) reached only after collecting all pertinent information and evaluating the problem carefully.   6. _____

7. All of our representatives (is, are) trained on troubleshooting technical problems. 7. _____

8. Customer satisfaction (is, are) the ultimate goal.   8. _____

Your Total Score _____ /8

53 | Writing Improvement

A | **Directions** Revise the paragraph so it has unity. All sentences need to be related to the main topic of the paragraph. Delete any unrelated sentences, and put the sentences in a logical order. Your final paragraph should flow smoothly and should be clear and concise.

When I visit the San Diego Zoo, my first stop is always the Giant Panda Research Station. I also like Ituri Forest. The zoo has more giant pandas than any other zoo in the United States. The first giant pandas were sent to the zoo in 1987 from China. Hua Mei, the first panda born in North America to survive to adulthood, was born there. Pandas weigh only about 4 ounces at birth. I used to watch Hua Mei on the zoo's Panda Cam. She was so cute. The panda exhibit is just one of the exhibits that feature endangered species. The line to see the pandas is usually very long. They live in enclosures carefully designed to resemble their habitat in the wild.

_____

_____

_____

_____

B | **Directions** Write a short paragraph (four to five sentences) in response to the following possible interview question. Use clear, concise sentences, and make sure all verbs agree with their subjects.

What is your energy level? Describe a typical day. (Your answer should demonstrate that you use your time well, that you believe in planning, and that when a day is done you review your performance.)

_____

_____

_____

_____

_____

 **Give your completed application to your instructor for evaluation.**

54 | Comprehensive Review

Directions Underline the correct noun, pronoun, or verb in parentheses. Score one point for each correct answer.

Your Score

1. Everyone but Conrad and two others workers (is, are) taking inventory this weekend. 1. _____

2. There (is, are) hundreds of people applying for each job opening. 2. _____

3. (Who, Whom) knows what protocol is being used for issuing company credit cards? 3. _____

4. (Has, Have) any of the work orders for Ajax Inc. been completed? 4. _____

5. We value (customer's customers') suggestions for improving our products and services. 5. _____

6. (She, Her) and Kazuo prefer automatic deposit of their paychecks. 6. _____

7. Some (company's, companies) offer caregiver benefits. 7. _____

8. The report on flexible work schedules (is, are) making (it's, its) way through the committee. 8. _____

9. Many of our employees (has, have) inquired about telecommuting. 9. _____

10. Members of senior management (is, are) speaking to the visitors from India. 10. _____

11. Business (is, are) done when the workday is done. 11. _____

12. Rashid gave Suzie and (I, me) some suggestions on things to do this weekend. 12. _____

13. Please arrange the new products on those (shelfs, shelves). 13. _____

14. Was it (he, him) who did the research for the proposal? 14. _____

15. (You, He) never completes proposals without careful research. 15. _____

16. It (was, were) sometimes difficult for Jonathon to determine Mr. Worth's reaction to his proposals. 16. _____

17. The committee (is, are) recommending diversity training for all employees. 17. _____

18. The (women's, womens') aerobics class starts at 4 p.m. 18. _____

19. There (is, are) several ways of calling a server over to your table when dining in a restaurant. 19. _____

20. The traffic laws may cause him and (they, them) some confusion. 20. _____

Your Total Score _____ /21

PROOF IT!

Directions Proofread the flyer. Mark any changes that are needed using the proofreaders' marks on page 317. Then key the flyer, making all necessary corrections. Center it vertically and horizontally. Proofread your work, and make any corrections that are needed. Turn in both this page and your finished flyer to your instructor.

Welcome Back to School Picnic an Beach Party

Saturday, September 4

Powerhouse Park, Solana Beach

1 p.m. to 7p.m.

Food and refreshments is provided.

Look for the balloons to to lead you to the Collins College picnic site

Please RSVP to adela johnson in the Student Affairs Office, Room H105,

be fore 4 p.m. own August 29 (or call Extension 1146).

Posttest

A | **Directions** Underline each verb. In the blank at the right, write *S* if the verb makes a statement, *Q* if it asks a question, or *C* if it gives a command.

1. Meet me after the Fourth of July parade.   1. _____

2. Brock marches with his Boy Scout troop.   2. _____

3. Who is the grand marshal?   3. _____

4. People on the floats toss candy to the crowd.   4. _____

5. Our class won the prize for the best float.   5. _____

B | **Directions** Identify the helping verbs by underlining them once. Identify the main verbs by underlining them twice.

1. Chloe has attended a CPR training session.

2. All lifeguards must pass a rigorous test.

3. Jacob should lift weights every morning.

4. I can hold my breath underwater for more than two minutes.

5. The manager of the city swimming pool will administer the lifeguard exam.

C | **Directions** Underline the correct verb form in parentheses. Make the verb agree in person and number with the subject.

1. Many of your classmates (has, have) donated money to the relief efforts.

2. Neither Marla nor Fran (is, are) helping out at the local hospital.

3. There (is, are) volunteer firefighters from all over the state.

4. Soup and sandwiches (is, are) available to the firefighters on the scene.

5. Our community (is, are) known for helping those in need.

unit 5
The Time of Verbs

Objectives

1. To recognize and use the present, past, and future tenses of verbs
2. To recognize and use the perfect tenses of verbs
3. To recognize and use verbs according to person, number, tense, and voice
4. To recognize and use topic sentences

Sections

Pretest

A | **Directions** If the underlined verb is correct, write *C* in the blank at the right. If it is incorrect, write the correct verb.

1. Constance <u>carrys</u> her planner with her everywhere she goes.   1. _____

2. They <u>will have eaten</u> dinner by the time I get there.   2. _____

3. <u>Will</u> we <u>sign</u> the papers tomorrow morning?   3. _____

4. Grace still <u>hasn't worn</u> the suit we bought her.   4. _____

5. Catalina often <u>forgets</u> to turn on her cell phone.   5. _____

6. Ervin <u>read</u> the play, so he knew what was going to happen.   6. _____

7. She <u>were</u> at the game last night, too.   7. _____

8. Woody <u>don't</u> work at the mall anymore.   8. _____

9. Roberta <u>slipped</u> on the stairs and broke her ankle.   9. _____

10. She <u>owned</u> a house in Chelsea for several years.   10. _____

B | **Directions** If the underlined verb is in the active voice, write *A* in the blank at the right. Write *P* if it is in the passive voice.

1. The concert <u>was canceled</u> because of the snow.   1. _____

2. Dr. Shih <u>admitted</u> her to the hospital this morning.   2. _____

3. Travis <u>divided</u> the work among the volunteers.   3. _____

4. Our high school band <u>was selected</u> to march in the Tournament of Roses Parade.   4. _____

5. Several boys <u>dove</u> off the cliff, disregarding the sign.   5. _____

Business Dress

A good guide for business attire is to select a few co-workers who dress in a way you like and to model your style on theirs. In many organizations, the standard for men is nice slacks, a shirt and tie, and sometimes a sweater. For women, skirts, dresses, slacks, blouses, and sweaters are acceptable. If your company has casual days, follow any rules established for those days. Even on casual days, if you will be meeting with customers or clients, dress for the meeting.

Some clothes are never appropriate at work. They include clothes that show your midriff or back, tops that are cut too low, skirts that are too short, clothes that let your underwear show, and clothes with words that could be offensive.

Pay attention to details. Your nicest shirt won't impress if it's wrinkled or stained. Get your clothes ready the night before. Press them, if necessary (buy wrinkle-free clothes to minimize ironing). Examine them in a good light. Look for stray threads, lint, pulls, and spots. Your shoes should be shined and your hair neat and clean. Keep jewelry and makeup subtle. Before you leave for work, check your appearance in a mirror. Make sure the impression you give is always a positive one.

Section 13 Present Tense

Verbs are used to express the time at which events occur. Some events take place in the present, some took place in the past, and others will take place in the future.

The form of a verb that is used to indicate the time of an event is called tense. There are three primary tenses: the present, the past, and the future.

Verbs in the Present Tense

The present tense tells what is happening now. It is also used to indicate habitual action and to express a general truth.

> Melissa <u>walks</u> briskly through the crowd.
>
> > <u>walks</u>—present tense because the subject *Melissa* is doing it now
>
> Justin <u>checks</u> for downloads every few days.
>
> > <u>checks</u>—present tense because it indicates habitual action
>
> "Change <u>is</u> inevitable, except from vending machines."
>
> > <u>is</u>—present tense because it expresses a general truth

To form the present tense of most verbs, use the verb in its original form for all persons except the third-person singular. In the third-person singular, add the letter *s* to the verb.

	Singular	**Plural**
1st person	I stay	we stay
2nd person	you stay	you stay
3rd person	he, she, it stays	they stay

Study the verbs *close* and *look*, for example, to see how they are formed in the present tense.

I close	we close
you close	you close
he, she, it closes	they close

I look	we look
you look	you look
he, she, it looks	they look

Some verbs have a slightly different ending in the third-person singular. For verbs ending in *y* preceded by a consonant, change the *y* to *i* and add *es* (*study/studies*). For verbs ending in *s*, *ch*, or *sh*, add *es* (*pass/passes, catch/catches, wash/washes*).

The Verb *Be* in the Present Tense

Perhaps the most frequently used verb in the English language is the verb *be*. Unlike the verbs mentioned before, this verb changes forms in the first-, second-, and third-person singular.

	Singular	**Plural**
1st person	I am	we are
2nd person	you are	you are
3rd person	he, she, it is	they are

(See page 100 for a discussion of agreement of subjects with the forms of the verb *be*.)

When you proofread, check for consistency of verb tense, facts, and format.

- Is the verb tense the same where it should be, or does it sometimes change with no reason?

- Are the facts consistent? For example, if the time of a meeting is 10:30 on the first page of a memo and 1:30 on the second page, which is correct?

- Is the format the same throughout?

The Verb *Have* in the Present Tense

Have is the next-most-used verb. This verb is easy to learn because it is the same in almost all forms. The only change takes place in the third-person singular, where the form *has* is used. *Have* is used with all other singular and plural subjects.

	Singular	**Plural**
1st person	I have	we have
2nd person	you have	you have
3rd person	he, she, it has	they have

(See page 101 for a discussion of agreement of subjects with the forms of the verb *have*.)

The Verb *Do* in the Present Tense

A frequent mistake is using the wrong form of the verb *do* in the third-person singular. Always be sure to use *does* with third-person singular subjects. Do not use *he don't*. Use the correct form, *he doesn't*.

	Singular	**Plural**
1st person	I do	we do
2nd person	you do	you do
3rd person	he, she, it does	they do

Incorrect	She <u>don't</u> play the piano.
Correct	She <u>doesn't</u> play the piano.
Incorrect	It <u>don't</u> taste good.
Correct	It <u>doesn't</u> taste good.

TRY IT!

Directions If the underlined verb is correct, write C in the blank at the right. If it is incorrect, write the correct verb. Check your answers on page 319 or with your instructor before continuing with your assignment.

1. We usually <u>shop</u> for fruit and vegetables at the farmers' market.　　1. _____

2. Amanda <u>trys</u> to read one good book a month.　　2. _____

3. We can't serve sushi because Hector <u>don't</u> like it.　　3. _____

4. <u>Is</u> Jenna the first person in her family to go to college?　　4. _____

5. Nicholas <u>has</u> a new digital camera.　　5. _____

6. After supper, Sarah <u>watchs</u> the news.　　6. _____

7. Please <u>introduce</u> me to the rest of the team.　　7. _____

8. <u>Does</u> it make sense for us to get disability insurance?　　8. _____

Verbs in the Past Tense

The **past tense** tells what has already happened. The past tense of most verbs is formed by adding *ed* to the verb regardless of number (singular or plural) or person. If the verb ends with the letter *e*, add *d* to form the past tense.

> With a few simple changes, the company <u>reduced</u> its water use by 30 percent.

<u>reduced</u>—past tense of the verb *reduce*—tells that the subject *company* has already completed the act of reducing

> Andrew <u>cheered</u> when his team <u>scored</u> a touchdown.

<u>cheered</u>—past tense of the verb *cheer*—tells that the subject *Andrew* has already completed the act of cheering

<u>scored</u>—past tense of the verb *score*—tells that the subject *team* has already completed the act of scoring

Some verbs have a minor change at the end before *ed* or *d* is added. For verbs ending in *y* preceded by a consonant, change the *y* to *i* and add *ed* (*carry/carried*). For one-syllable verbs ending in a consonant preceded by a short vowel, double the final consonant before adding *ed* (*drop/dropped*). Do the same for two-syllable verbs in which the second syllable is accented (*occur/occurred*).

The Verb *Be* in the Past Tense

The verb form *was* is used with all singular subjects except *you*. Always say and write *you were*. The verb form *were* is used with all plural subjects.

	Singular	**Plural**
1st person	I was	we were
2nd person	you were	you were
3rd person	he, she, it was	they were

The Verb *Have* in the Past Tense

The past tense of *have* has only one form. It is *had*. Use *had* with all subjects, singular and plural, in the past tense.

	Singular	**Plural**
1st person	I had	we had
2nd person	you had	you had
3rd person	he, she, it had	they had

TRY IT!

Directions Complete each sentence by writing in the blank at the right the past tense of the verb in parentheses. Check your answers on page 319 or with your instructor before continuing with your assignment.

1. Our football team (play) for the conference championship.

2. (Be) you at the convention in Dallas last week?

3. They (open) a 529 college savings plan.

4. Louise (have) five interviews before accepting a job.

5. Santiago (copy) the managers on that e-mail.

6. We (ship) the order two days ago.

7. The voters (approve) a proposition for a mass transit system.

8. At first, I (regret) selling my truck, but now I'm glad I did.

1. _____

2. _____

3. _____

4. _____

5. _____

6. _____

7. _____

8. _____

WRITE NOW!

The Topic Sentence

A topic sentence expresses the central thought of a paragraph. The first sentence in a paragraph is usually the topic sentence. Sometimes the topic sentence is restated in a summary sentence to conclude the paragraph. Occasionally, for a particular effect, experienced writers prefer to place the topic sentence at the end of the paragraph. Wherever it is placed, the topic sentence should catch the reader's interest so that he or she will want to continue reading.

Once the topic sentence has been written, the paragraph should be developed with other sentences that expand on the topic sentence. Ideas should be presented concisely, in a sensible, natural order. Each sentence should include additional details that keep to the point.

Future Tense

The future tense tells what will happen in the time to come.

> Ryan <u>will hike</u> across the Presidential Range in August.
>
>> <u>will hike</u>—future tense because the subject *Ryan* will hike across the range in the time to come

To express the future, use the helping verb *will* before the main verb in all persons, except in questions. For the first person (*I, we*) in questions, use the helping verb *shall* before the main verb.

> <u>Shall</u> we <u>dance</u>?
>
> <u>Shall</u> I <u>wait</u> for you?
>
> <u>Will</u> they <u>reveal</u> the plans next week?

	Singular	**Plural**
1st person	I will start	we will start
(questions)	Shall I start?	Shall we start?
2nd person	you will start	you will start
3rd person	he, she, it will start	they will start

Some people use *shall* in the first-person singular and plural in declarative sentences (*I shall rest. We shall rest.*). This usage, however, is seldom heard today in speech and is considered formal rather than general English usage.

TRY IT!

Directions Underline the correct future tense helping verb in parentheses. Check your answers on page 320 or with your instructor before continuing with your assignment.

1. (Shall, Will) I tell Anita we'll be there at 7?

2. (Shall, Will) Ehab want to go with us?

3. (Shall, Will) we go to the Festival of Lights?

4. I (shall, will) fly to New York this time.

APPLICATION Complete Applications 55–56, pages 125–126, at this time.

55 | Present and Past Tenses

A | **Directions** If the underlined verb is correct, write *C* in the blank at the right. If it is incorrect, write the correct verb. Score one point for each correct answer.

Answers

1. The sun's energy <u>heats</u> the surface of the earth.

    1. _____

2. The earth <u>radiates</u> energy back into space.

    2. _____

3. The outgoing energy <u>don't</u> all return to space, however.

    3. _____

4. Atmospheric greenhouse gases <u>traps</u> most of it.

    4. _____

5. The gases <u>are</u> like the glass panels on a greenhouse.

    5. _____

6. This greenhouse effect <u>pushs</u> the earth's temperature higher.

    6. _____

7. Scientists have found that an increase of just 1 degree Fahrenheit <u>has</u> profound effects.

    7. _____

8. As the concentration of greenhouse gases <u>reachs</u> higher levels, more energy is retained.

    8. _____

9. Human activities such as burning fossil fuels <u>contributes</u> to this increase.

    9. _____

10. The Red List, produced by the International Union for Conservation of Nature and Natural Resources, <u>identifys</u> species threatened by climate change and other dangers.

    10. _____

Your Total Score _____ /10

If your score was 7 or less, review Section 13, pages 119–121, before continuing.

B | **Directions** Complete each sentence by writing in the blank at the right the past tense of the verb in parentheses. Score one point for each correct answer.

1. The students in my class (decide) to research some things they could do to reduce global warming.

    1. _____

2. Erica (replace) all her lightbulbs with compact fluorescent bulbs.

    2. _____

3. When the Ernsts (have) to buy a new dishwasher, they chose one with an ENERGY STAR rating.

    3. _____

4. Stan (learn) that keeping your tires properly inflated helps.

    4. _____

5. I (ask) my utility company for a free energy audit.

    5. _____

6. Fatima (prefer) riding the bus to fighting rush-hour traffic.

    6. _____

7. Mr. Hakimi (wrap) his water heater with an insulating blanket.

    7. _____

8. Lydia (try) lowering her thermostat at night and during work hours.

    8. _____

9. (Are) you online, researching fuel-efficient cars?

    9. _____

10. If people (recycle) half their household waste, they could save 1.2 tons of carbon dioxide a year.

    10. _____

Your Total Score _____ /10

If your score was 7 or less, review Section 14, pages 122–123, before continuing.

56 | Present, Past, and Future Tenses

A | **Directions** Underline the correct future tense helping verb in parentheses. Score one point for each correct answer.

Your Score

1. As energy prices rise, more homes (shall, will) have green features. 1. _____

2. They (shall, will) use less energy and water and fewer natural resources. 2. _____

3. (Shall, Will) we choose a green design for our new house? 3. _____

4. We (shall, will) begin by planning a smaller-than-average home. 4. _____

5. The contractor (shall, will) recycle from 40 to 70 percent of construction waste, which would have gone to a landfill. 5. _____

6. Installing storm doors and double-pane windows (shall, will) cut energy spending. 6. _____

7. Properly insulating a home (shall, will) lower utility bills. 7. _____

8. Shade trees (shall, will) save the average household $100 to $250 in energy costs each year. 8. _____

9. I (shall, will) replace most of my lawn with a native groundcover. 9. _____

10. (Shall, Will) I start composting yard waste, too? 10. _____

Your Total Score _____ /10
If your score was 7 or less, review Section 15, page 124, before continuing.

B | **Directions** Complete each sentence by writing in the blank at the right the correct form of the verb in parentheses. Score one point for each correct answer.

Answers

1. The greenhouse effect (present tense of *be*) a natural phenomenon. 1. _____

2. By keeping the earth warm, the greenhouse gases in the atmosphere (present tense of *support*) life. 2. _____

3. Svante Arrhenius, a Swedish scientist, first (past tense of *recognize*) the greenhouse effect. 3. _____

4. He (past tense of *study*) possible effects of changes in carbon dioxide levels in the atmosphere on the earth's climate. 4. _____

5. Scientists are searching for ways to capture and store carbon dioxide before it (present tense of *reach*) the atmosphere. 5. _____

6. Under a cap-and-trade system, a government that (past tense of *cap*) greenhouse gases would let companies trade credits for emitting them. 6. _____

7. Companies bringing their emissions below the cap could sell credits and offset any costs they (past tense of *incur*). 7. _____

8. The responsibility for reducing greenhouse gases (present tense of *rest*) with individuals as well as big organizations. 8. _____

9. I (future tense of *determine*) my carbon footprint with an online calculator. 9. _____

10. Your carbon footprint (future tense of *show*) how many pounds of carbon dioxide and other greenhouse gases your activities generate. 10. _____

Your Total Score _____ /10
If your score was 7 or less, review Sections 13–15, pages 119–124, before continuing.

Perfect Tenses

All the perfect tenses have to do with the completion of an action. Although we use the perfect tenses less often, an understanding of them is essential to good English. You will find that the perfect tenses are easy to learn.

Present Perfect Tense

The present perfect tense is used to show that something started in the past and has continued to the present. It is also used to show that an action was completed recently or at some indefinite time in the past.

The present perfect tense is formed by using the present tense of the verb *have* before the past participle of the main verb. A participle is a verb form usually ending in *ing, ed, t,* or *en* that is combined with a helping verb to form certain tenses and is sometimes used as an adjective.

For most verbs, the past tense form of the verb and the past participle are the same. Most of the irregular past participles can be found on pages 133–134.

When you are forming the present perfect tense, be careful to make the subject and verb agree. Use *has* only when the subject is third-person singular. Use *have* with all other singular and plural subjects.

	Singular	**Plural**
1st person	I have finished	we have finished
2nd person	you have finished	you have finished
3rd person	he, she, it has finished	they have finished

Ms. Taggert has managed our Information Technology Department for the past eight years.

> has managed—present perfect tense—indicates an action that started in the past and that has continued to the present

They have filled two dozen orders since lunchtime.

> have filled—present perfect tense—indicates an action that was completed recently

I have changed my career plans.

> have changed—present perfect tense—indicates an action that was completed at some indefinite time in the past

TRY IT!

Directions Complete each sentence by writing in the blank at the right the correct form of the verb in parentheses: present perfect tense or past tense. Check your answers on page 320 or with your instructor before continuing with your assignment.

1. I (remember) my new dress after boarding the plane. 1. _____

2. Since starting her own business, Veda (contribute) $4,500 every year to her SEP IRA. 2. _____

3. We (have) a severe drought last summer. 3. _____

4. He (publish) five novels so far. 4. _____

5. Sean and I (work) together for the past 15 years. 5. _____

6. Suki (arrange) the meeting three months ago. 6. _____

Past Perfect Tense

The **past perfect tense** refers to something that was completed in the past before another past action or event. It is formed in all numbers and persons by using *had* with the past participle of the main verb.

	Singular	**Plural**
1st person	I had learned	we had learned
2nd person	you had learned	you had learned
3rd person	he, she, it had learned	they had learned

I asked Carson's advice because he <u>had lived</u> in France for a year.

> <u>had lived</u>—past perfect tense—indicates an action that was completed before another past action

Alexis called to let us know that she <u>had arrived</u>.

> <u>had arrived</u>—past perfect tense—indicates an action that was completed before another past action

Future Perfect Tense

The **future perfect tense** is used when an action begun at any time will be completed by or before a specific time in the future. It is formed by using *will have* with the past participle of the main verb. Use *shall have* instead of *will have* for the first person in questions.

	Singular	**Plural**
1st person	I will have studied	we will have studied
2nd person	you will have studied	you will have studied
3rd person	he, she, it will have studied	they will have studied

Liza <u>will have completed</u> all her course work by December.

> <u>will have completed</u>—future perfect tense—indicates an action that will be completed by a specific time in the future

<u>Will</u> Mateo <u>have prepared</u> the financial reports before he leaves for the conference?

> <u>Will have prepared</u>—future perfect tense—indicates an action that will be completed before a specific time in the future

TRY IT!

Directions Complete each sentence by writing in the blank at the right the correct form of the verb in parentheses. Check your answers on page 320 or with your instructor before continuing with your assignment.

1. By the time he was 16, Wolfgang Amadeus Mozart (past perfect tense of *compose*) three operas and 25 symphonies.   1. _____

2. They (future perfect tense of *test*) the software before we meet.   2. _____

3. Tran said that he (past perfect tense of *collect*) 2,500 signatures.   3. _____

4. By Friday, we (future perfect tense of *calculate*) the sales bonuses for this year.   4. _____

APPLICATION ▶ Complete Applications 57–58, pages 129–130, at this time.

57 | Perfect Tenses

Directions Underline each perfect tense verb. In the blank at the right, write *present perfect, past perfect,* or *future perfect.* If the sentence does not contain a perfect tense verb, do not underline or write anything. Score one point for each correctly underlined verb and one point for each correct identification.

Answers

1. Some people have several careers during their lives.

1. _____

2. Max has changed careers four times.

2. _____

3. He had always loved sports, so he planned to be a physical education teacher.

3. _____

4. Before he went to college, Max had worked part-time in a fitness center.

4. _____

5. By the time he graduated, Max and a friend had decided to open a gym.

5. _____

6. After they had operated it for several years, Max wanted a change.

6. _____

7. He went back to school to become an exercise physiologist.

7. _____

8. Max had completed several interviews when he found a job he really wanted: exercise physiologist in a cardiopulmonary rehabilitation program.

8. _____

9. He designed exercise programs for heart patients and worked with them one-on-one with the goals of speeding recovery and improving health.

9. _____

10. After nine years had passed, Max started taking classes to become a registered nurse.

10. _____

11. He liked working in the emergency room and intensive care the best.

11. _____

12. Then the job of cardiac rehabilitation clinical manager opened.

12. _____

13. For the past two years, Max has managed the day-to-day operations of the cardiac rehabilitation clinic.

13. _____

14. At the same time, as a certified diabetes educator, he has talked to people about how to live well with this disease.

14. _____

15. Max has enjoyed the challenges, benefits, and opportunities that working in allied health care and nursing offers.

15. _____

16. The Bureau of Labor Statistics projects that, by 2016, the health care and social assistance sector will have added 4 million jobs.

16. _____

17. In that year, the total number of jobs in that sector will have reached 19 million.

17. _____

Your Total Score _____ /24
If your score was 18 or less, review Section 16, pages 127–128, before continuing.

58 | Perfect Tenses

Directions Complete each sentence by writing in the blank at the right the correct perfect tense form of the verb in parentheses. Score one point for each correct answer.

Answers

1. Two companies (offer) Lucia a job. 1. _____

2. Wesley (accept) an offer from a multinational corporation. 2. _____

3. They (pick) their benefits by next Monday. 3. _____

4. Traditionally, employee benefits (include) a retirement plan, life and health insurance, and vacation and sick days. 4. _____

5. When she was sick and couldn't work, Raja was able to meet her expenses because she (purchase) disability insurance. 5. _____

6. There is a 30 percent chance that a 20-year-old worker (suffer) a disability before he or she retires. 6. _____

7. Russell showed us how he (compare) the features of various health plans. 7. _____

8. Before we schedule the next open enrollment period, we (add) dental and vision coverage to our benefits package. 8. _____

9. He (enroll) in the company's dental plan. 9. _____

10. At lunch last Tuesday, Greta described how she (reduce) her taxable income by $2,000 with a flexible spending account. 10. _____

11. Once she (calculate) her likely medical expenses for the next year, she knew how much money to put into the account. 11. _____

12. Since 2004, the company (provide) free health screenings and gym memberships as part of its wellness program. 12. _____

13. The flexible work schedule and paid personal days his employer offers (enable) Austin to care for his father. 13. _____

14. By this time next year, Isabella (earn) her master's degree through a company-sponsored education plan. 14. _____

15. For the past three years, we (allow) our employees up to 20 hours of paid time off for community service. 15. _____

16. Deborah (consider) the value of the benefits—40 percent of her salary—before she agreed to take the job. 16. _____

17. Dustin (e-mail) us his recommendations by the time we meet. 17. _____

18. So far, Jack (save) $40,000 toward retirement through his employer's dollar-for-dollar matching 401(k) plan. 18. _____

19. Linda knew about the employee stock options because she (research) the company on the Internet. 19. _____

20. She (finish) the paperwork by tomorrow morning. 20. _____

Your Total Score _____ /20

If your score was 15 or less, review Section 16, pages 127–128, before continuing.

Conjugation, Voice, and Irregular Verbs

Conjugation of Verbs

Conjugation means breaking a verb down into its different forms to show person, number, tense, and voice. Page 132 shows the conjugation of a regular verb.

All verbs have three basic forms, which are called their principal parts. From these basic forms, you can make up the tense of any verb. The first principal part is the verb itself. This is the part with which you are most familiar: *form, change, discuss*. The second principal part is the past tense form. The third principal part is the past participle. Remember that the past tense and past participle for most verbs are formed the same way: by adding *d* or *ed* to the verb.

Verb	Past Tense	Past Participle
form	formed	formed
change	changed	changed
discuss	discussed	discussed

Some people consider the present participle a fourth principal part. The present participle is formed, for most verbs, by adding *ing* to the verb (*forming, changing, discussing*). Note that in *changing*, the final *e* was dropped before *ing* was added.

Here is how you can use the principal parts of verbs to form different tenses:

Present tense

The verb, with *s* added in the third-person singular

Past tense

The past tense of the verb

Future tense

Shall or *will* plus the verb

Present perfect tense

Have or *has* plus the past participle

Past perfect tense

Had plus the past participle

Future perfect tense

Shall have or *will have* plus the past participle

The chart on page 132 simplifies conjugation as much as possible, but the only way to learn how to conjugate verbs is to use them repeatedly.

Voice

Verbs may be in either the active voice or the passive voice. A verb is in the active voice when the subject performs the action. A verb is in the passive voice when the action is done to the subject by something or someone else. Some form of the helping verb *be* and a past participle are necessary with the passive voice.

Old Faithful <u>erupts</u> about 20 times a day.

<u>erupts</u>—active voice—the subject *Old Faithful* performs the action

The eruptions <u>are witnessed</u> by thousands of tourists.

<u>are witnessed</u>—passive voice—action is done to the subject *eruptions* by tourists

The fire <u>burned</u> for three hours.

<u>burned</u>—active voice—the subject *fire* performed the action

Seven homes <u>were destroyed</u> by the fire.

<u>were destroyed</u>—passive voice—action was done to the subject *homes* by the fire

Old Faithful erupts about 20 times a day.

The eruptions are witnessed by thousands of tourists.

ACTIVE   PASSIVE

Sentences with verbs in the active voice are usually stronger and more concise than sentences with verbs in the passive voice. When you write, use the active voice most of the time. Use the passive voice when you don't know, or when it doesn't matter, who or what performed the action. The passive voice is also appropriate when you want to emphasize the receiver of the action or to avoid sounding as if you are assigning blame.

The display <u>was removed</u> after repeated complaints.

<u>was removed</u>—passive voice—it doesn't matter who removed the display

My nephew <u>was selected</u> for the All State Orchestra.

<u>was selected</u>—passive voice—emphasizes the receiver of the action, *my nephew*

The entry <u>was received</u> two weeks after the deadline.

<u>was received</u>—passive voice—avoids sounding as if you are assigning blame

Conjugation of the Verb *Turn*

The following chart can be used as a guide and check in deciding how a verb is broken down into its different parts. Use and refer to this chart often.

Verb	Present Participle	Past Tense	Past Participle
turn	turning	turned	turned

Active Voice (action done by the subject)		Passive Voice (action done to the subject)	
Singular	**Plural**	**Singular**	**Plural**
Present Tense		**Present Tense**	
I turn	we turn	I am turned	we are turned
you turn	you turn	you are turned	you are turned
he, she, it turns	they turn	he, she, it is turned	they are turned
Past Tense		**Past Tense**	
I turned	we turned	I was turned	we were turned
you turned	you turned	you were turned	you were turned
he, she, it turned	they turned	he, she, it was turned	they were turned
Future Tense		**Future Tense**	
I will turn	we will turn	I will be turned	we will be turned
you will turn	you will turn	you will be turned	you will be turned
he, she, it will turn	they will turn	he, she, it will be turned	they will be turned
Present Perfect Tense		**Present Perfect Tense**	
I have turned	we have turned	I have been turned	we have been turned
you have turned	you have turned	you have been turned	you have been turned
he, she, it has turned	they have turned	he, she, it has been turned	they have been turned
Past Perfect Tense		**Past Perfect Tense**	
I had turned	we had turned	I had been turned	we had been turned
you had turned	you had turned	you had been turned	you had been turned
he, she, it had turned	they had turned	he, she, it had been turned	they had been turned
Future Perfect Tense		**Future Perfect Tense**	
I will have turned	we will have turned	I will have been turned	we will have been turned
you will have turned	you will have turned	you will have been turned	you will have been turned
he, she, it will have turned	they will have turned	he, she, it will have been turned	they will have been turned

Principal Parts of Irregular Verbs

Irregular verbs do not follow the rules for forming the past tense and the past participle. They are, however, the most-used verbs in the English language. Learning them involves practice and memorization. Review them now, and study any that are unfamiliar to you.

Frequently Used Irregular Verbs

Irregular Verb	Past Tense	Past Participle
be (am, is, are)	was (were)	been
become	became	become
begin	began	begun
bite	bit	bitten
break	broke	broken
bring	brought	brought
build	built	built
come	came	come
do	did	done
drink	drank	drunk
drive	drove	driven
eat	ate	eaten
fall	fell	fallen
fight	fought	fought
find	found	found
fly	flew	flown
get	got	gotten or got
give	gave	given
go	went	gone
grow	grew	grown
hear	heard	heard
hide	hid	hidden
hit	hit	hit
keep	kept	kept
know	knew	known
lay	laid	laid
lead	led	led
leave	left	left
let	let	let
lie (recline)	lay	lain
lose	lost	lost
make	made	made
put	put	put
ride	rode	ridden
ring	rang	rung
run	ran	run
say	said	said
see	saw	seen
show	showed	shown or showed
sing	sang	sung
sit	sat	sat
sleep	slept	slept
speak	spoke	spoken
take	took	taken
teach	taught	taught
tell	told	told
think	thought	thought
throw	threw	thrown
wear	wore	worn
write	wrote	written

The following list contains 31 additional irregular verbs. They are important for you to learn as well.

Less Frequently Used Irregular Verbs

Irregular Verb	Past Tense	Past Participle
arise	arose	arisen
awake	awoke or awaked	awoken, awaked, or awoke
bear	bore	borne
beat	beat	beaten
blow	blew	blown
burst	burst or bursted	burst or bursted
catch	caught	caught
choose	chose	chosen
cling	clung	clung
cost	cost	cost
dive	dived or dove	dived
draw	drew	drawn
fling	flung	flung
forget	forgot	forgotten or forgot
freeze	froze	frozen
hang	hung or hanged	hung or hanged
hurt	hurt	hurt
pay	paid	paid
read	read	read
rise	rose	risen
set	set	set
shake	shook	shaken
shine	shone or shined	shone or shined
sink	sank or sunk	sunk
spring	sprang or sprung	sprung
steal	stole	stolen
swear	swore	sworn
swim	swam	swum
swing	swung	swung
tear	tore	torn
wake	woke or waked	woken, woke, or waked

TRY IT!

Directions Complete each sentence by writing in the blank at the right the correct form of the verb in parentheses. Check your answers on page 320 or with your instructor before continuing with your assignment.

1. We (past tense of *see*) Nolan Ryan pitch his last game.   1. _____

2. We recalled how he (past perfect tense of *break*) Sandy
   Koufax's single-season strikeout record 20 years before.   2. _____

3. Few pitchers have achieved as much as he (past tense of *do*).   3. _____

 **APPLICATION** **Complete Applications 59–65, pages 135–139 and 141–142, at this time.**

59 | Active and Passive Voices

A | **Directions** If the underlined verb is in the active voice, write *A* in the blank at the right. Write *P* if it is in the passive voice. Score one point for each correct answer.

Answers

1. Our corporate headquarters <u>will be designed</u> by Foyle and Grimsby.

2. They <u>have built</u> a dozen structures downtown in the past several years.

3. We <u>serve</u> clients in many different industries.

4. The parts <u>are flown</u> to our plants in Toledo and Detroit.

5. Lamar <u>trains</u> new employees on handling customer complaints.

6. The package <u>had been delivered</u> to the wrong address.

7. Our self-directed work team <u>produced</u> more parts per hour this year than any other.

8. The commission <u>was represented</u> by its chair, Victorrie Scott.

9. We <u>will supply</u> tablets and GPS systems for all our sales agents.

10. Everyone <u>has been invited</u> to the dedication ceremony.

1. _____

2. _____

3. _____

4. _____

5. _____

6. _____

7. _____

8. _____

9. _____

10. _____

B | **Directions** Rewrite active-voice sentences to be in the passive voice. Rewrite passive-voice sentences to be in the active voice. Score one point for each correct rewrite.

Example A person on our staff will contact successful candidates by June 30.

Successful candidates will be contacted by June 30.

Your Score

1. You sent an e-mail with confidential information.

_____

2. The annual sales figures were explained by the vice president.

_____

3. Someone in the office will answer questions within 24 hours.

_____

4. The data were examined by a team of experts.

_____

5. They recognized Craig Beardsley for 25 years of service.

_____

1. _____

2. _____

3. _____

4. _____

5. _____

Your Total Score _____ /15

If your score was 11 or less, review "Voice," pages 131–132, before continuing.

60 | Irregular Verbs

Directions Complete each sentence by writing in the blank at the right the correct form of each verb in parentheses. Refer to the lists on pages 133–134 if necessary. Score one point for each correct answer.

Answers

1. The story of the Berlin Airlift (present tense of *begin*) after World War II, with the division of Germany between the Soviet Union and the Western allies.

1. _____

2. Over the next few years, Cold War tensions (past tense of *grow*).

2. _____

3. In June 1948, the Soviets (past tense of *set*) a blockade of West Berlin, the part of the city controlled by France, the United Kingdom, and the United States.

3. _____

4. To keep people from starving, the Western allies (past tense of *choose*) to fly food, fuel, medicines, and other supplies into West Berlin.

4. _____

5. They (past tense of *know*) that the operation would be dangerous and that bringing in enough supplies would be nearly impossible.

5. _____

6. Planes (past tense of *take*) off and landed at the city's two airports every 90 seconds.

6. _____

7. In the first weeks, crews worked long hours and (past tense of *sleep*) little, yet they could provide less than half of what was needed.

7. _____

8. The Americans (past tense of *bring*) in bigger C-54 airplanes.

8. _____

9. More than 17,000 Berlin citizens (past tense of *make*) a third airfield in just 92 days.

9. _____

10. Between takeoffs and landings, men and women (past tense of *run*) onto the runways to work some more.

10. _____

11. When the Soviets refused to take down a radio transmitting tower that was in the way, the French (past tense of *blow*) it up.

11. _____

12. Slowly, the quantities of supplies provided (past tense of *rise*).

12. _____

13. The pilots (past tense of *speak*) of the mission as Operation Vittles.

13. _____

14. In Operation Little Vittles and Operation Santa Claus, they (past tense of *give*) children candy and Christmas toys, dropped by parachute and (past tense of *pay*) for with their own money.

14. _____
_____

15. The planes (past tense of *bear*) sick children out of the city.

15. _____

16. When the siege was over, 39 Britons, 31 Americans, and at least five Germans (past perfect tense of *lose*) their lives.

16. _____

17. In 15 months, the pilots (past perfect tense of *fly*) more than 250,000 missions.

17. _____

18. They (past perfect tense of *take*) in more than 2 million tons of supplies.

18. _____

19. All together, 60,000 men and women, Western allies and their former enemies, (past perfect tense of *keep*) the airlift going.

19. _____

20. In 2008, American, British, and French veterans (past tense of *go*) back to Germany to commemorate the sixtieth anniversary of the airlift.

20. _____

Your Total Score _____ /21

If your score was 16 or less, review "Principal Parts of Irregular Verbs," pages 133–134, before continuing.

61 | Unit Review

A | **Directions** Underline the correct verb in parentheses. Score one point for each correct answer.

Your Score

1. (Shall, Will) we meet again next Wednesday at 1:30?

1. _____

2. It (doesn't, don't) seem likely that sales will improve in the next quarter.

2. _____

3. Yvonne (teachs, teaches) a class in advanced accounting.

3. _____

4. The schedule for that project (worrys, worries) me.

4. _____

5. I (shall, will) finish the report this afternoon.

5. _____

6. She (was, were) in meetings all day.

6. _____

7. Mr. Wright (refered, referred) me to your office.

7. _____

8. They (has, have) an idea for a new product line.

8. _____

B | **Directions** Complete each sentence by writing in the blank at the right the correct form of the verb in parentheses. Score one point for each correct answer.

Answers

1. Speaking in public (present tense of *be*) many people's greatest fear.

1. _____

2. Ziba (present tense of *do*) demonstrations at shows and conventions.

2. _____

3. She (present tense of *believe*) that a thorough knowledge of your topic and plenty of practice (present tense of *lead*) to success.

3. _____
_____

4. Many people (present tense of *record*) their practice presentations and then (present tense of *review*) the recordings.

4. _____
_____

5. Sally always (present tense of *practice*) in front of a mirror.

5. _____

6. Wendell (present tense of *imagine*) questions the audience might ask and (present tense of *develop*) answers for them.

6. _____
_____

7. He (past tense of *encourage*) me to make an outline.

7. _____

8. At the beginning of her speech, Miriam (past tense of *relate*) a story that the audience (past tense of *enjoy*).

8. _____
_____

9. She (past tense of *have*) an electronic presentation and handouts.

9. _____

10. Gunter (past tense of *warn*) me not to turn my back to the audience.

10. _____

11. Rachel (past tense of *hurry*) too much.

11. _____

12. Pedro (future tense of *use*) visualization techniques to help with stage fright.

12. _____

Your Total Score _____ /24
If your score was 18 or less, review Sections 13–15, pages 119–124, before continuing.

62 | Unit Review

Directions Complete each sentence by writing in the blank at the right the correct perfect tense form of the verb in parentheses. Score one point for each correct answer.

Answers

1. By the end of his junior year in high school, Josh (decide) to become a dental assistant.

    1. _____

2. Before making his decision, he (visit) several schools to learn about their dental assisting programs.

    2. _____

3. Josh (work) in Dr. Chopra's office since 2006.

    3. _____

4. Since he started, his work (involve) routine tasks such as sterilizing and disinfecting instruments and arranging them for Dr. Chopra's use.

    4. _____

5. He (assist) her by handing her instruments and materials and using a suction hose to keep the patient's mouth dry.

    5. _____

6. Dr. Chopra (allow) Josh to take X-rays as well.

    6. _____

7. In addition, he (remove) sutures and (place) rubber dams on teeth.

    7. _____

    _____

8. For the past few months, Josh (order) all the dental supplies for the office.

    8. _____

9. By the time of his next performance review, Josh (perform) many of the tasks that dental assistants typically do.

    9. _____

10. The Bureau of Labor Statistics projects that by 2016, the rate of growth in dental assistant jobs (increase) by 29 percent.

    10. _____

_____

_____

11. By this time next year, Judy (return) to the workforce.

    11. _____

12. She (plan) to go back to work when her youngest child started grade school.

    12. _____

13. She remembered that a friend (suggest) becoming a dental hygienist.

    13. _____

14. This (result) in Judy's enrolling in college part-time, where she began working toward an associate's degree in dental hygiene.

    14. _____

15. Before she decided to go back to school, Judy (look) for a job with a flexible schedule.

    15. _____

16. She (want) good pay and benefits and excellent employment prospects.

    16. _____

17. Since starting her internship at a pediatric dentist's office, Judy (care) for many patients, cleaning their teeth and teaching them to brush and floss.

    17. _____

18. She (treat) dozens of children, from toddlers to high school students.

    18. _____

19. Judy (like) spending extra time with the youngest patients.

    19. _____

20. Already, Judy (receive) three job offers.

    20. _____

Your Total Score _____ /21

If your score was 16 or less, review Section 16, pages 127–128, before continuing.

63 | Unit Review

A | **Directions** Rewrite active-voice sentences to be in the passive voice. Rewrite passive-voice sentences to be in the active voice. Score one point for each correct rewrite.

Example   We will set aside 300 acres for a new state park.

Three hundred acres will be set aside for a new state park.

Your Score

1. You missed several errors in the report.

_____   1. _____

2. The printer and shredder were paid for by him.

_____   2. _____

3. Cormac McCarthy wrote *The Road*.

_____   3. _____

4. The results of the study were presented by Quang and me.

_____   4. _____

5. We will release a new version of the software in May.

_____   5. _____

Your Total Score _____ /5
If your score was 3 or less, review "Voice," pages 131–132, before continuing.

B | **Directions** Underline the correct irregular verb in parentheses. Score one point for each correct answer.

1. My friend Ava (become, became) a radiation therapist.   1. _____

2. I (saw, seen) her at our high school reunion last week.   2. _____

3. We (drank, drunk) coffee while she talked about her work.   3. _____

4. Ava had (went, gone) through a two-year program leading to an associate's degree.   4. _____

5. She had (took, taken) a certification exam administered by the American Registry of Radiologic Technologists.   5. _____

6. Then Ava had (got, gotten) a job giving radiation treatments to people with cancer.   6. _____

7. As part of her job, she has (spoke, spoken) to many patients, explaining the treatment and side effects.   7. _____

8. She (told, told) me that a machine called a simulator is used to pinpoint the treatment area.   8. _____

9. The patient is (gave, given) doses of radiation designed specifically to kill the particular type of cancer cell.   9. _____

10. Recently, Ava (began, begun) applying for jobs managing radiation therapy programs.   10. _____

Your Total Score _____ /10
If your score was 7 or less, review "Principal Parts of Irregular Verbs," pages 133–134, before continuing.

ENGLISH ON THE JOB /
Physical Therapist Assistant

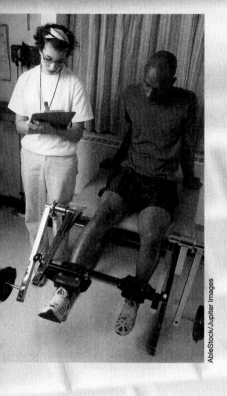

AbleStock/Jupiter Images

Dustin Forney is a physical therapist assistant, or PTA. He works with accident victims and people with disabling conditions to improve or restore function or mobility, to relieve pain, or to prevent or lessen physical disabilities. People needing physical therapy include injured athletes, people hurt in car accidents, people who have had hip or knee replacements, people with arthritis or back pain, and many others.

After a physical therapist evaluates a patient and prepares a treatment plan, the PTA executes the plan. Dustin works with patients from the first to the final day of their rehabilitation. For a person with a knee injury, for example, treatment might begin with passive range of motion exercises, with Dustin straightening the leg and helping the patient bend it. He might also massage the knee to reduce swelling. As time passes and the knee improves, Dustin takes the patient through a changing regimen of exercises carefully chosen to increase muscle strength and restore balance and full range of motion. After each session, he makes notes on the patient's progress, and he does periodic rechecks for range of motion, strength, and other factors.

Job prospects for PTAs are very good. The Bureau of Labor Statistics projects that 20,000 jobs for PTAs will be created between 2000 and 2016, an increase of 32 percent.

What skills do PTAs need? They must be able to communicate clearly with patients and other employees and to listen carefully to feedback and instructions. In addition, PTAs must write progress notes that are clear, accurate, and detailed. They need to be well organized and detail-oriented to work effectively with many patients and to manage their treatment plans. Dustin, who works closely with a physical therapist and an athletic trainer, describes his workplace as "very much a team environment." Good teamwork skills are essential.

Directions Complete each sentence by writing in the blank at the right the correct form of the verb in parentheses. Score one point for each correct answer.

Answers

1. Most PTAs (present tense of *work*) in physical therapists' offices or hospitals.   1. _____

2. Cheri (past tense of *take*) algebra, anatomy, physiology, biology, chemistry, and psychology in her PTA degree program.   2. _____

3. Many states (present tense of *demand*) an associate's degree or higher; some (present tense of *require*) licensing or registration.   3. _____   _____

4. In May 2006, the median annual earnings of PTAs (past tense of *be*) $41,360.   4. _____

5. Terri (present tense of *specialize*) in geriatric patients; Malcolm, in sports injuries.   5. _____

Your Total Score _____ /6

64 | Writing Improvement

A | **Directions** Write a topic sentence for each paragraph topic. Pay special attention to your use of tense, voice, and irregular verbs.

1. cell phones _____
_____

2. blogs _____
_____

3. a professional attitude at work _____
_____

4. planning a career _____
_____

5. the best movies _____
_____

6. social networking websites _____
_____

B | **Directions** Underline the three statements that support each topic sentence.

1. Good climbing techniques will allow you to ascend mountains safely and efficiently.
    a. Keep your arms straight when climbing.
    b. When you reach the summit of a mountain, you will experience a great sense of accomplishment.
    c. Try not to grip any harder than you have to; grip only hard enough not to slip.
    d. Basic equipment for climbing includes a harness, a helmet, chalk, and climbing shoes.
    e. El Capitan in Yosemite Valley, California, is a favorite climbing spot.
    f. When you are reaching for a hold, twist your hips into the wall; this will increase your reach.

2. Oceanic trenches are the deepest parts of the ocean.
    a. Many deep ocean fish have special organs on their bodies that generate light.
    b. They occur where two tectonic plates collide.
    c. *Submersibles*—small underwater research vessels—can penetrate parts of the ocean too deep or dangerous to explore by other means.
    d. The study of the deep ocean (and oceanography itself) began with the voyage of HMS *Challenger* from 1872 to 1876.
    e. The deepest, Challenger Deep in the Mariana Trench east of the Philippines, is 11,034 meters (36,201 feet) below sea level.
    f. The heavier plate is forced below the lighter one, carving the trench.

APPLICATION ⟩ **Give your completed application to your instructor for evaluation.**

65 | Comprehensive Review

Directions If the underlined noun, pronoun, or verb is correct, write *C* in the blank at the right. If it is incorrect, write the correct word or words. Score one point for each correct answer.

Answers

1. The President's Council on Physical Fitness and Sports <u>recommend</u> four types of exercise for overall fitness.

1. _____

2. They <u>are</u> muscular strength, muscular endurance, cardiorespiratory endurance, and flexibility.

2. _____

3. Elijah <u>lifts</u> weights for 20 minutes twice a week to build muscular strength.

3. _____

4. Kayla <u>read</u> that calisthenics, push-ups, pull-ups, and sit-ups are muscular endurance exercises.

4. _____

5. Many ways of exercising that people enjoy <u>builds</u> cardiorespiratory endurance.

5. _____

6. Julia <u>will have done</u> cross-country skiing before she moved to Denver.

6. _____

7. <u>Whom</u> do you think will teach the intermediate skiing class?

7. _____

8. Paula and Diego <u>have rode</u> their bikes on the Mount Vernon Trail many times.

8. _____

9. Their family <u>are</u> going cycling in Ontario next summer.

9. _____

10. Eva <u>joined</u> a water aerobics class.

10. _____

11. She <u>swum</u> three times a week and <u>lost</u> 25 pounds.

11. _____
_____

_____

_____

12. <u>Him</u> and Debbie walk 10,000 steps a day.

12. _____

13. That pedometer is <u>her's</u>.

13. _____

14. They walk about 3,500 steps in their daily <u>activitys</u>.

14. _____

15. An <u>hour's</u> walk in their neighborhood or a park does the rest.

15. _____

16. Vincent rowed with Jordan and <u>me</u>.

16. _____

17. It must have been <u>her</u> who showed you those stretches for flexibility.

17. _____

18. <u>What</u> trail do you recommend?

18. _____

19. You <u>was</u> doing the parcours trail at Sharon Woods last weekend.

19. _____

20. Destiny is training for the <u>women's</u> marathon in September.

20. _____

21. One of the boys left <u>their</u> skates in the locker room.

21. _____

22. Jayden <u>don't</u> play racquetball anymore; he switched to squash.

22. _____

23. Kelly <u>jumps</u> rope for ten minutes to burn a quick 100 calories.

23. _____

24. <u>Does</u> any of you know what bushwalking is?

24. _____

25. A good workout session <u>includes</u> brief warm-up and cool-down periods.

25. _____

Your Total Score _____ /26

PROOF IT!

Directions Proofread the Internet job posting. Mark any changes that are needed using the proofreaders' marks on page 317. Watch especially for errors in consistency in verb tense, format, and content. For help, see the Proofreading Tips on page 120. Key the posting, making all necessary corrections, and proofread your work. Turn in both this page and your finished posting to your instructor.

Physical Therapist Assistant

Job ID: 34-01389

Company Name: Newport General Hospital

Location: Newport, R.I.

▶ **Apply Now!**

Hours: Full-time (40)

Experience: 0–2 years

Education: Associate's degree from an accredited PTA program

Certification: License (R.I. PTA); CPR

Date: June 30, 20–

We seek an outstanding PT to join our award-winning PT program. At Newport General Hospital, you will serve as a valued member OF A multidisciplinary team. You will work with all types of patients under the supervision of a physical therapist. You assist and supervise patients in rehabilitative exercises. You will also provide heat, light, ultrasound, and massage treatments.

This position requires good written an verbal communication skills. Interpersonal skills will be essential, and teamwork skills are also required. We offer a competitive starting salary, excellent *benefits, and* outstanding advancement opportunities. Interested candidates should submit a resume to Wade Tully, Human Resources Director, New Port General Hospital, 103 Front St., Newport, RI 02841-1419.

Posttest

A | **Directions** If the underlined verb is correct, write *C* in the blank at the right. If it is incorrect, write the correct verb.

1. <u>Will</u> the rain <u>have ended</u> by tomorrow morning?

1. _____

2. The clerks <u>counted</u> about half the items by the time we arrived.

2. _____

3. Oren <u>wishes</u> he could be here with us.

3. _____

4. Nakeisha <u>has visited</u> the museum many times.

4. _____

5. Mrs. Craig and Mr. Alighieri <u>shall organize</u> the field trip.

5. _____

6. Salena <u>translates</u> articles from Spanish into English.

6. _____

7. The coins <u>were hid</u> at the back of the closet.

7. _____

8. The store <u>don't</u> open until 9:30.

8. _____

9. My friends and I <u>shopped</u> all afternoon.

9. _____

10. She <u>were</u> the last person I expected to see.

10. _____

B | **Directions** If the underlined verb is in the active voice, write *A* in the blank at the right. Write *P* if it is in the passive voice.

1. Our flight <u>was delayed</u> for two hours.

1. _____

2. People <u>stood</u> patiently in line, hoping for tickets.

2. _____

3. The repairperson <u>fixed</u> both the dryer and the refrigerator.

3. _____

4. Some of our personal belongings <u>were left</u> behind.

4. _____

5. Those players <u>don't understand</u> the rules.

5. _____

unit 6
Misused Verbs

Objectives

1. To use commonly misused verbs correctly
2. To use less troublesome verbs correctly
3. To recognize and use linking words and phrases

Sections

Pretest

Directions Underline the correct word in parentheses.

1. We (might, could) always use more rain.
2. Please (bring, take) me home.
3. They (rise, raise) wheat, corn, and soybeans on their farm.
4. Robert Gould Shaw (lead, led) the Massachusetts 54th Regiment.
5. (Should, Would) you write down the directions for me?
6. Kira usually (sits, sets) in the front row.
7. A. J. (lay, laid) on the cot in the spare room.
8. (May, Can) I speak with you for a few minutes?
9. The journal (accepted, excepted, expected) three of her poems.
10. Everyone needs to (bring, take) a yoga mat to our next class.
11. The sun, moon, planets, and stars all (rise, raise) in the east.
12. The wreck (lay, laid) undisturbed for more than 200 years.
13. Brigid is (teaching, learning) me to knit.
14. (Should, Would) we (borrow, lend) him the truck?
15. Please (sit, set) everything you'd like me to pack on the bed.

WORKPLACE FOCUS

Diversity

A portrait of the nation (and workplace) today would be different than many people imagine. The population age 65 and over is rising—one in eight at the moment—and so is the population of older workers. Fifteen percent of us are Hispanic, and one in three belongs to some minority group. Huge numbers of immigrants have arrived since the 1990s, and they have settled not just in traditional high-immigration states but in places that never had any immigrants or that haven't had many for decades. As a result of *globalization*—the growth of markets and manufacturing across borders—U.S. employees increasingly work with employees from other countries. Business travel has risen, and so has the number of employees working in foreign countries. For U.S. businesses, customers and clients have become more international.

In your career, you will work with many different kinds of people. To be successful in your career, you will need to work effectively with all kinds of people. There will be people you don't understand, disagree with, or personally dislike. An inability to get along with others is one of the most common reasons people are fired. It can affect your ability to enjoy your work and your chances for advancement.

To work well with different kinds of people, you need to be open to different ways of doing things. You need to be respectful and tolerant of differences in others. You need to avoid making assumptions or being judgmental. You need to show people respect the way they understand it. In short, you need a professional attitude. If your work takes you to foreign countries or brings you in contact with people from different cultures, take the time to learn about those countries or cultures. Get to know people, and get to know about them, too.

Commonly Misused Verbs

A few verbs can be troublesome. Special attention should be given when you use them. Some of the most troublesome verbs are *lie* and *lay* and *sit* and *set*.

Lie and *Lay*

Uses of the Verb *Lie*

The verb *lie* means to rest or recline. With *lie*, the subject usually takes a position or is in a position. *Lie* never has an object (a noun or pronoun that receives the action of the verb and answers the question *what, whom, to* or *for what,* or *to* or *for whom*). The principal parts of *lie* are *lie* (verb), *lay* (past tense), and *lain* (past participle).

LIE REST OR RECLINE (NO OBJECT)

I lie on the couch.

I lay the remote control on the table.

LAY PLACE OR PUT (TAKES OBJECT)

Present Tense

I lie	we lie
you lie	you lie
he, she, it lies	they lie

Past Tense

I lay	we lay
you lay	you lay
he, she, it lay	they lay

Present Perfect Tense

I have lain	we have lain
you have lain	you have lain
he, she, it has lain	they have lain

I lie in my hammock reading during summer afternoons.

    lie—present tense—means to rest or recline—does not have an object

For a CT scan, the patient lies on a movable table.

    lies—present tense—means to rest or recline—does not have an object

We lay in our sleeping bags on the low roof and watched the night sky.

    lay—past tense—means to rest or recline—does not have an object

The stones must have lain there for a long time.

    have lain—present perfect tense—means to rest or recline—does not have an object

Uses of the Verb *Lay*

The verb *lay* is often confused with the verb *lie*. Lay means to place or put something down. It always takes an object (a noun or pronoun that receives the action of the verb and answers the question *what, whom, to* or *for what,* or *to* or *for whom*). The principal parts of *lay* are *lay* (verb), *laid* (past tense), and *laid* (past participle).

Present Tense

I lay	we lay
you lay	you lay
he, she, it lays	they lay

Past Tense

I laid	we laid
you laid	you laid
he, she, it laid	they laid

Present Perfect Tense

I have laid	we have laid
you have laid	you have laid
he, she, it has laid	they have laid

I <u>lay</u> the map on the front seat.

> <u>lay</u>—present tense—means to place or put something down—has an object, *map*

She <u>lays</u> the shirts next to the other sale merchandise.

> <u>lays</u>—present tense—means to place or put something down—has an object, *shirts*

The roofers <u>laid</u> the shingles in neat piles on the pallet.

> <u>laid</u>—past tense—means to place or put something down—has an object, *shingles*

They <u>have laid</u> the boxes by the front door.

> <u>have laid</u>—present perfect tense—means to place or put something down—has an object, *boxes*

How can you be sure when to use *lie* or *lay*? If you can use *place* or *put* instead of the verb, you know that some form of the verb *lay* is correct.

Beverly (<u>lies</u> or <u>lays</u>?) northeast of Boston.

(Substitute *place* or *put* for the verb: *Beverly places* [or *puts*] *northeast of Boston.* Does the sentence make sense? If not, the appropriate form of *lie* is correct: *Beverly lies northeast of Boston.*)

Review

Verb	Present Participle	Past Tense	Past Participle
lie (to rest or recline)	lying	lay	lain (no object)
lay (to put or place)	laying	laid	laid (always has an object)

TRY IT!

Directions Underline the correct verb in parentheses. Check your answers on page 320 or with your instructor before continuing with your assignment.

1. I (lie, lay) my school clothes on the chair every evening.

2. Gabrielle (lay, laid) her purchases on the coffee table.

3. Most of an iceberg's mass (lies, lays) under the water.

4. Jayla took off her shoes and (lay, laid) them in a gray plastic bin.

5. He (lay, laid) in bed all day yesterday.

6. The volcanoes have (lain, laid) dormant for many years.

7. Did you (lie, lay) the programs on the seats?

8. President Washington (lay, laid) the cornerstone of the U.S. Capitol in 1793.

APPLICATION **Complete Application 66, page 151, at this time.**

Sit and Set

SIT TO HAVE A SEAT OR OCCUPY A POSITION

She <u>sits</u> at the table.

He <u>sets</u> plates and silverware on the table.

SET TO PUT OR PLACE

The verbs *sit* and *set* are also troublesome. Now that you have learned the use of *lie* and *lay*, *sit* and *set* will be easy. *Sit* and *lie* are governed by the same rules, while *set* and *lay* have the same rules.

Uses of the Verb *Sit*

Sit means to have a seat or occupy a position. It never has an **object** (a noun or pronoun that receives the action of the verb and answers the question *what, whom, to* or *for what*, or *to* or *for whom*). The principal parts of *sit* are *sit* (verb), *sat* (past tense), and *sat* (past participle).

Present Tense

I sit	we sit
you sit	you sit
he, she, it sits	they sit

Past Tense

I sat	we sat
you sat	you sat
he, she, it sat	they sat

Present Perfect Tense

I have sat	we have sat
you have sat	you have sat
he, she, it has sat	they have sat

When I fly, I always <u>sit</u> on the aisle.

> <u>sit</u>—present tense—means to have a seat or occupy a position—does not have an object

Liesl <u>sits</u> beside me at the office.

> <u>sits</u>—present tense—means to have a seat or occupy a position—does not have an object

They <u>sat</u> by the river under a cypress tree.

> <u>sat</u>—past tense—means to have a seat or occupy a position—does not have an object

Those books <u>have sat</u> on the shelves for years.

> <u>have sat</u>—present perfect tense—means to have a seat or occupy a position—does not have an object

Uses of the Verb *Set*

Set means to put or place (it has some other meanings, but these are rarely confused with *sit*). *Set* always has an object. The principal parts of *set* are *set* (verb), *set* (past tense), and *set* (past participle).

Present Tense

I set	we set
you set	you set
he, she, it sets	they set

Past Tense

I set	we set
you set	you set
he, she, it set	they set

Present Perfect Tense

I have set	we have set
you have set	you have set
he, she, it has set	they have set

I <u>set</u> my phone in the charger.

> <u>set</u>—past tense—means to put or place—has an object, *phone*

Ethan <u>sets</u> his messenger bag to the side.

> <u>sets</u>—present tense—means to put or place—has an object, *messenger bag*

The workers <u>set</u> the posts in concrete.

> <u>set</u>—past tense—means to put or place—has an object, *posts*

She <u>has set</u> flowers on all the tables.

> <u>has set</u>—present perfect tense—means to put or place—has an object, *flowers*

How can you be sure when to use *sit* or *set*? If you can use *put* or *place* instead of the verb, you know that some form of *set* is correct.

Please (*sit* or *set*?) the CDs in that rack.

> (Substitute *put* or *place* for the verb: *Please put* [or *place*] *the CDs in that rack.* Does the sentence make sense? If so, the appropriate form of *set* is correct: *Please set the CDs in that rack.*)

Review

Verb	Present Participle	Past Tense	Past Participle
sit (have a seat or occupy a position)	sitting	sat	sat (no object)
set (place or put)	setting	set	set (always has an object)

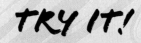

Directions Underline the correct verb in parentheses. Check your answers on page 320 or with your instructor before continuing with your assignment.

1. I (sit, set) my keys on the dresser.

2. Would you like to (sit, set) outside?

3. Please (sit, set) those files on the counter.

4. Will you (sit, set) with Mr. Granby for a while?

5. My brother and I (sat, set) by the pond and talked for hours.

6. Let's (sit, set) in the balcony.

7. The loan officer (sat, set) a stack of forms before us.

8. Have you ever (sat, set) in a skybox for a game?

APPLICATION ▶ Complete Application 67, page 152, at this time.

66 | *Lie–Lay*

A | **Directions** Complete each sentence by writing in the blank at the right the correct form of the verb in parentheses. Score one point for each correct answer.

Answers

1. The night shift (past perfect tense of *lie*) asleep for several hours when the alarm sounded.   1. _____

2. The car (past tense of *lie*) on its side over an embankment.   2. _____

3. The victim (present perfect tense of *lie*) there for an hour.   3. _____

4. Bernie (past tense of *lay*) the medical supplies and equipment on the ground.   4. _____

5. Diane (present tense of *lay*) the IV bag next to the victim.   5. _____

6. Please (present tense of *lie*) still while I take your pulse.   6. _____

7. The victim (present tense of *lie*) on a stretcher, waiting to be transported.   7. _____

8. They (future tense of *lay*) the stretcher in the back of the ambulance.   8. _____

9. Did Mikah (present tense of *lay*) his case notes on the captain's desk?   9. _____

10. We (past perfect tense of *lay*) breakfast on the table, but then we got another call.   10. _____

B | **Directions** Underline the correct verb in parentheses. Score one point for each correct answer.

Your Score

1. The salesclerk (lay, laid) the watches on the counter.   1. _____

2. He had (lain, laid) aside his work to join us.   2. _____

3. These pages won't (lie, lay) flat.   3. _____

4. For a week, the street had (lain, laid) under two feet of water.   4. _____

5. Could you (lie, lay) the coats on the bed?   5. _____

6. Brent likes to (lie, lay) on the sleeping porch on summer evenings.   6. _____

7. Do you mean the report has (lain, laid) in her inbox all this time?   7. _____

8. Why don't we (lie, lay) beside the pool this afternoon?   8. _____

9. The mantle (lies, lays) beneath the earth's crust.   9. _____

10. We (lay, laid) tarps over the furniture.   10. _____

11. The development will (lie, lay) alongside the river.   11. _____

12. Mel hasn't (lain, laid) the tile yet.   12. _____

13. When Consuelo (lies, lays) in the sun, she always uses sunscreen.   13. _____

14. Camilla (lay, laid) on a blanket and watched the fireworks.   14. _____

15. The landscapers will (lie, lay) the sod tomorrow.   15. _____

Your Total Score _____ /25

If your score was 19 or less for A and B, review "*Lie* and *Lay*," pages 147–148, before continuing.

67 | *Sit–Set*

A | **Directions** Complete each sentence by writing in the blank at the right the correct form of the verb in parentheses. Score one point for each correct answer.

Answers

1. Kristi (past tense of *set*) her grandmother's china and crystal on the table.   1. _____

2. My nephews (future tense of *set*) the punch glasses by the bowl.   2. _____

3. I usually (present tense of *sit*) at the head of the table for family dinners.   3. _____

4. We (past perfect tense of *sit*) by the fireplace talking the night before.   4. _____

5. Joni (future tense of *set*) three pitchers of apple cider on the buffet.   5. _____

6. Let's (present tense of *sit*) down so we can begin.   6. _____

7. Melinda (present perfect tense of *sit*) with the children for the past two years.   7. _____

8. The children (past tense of *sit*) very patiently during the meal.   8. _____

9. Bud (past tense of *set*) the dishes in the kitchen.   9. _____

10. After everyone left, I (past tense of *sit*) in the recliner and closed my eyes to rest.   10. _____

B | **Directions** Underline the correct verb in parentheses. Score one point for each correct answer.

Your Score

1. Will you (sit, set) the cages in the back room to be cleaned?   1. _____

2. Use a food bowl small enough that your sugar gliders can't (sit, set) in it.   2. _____

3. Has anyone (sat, set) down with Mrs. Milner and explained the procedure?   3. _____

4. Ms. James wants to know how long her cockatiel will (sit, set) on its eggs.   4. _____

5. After I take and develop the X-ray, I (sit, set) it on the viewer.   5. _____

6. The technician (sat, set) the sediment under the microscope.   6. _____

7. A ferret never (sits, sets) still for long.   7. _____

8. We had (sat, set) a humane trap for the feral cat that morning.   8. _____

9. Those two have (sat, set) food in the vacant lot for feral cats for years.   9. _____

10. Cokie (sat, set) the supplies in that corner.   10. _____

11. Ask Jody to (sit, set) the instruments in the autoclave.   11. _____

12. Snakes often (sit, set) in their water bowls, so you'll want to change the water daily.   12. _____

13. The technologist (sat, set) with the animals and talked quietly to them.   13. _____

14. (Sit, Set) next to your gerbil's cage to help it get used to you.   14. _____

15. Please (sit, set) your dog on the exam table.   15. _____

Your Total Score _____ /25

If your score was 19 or less for A and B, review "*Sit* and *Set*," pages 149–150, before continuing.

Now that you understand *lie/lay* and *sit/set,* we'll look at some less troublesome verbs. Most of these verbs you already know; however, all of us misuse them occasionally.

Shall, Should, Will, and *Would*

You have already learned to use *shall* and *will* in the future tense. The helping verb *will* is used before the main verb in all persons, except in questions. For the first person (*I, we*) in questions, the helping verb *shall* is used.

> They <u>will</u> fly to Chicago this afternoon.
>
> <u>Shall</u> I check the airline website to see if the flight is on time?

Would is used in sentences that convey willingness but some doubt or uncertainty about the statement being made.

> Denzel <u>would</u> sell his bike, if he got a good offer.
>
> I <u>would</u> like to go with you.

Should is used with all subjects to indicate obligation. In such sentences, *should* is used in the sense of *ought.*

> He <u>should</u> change the oil in his car this week.
>
> They <u>should</u> tear down that building.

Would is used in polite requests or expressions of willingness.

> <u>Would</u> you sit in on the meeting?
>
> I <u>would</u> be glad to help.

May, Might, Can, and *Could*

May and *might* are used to express permission or possibility.

> You <u>may</u> have the condo next weekend.
>
> My sister <u>might</u> like that exhibit.

Can and *could* are used to express the ability or power to do something.

> Richard <u>can</u> fix almost anything.
>
> Pamela <u>could</u> authorize those expenditures. She heads the committee.

Leave and *Let*

Leave is often confused with *let. Leave* means to depart. It also means to cause or allow to remain.

> Kyle <u>leaves</u> the house at 7:30 every morning.
>
> Dominique <u>leaves</u> her baby at the day-care center at work.
>
> I'll <u>leave</u> you some money in case you need it.

Let means to permit or allow.

> Will Ms. Valdes <u>let</u> us switch shifts?
>
> Mahmad <u>let</u> Jocelyn borrow his biology notes.

Only with *alone,* meaning to stop disturbing, can either verb be used.

> Please <u>leave</u> (or let) me alone for a while so I can study.

Teach and *Learn*

Teach means to instruct or to show someone how something is done.

> Efrem <u>teaches</u> a course in appellate practice and procedure.

> Would you <u>teach</u> me to make naan bread?

Learn means to acquire knowledge.

> You'll <u>learn</u> how to design a website in this class.

Borrow and *Lend*

Borrow means to obtain something from someone else on loan. You do not have it, so you borrow it.

> May I <u>borrow</u> your lawn mower?

> Eddie might <u>borrow</u> the car tomorrow.

Lend means to let someone use something of yours for a period of time. You have it, and you allow the other person to use it.

> I'll be glad to <u>lend</u> you my GPS system for the trip.

> Would you <u>lend</u> me $20?

WRITE NOW!

Linking Words and Phrases

Linking words and phrases make writing easier to understand. They lead readers through a piece of writing, helping them identify and understand the connections between ideas. Here are some examples:

Add	in addition, besides, also, furthermore
Compare and/or contrast	however, yet, likewise
Give an example	for example, for instance
Describe a consequence	therefore, as a result
List in order	first, second, third, then, next, at first, later, finally
Describe a location	near, next to, above, below, beside, behind, in front of, between

> <u>In the past two weeks</u>, two employees have left, and another has gone on disability leave. <u>As a result</u>, Tenille has had to take on more than her share of work.
>
> > <u>In the past two weeks</u>—**gives the time frame of the situation**
> >
> > <u>As a result</u>—**states the effect of the situation**

> There are many ways to get better results from online searches. <u>For example</u>, if you key words in quotation marks, the search engine will find that exact sequence of words.
>
> > <u>For example</u>—**gives an example for the idea in the previous sentence**

> <u>At first</u>, I simply answered questions as they arose. <u>Later</u>, I started writing down the questions that were asked the most often. <u>Finally</u>, I developed an FAQ for those questions.
>
> > <u>At first</u>, <u>Later</u>, <u>Finally</u>—**show the order in which the actions were taken**

TRY IT!

Directions Underline the correct verb in parentheses. Check your answers on page 320 or with your instructor before continuing with your assignment.

1. (May, Can) I take your picture?

2. Dana (might, could) paint a room in one afternoon.

3. I hope Sensei (shall, will) (teach, learn) us a new kata tonight.

4. Why don't you (leave, let) it be for now?

5. Would you (borrow, lend) us your tent for our vacation?

6. Nobuhiro (should, would) give us some lessons, if he had the time.

Bring and *Take*

Bring means to carry something toward a person, place, or thing or to *come* carrying something.

> Would you please <u>bring</u> me the scissors?

> I hope Pat will <u>bring</u> her potato salad to the cookout.

Take means to carry something away from a person, place, or thing or to *go* carrying something.

> Shall I <u>take</u> these suitcases up to your room?

> The Wilsons always <u>take</u> their dog with them when they go away.

Rise and *Raise*

Rise means to get or go up. It never has an object.

> Liliam <u>rises</u> early every morning.

> As the curtain <u>rises</u>, we see Willy Loman sitting at his kitchen table.

Raise means to lift something. It has an object.

> We need to <u>raise</u> the window a few more inches.

> I hope my landlord doesn't <u>raise</u> the rent.

 To proofread a document against an original, place the documents side by side. Get two file cards, envelopes, or similar items. Holding one in each hand, move through the documents, comparing them line by line.

Lead and *Led*

Lead is often used when *led* should be. The verb *lead* means to be first or in charge, to take to, or to carry on.

Julian will <u>lead</u> the way up the trail.

That road <u>leads</u> to Wenham.

My grandparents <u>lead</u> a quiet life in the country.

Led is the past tense and past participle of *lead*.

Our team <u>led</u> the division in goals last year.

That committee is <u>led</u> by Missy Niles.

Lead (pronounced *led*) is also a noun, sometimes used as an adjective, which refers to an element.

The symbol for <u>lead</u> is Pb.

Accept, *Except*, and *Expect*

Accept is a verb. It means to take willingly or agree with.

I <u>accept</u> your nomination for the presidency of the United States.

The heliocentric theory was not widely <u>accepted</u> for many years.

Except is rarely a verb; it is usually a preposition. As a verb, it means to leave out or object to. As a preposition, it means not including. (See pages 197–198 for a detailed discussion of prepositions.)

Everyone must park in the lower lot. People with disabilities and parents with small children are <u>excepted</u> from this rule.

Everyone <u>except</u> Charity is going to the party.

Expect is a verb. It means to believe something is going to happen or arrive.

We <u>expect</u> an answer by noon tomorrow.

TRY IT!

Directions Underline the correct verb in parentheses. Check your answers on page 320 or with your instructor before continuing with your assignment

1. You had better (bring, take) this umbrella with you.

2. As public awareness (rises, raises), we'll see some action on the issue.

3. A guide (lead, led) us to the main gallery, where the tour had already started.

4. Employers want employees who (accept, except, expect) responsibility for their actions.

5. When I come, I'll (bring, take) the new schedule with me.

APPLICATION > **Complete Applications 68–74, pages 157–161 and 163–164, at this time.**

68 | *Shall–Will, Should–Would*

Directions Underline the correct verb in parentheses. Score one point for each correct answer.

Your Score

1. Which movie (shall, will) we see today?

   1. _____

2. I (shall, will) make a dinner reservation for afterwards.

   2. _____

3. They (shall, will) meet us at the movie theater.

   3. _____

4. Marie (shall, will) get us tickets for *August: Osage County*.

   4. _____

5. (Shall, Will) I call you before I leave for the theater?

   5. _____

6. The house (shall, will) open at 7:30.

   6. _____

7. (Shall, Will) we go out for dessert and coffee after the play?

   7. _____

8. The next production (shall, will) be *Rabbit Hole*.

   8. _____

9. (Shall, Will) you buy the tickets online?

   9. _____

10. By purchasing online, we (shall, will) save $16.

   10. _____

11. Everyone (should, would) visit Alaska.

   11. _____

12. Anita (should, would) like to go, but she can't get away.

   12. _____

13. (Should, Would) you help me research cruise packages?

   13. _____

14. I (should, would) be glad to do that.

   14. _____

15. Do you think we (should, would) fly into Vancouver?

   15. _____

16. Taking a train through the Canadian Rockies (should, would) be wonderful,
but it's expensive.

   16. _____

17. Which (should, would) Ami prefer: working out in the gym or doing laps around the deck?

   17. _____

18. She (should, would) join us, but she's taking the children to the pool.

   18. _____

19. At Ketchikan, Dale (should, would) try a zipline tour of the Alaska Rainforest Sanctuary.

   19. _____

20. I (should, would) be happy to see downtown Juneau with you.

   20. _____

21. (Should, Would) you please ask about Skagway's history as a gold rush town?

   21. _____

22. If Claudia (should, would) let us, we could take her picture.

   22. _____

23. If I could find the words, I (should, would) describe to you the magnificence
of the glaciers in College Fjord.

   23. _____

24. They (should, would) rent a car and drive around Anchorage.

   24. _____

25. We (should, would) be pleased to give a talk about our trip.

   25. _____

Your Total Score _____ /25

If your score was 19 or less, review *"Shall, Should, Will,* and *Would,"* page 153, before continuing.

69 | *May–Can, Might–Could*

Directions Underline the correct verb in parentheses. Score one point for each correct answer.

Your Score

1. (May, Can) I speak to Ms. West, please? 1. _____

2. I'm sorry; she's not in today. (May, Can) I take a message? 2. _____

3. (May, Can) someone else help me? 3. _____

4. I (may, can) transfer you to her assistant, Anton Foucault. 4. _____

5. (May, Can) you take a call for Ms. West? 5. _____

6. Yes, I (may, can). 6. _____

7. This is Anton Foucault. How (may, can) I help you? 7. _____

8. This is Meredith Bayles. We (may, can) add some guests for our seminar on June 15, so I need a new quote. 8. _____

9. Certainly, Ms. Bayles, I (may, can) take care of that for you. How many guests are you thinking of adding? 9. _____

10. Let's say a dozen. (May, Can) I expect the quote this afternoon? 10. _____

11. I (may, can) fax it to you in an hour. 11. _____

12. That's excellent. We (may, can) give some demonstrations, too, so we might need several tables moved after the luncheon. 12. _____

13. That's no problem. I'll make a note. Our custodial staff (may, can) move them. 13. _____

14. Thanks very much. (May, Can) you transfer me back to the operator? 14. _____

15. Yes, of course. Before I do, (may, can) I have your fax number? 15. _____

16. We (might, could) need to buy a new lawn mower. 16. _____

17. Corinne (might, could) clean out the garage today, if she gets home early. 17. _____

18. I appreciate the help, but I (might, could) finish packing these boxes on my own. 18. _____

19. Valentina was the only person who (might, could) drive a stick shift, so she took the truck. 19. _____

20. She (might, could) witness the signing of the sale agreement because she's a notary public. 20. _____

21. Seth (might, could) paint the deck today, depending on the weather. 21. _____

22. Ask Stu if we (might, could) use his hand truck. 22. _____

23. I (might, could) keep it until tomorrow morning, if that's all right. 23. _____

24. With a lockbox, the realtor (might, could) show the house while we're away. 24. _____

25. Everything looks so nice; we (might, could) decide not to sell after all! 25. _____

Your Total Score _____ /25

If your score was 19 or less, review "*May, Might, Can,* and *Could*," page 153, before continuing.

70 | Leave/Let, Teach/Learn, Borrow/Lend, Bring/Take

Directions Underline the correct verb in parentheses. Score one point for each correct answer.

Your Score

1. Shall I (bring, take) you some file folders?

2. Ellie (brings, takes) her PDA with her everywhere she goes.

3. She is going to (teach, learn) me to use the scheduling software.

4. Let's (bring, take) these storage boxes down to the records room.

5. I'd be glad to (borrow, lend) you that article on time management.

6. Douglas (taught, learned) me a few of his methods, such as trying to handle an e-mail or a memo just once.

7. There must be a more efficient way to do this. (Leave, Let) me try again.

8. Would you (borrow, lend) me a hammer so I can put up this bulletin board?

9. Please (leave, let) me alone so I can finish this to-do list.

10. That task is lower-priority; (leave, let) it be until tomorrow.

1. _____
2. _____
3. _____
4. _____
5. _____

6. _____

7. _____

8. _____

9. _____

10. _____

11. She (brings, takes) insight and a fresh perspective to our team.

12. Mr. Brock is going to (teach, learn) us to use the new press.

13. Mr. Miyamoto asked to be (left, let) alone so he could finish going over the accounts.

14. We were hoping you would (borrow, lend) us the equipment for a couple of days.

15. If he leaves, he will (bring, take) some of our best workers with him.

16. My advice is to (leave, let) it go. It's not worth arguing about.

17. Someone needs to (teach, learn) those employees to follow safety procedures.

18. Please (bring, take) the records for next week's cases to me.

19. The policy statement would be fine if the committee would (leave, let) it alone and stop tinkering.

20. You could (bring, take) the new employees over to the credit union.

21. I'm (bringing, taking) my tablet when I go out of town next week.

22. They're asking if we would (borrow, lend) them a few of our people to work on inventory.

23. She promised to (teach, learn) me about the privacy procedures.

24. Have someone (bring, take) this report to Mr. Volpe at once.

25. Would you (borrow, lend) me your notes from the last meeting?

11. _____
12. _____
13. _____
14. _____
15. _____
16. _____
17. _____
18. _____

19. _____

20. _____
21. _____
22. _____
23. _____
24. _____
25. _____

Your Total Score _____ /25

If your score was 19 or less, review pages 153–155 before continuing.

71 | *Rise/Raise, Lead/Led, Accept/Except/Expect*

Directions Underline the correct word in parentheses. Score one point for each correct answer.

Your Score

1. The instructor (lead, led) us into a large kitchen.   1. _____

2. The class is (lead, led) by a chef from a popular restaurant.   2. _____

3. We (accepted, excepted, expected) to learn to make a few simple dishes.   3. _____

4. Set the bread dough in a warm area away from drafts to (rise, raise).   4. _____

5. Let's (rise, raise) some windows to cool the room.   5. _____

6. Everyone (accept, except, expect) Shreya has finished preparing the chicken.   6. _____

7. If you know how to make apple pie, (rise, raise) your hand.   7. _____

8. A delicious odor is (rising, raising) through the air.   8. _____

9. I (accepted, excepted, expected) a taste of the crème brûlée with pleasure.   9. _____

10. The class has (lead, led) us to experiment with new cuisines.   10. _____

_____

_____

11. Raisa (accepts, excepts, expects) a promotion this year.   11. _____

12. Does anyone know whether the price (rose, raised) or declined?   12. _____

13. The task force's recommendations (lead, led) to a 30 percent reduction in energy use.   13. _____

14. If you would like to ask a question, please (rise, raise) so that everyone can see you.   14. _____

15. Charlene (rises, raises) some important concerns.   15. _____

16. Every manager (accept, except, expect) him sees the merits of the plan.   16. _____

17. Customer suggestions have (lead, led) directly to the development of some of our best products.   17. _____

18. If we (accept, except, expect) his view of the situation, urgent action is needed.   18. _____

19. She (lead, led) the region in sales last year.   19. _____

20. The entire board, Marcelo (accepted, excepted, expected), will be at the meeting (he will be out of town on business).   20. _____

21. Are you going to (accept, except, expect) the offer?   21. _____

22. Charles (lead, led) the transition team.   22. _____

23. When can we (accept, except, expect) the new computers to arrive?   23. _____

24. Please (accept, except, expect) this award with our thanks.   24. _____

25. I think the stock is going to (rise, raise) in value.   25. _____

Your Total Score _____ /25

If your score was 19 or less, review pages 155–156 before continuing.

72 | Unit Review

Directions Underline the correct word in parentheses. Score one point for each correct answer.

Your Score

1. Ashley (taught, learned) me some skills for being a better listener.   1. _____

2. You (may, can) be thinking about other things.   2. _____

3. You (should, would) focus your attention on the speaker.   3. _____

4. Don't try to do something else; (leave, let) it wait.   4. _____

5. (Sit, Set) paper and a pen on your desk so you can take notes on key points.   5. _____

6. (Sit, Set) still, make eye contact, and nod to show you understand.   6. _____

7. You (may, can) check your understanding by paraphrasing or asking questions.   7. _____

8. Sometimes the meaning (lies, lays) in how something is said rather than the words.   8. _____

9. Listen, for example, for how the speaker's voice (rises, raises) and falls.   9. _____

10. I (should, would) like to talk with you some more, but I have an appointment.   10. _____

_____

11. (May, Can) I offer you water or coffee?   11. _____

12. (Should, Would) you (borrow, lend) me your handheld scanner?   12. _____

13. Joanie always (brings, takes) her laptop to these meetings.   13. _____

14. (Shall, Will) we order some catered food for the seminar?   14. _____

15. Ronnie (might, could) repair that machine in no time.   15. _____

16. We (accept, except, expect) all major credit cards.   16. _____

17. Have the talks (lead, led) to anything?   17. _____

18. She (might, could) get a new assignment tomorrow.   18. _____

19. I really (should, would) stay tonight and draw up the final plans.   19. _____

20. Shelby (lay, laid) the order tickets on the desk.   20. _____

21. When you go to the construction site, (bring, take) the blueprints with you.   21. _____

22. I (shall, will) have those prescriptions ready in an hour.   22. _____

23. A mediator (sat, set) down with them and helped them resolve the dispute.   23. _____

24. The poll (rises, raises) two issues we need to consider.   24. _____

25. We should probably (leave, let) them alone so they can talk.   25. _____

Your Total Score _____ /26

ENGLISH ON THE JOB /
Administrative Professional

Polka Dot Images/Jupiter Images

Administrative professionals work in schools, hospitals, corporate settings, government agencies, legal and medical offices, and many other places. Their duties vary widely, but there are two basic responsibilities that all administrative professionals share: performing and coordinating an office's administrative work and managing information.

Administrative professionals are communication managers. They plan and schedule meetings and appointments, manage projects, and obtain and supply information by phone, mail, e-mail, and website. Many provide training and orientation for new staff. Administrative professionals also may handle travel and guest arrangements.

It should be clear that good communication skills are essential in this occupation. Administrative professionals must be able to listen carefully and to speak effectively with others. They must also write clearly and accurately, with correct spelling, punctuation, and grammar.

Administrative professionals need several other important skills. At the top of the list are good customer service and interpersonal skills. Increasingly, employers look for a thorough knowledge of software applications, such as desktop publishing, project management, spreadsheets, and database management. For higher-level positions, time management, discretion, good judgment, initiative, and the ability to work independently are especially important.

Directions Underline the correct word in parentheses. Score one point for each correct answer.

Your Score

1. I (shall, will) spend the morning doing research on the Internet. 1. _____
2. Please (teach, learn) me to use the videoconferencing software. 2. _____
3. Maya (may, can) do desktop publishing; let's ask her to make the brochure. 3. _____
4. I (should, would) be glad to write those letters for you. 4. _____
5. Please (bring, take) me the agenda you developed. 5. _____
6. The reports have (lain, laid) there for weeks; let's have Liu read and prioritize them. 6. _____
7. Kelly (rose, raised) and greeted the visitors. 7. _____
8. Brianna (rose, raised) the idea of having the administrative professionals work as a team. 8. _____
9. Have you (accepted, excepted, expected) the executive secretary job? 9. _____
10. Adrian (lead, led) a discussion about dealing with difficult callers. 10. _____
11. Nate (sat, set) the packets on the registration table. 11. _____
12. Let's (bring, take) Elvira to the Denver conference. 12. _____
13. Minh (might, could) be a good candidate for office manager. 13. _____
14. Cristina (might, could) untangle these figures; she's very good at that. 14. _____
15. (Shall, Will) I ask Vladimir to troubleshoot the new software? 15. _____

Your Total Score _____ /15

73 | Writing Improvement

A | **Directions** Underline the linking words and phrases in the following paragraphs. For help, refer to the WRITE Now feature on page 154.

Research and practice are key to a successful job interview. First, research the organization to which you are applying so you are familiar with its history, products, and services. There are many resources for such information. For example, you can visit the organization's website. You can also talk with someone you know who works there. Next, make a list of questions you think the interviewer will ask, and develop answers. Your answers should show how your skills, abilities, and qualifications match the organization's needs. Finally, practice. Ask a friend or family member to play the interviewer. Practice until you can answer the questions with poise and confidence.

I'll never forget my first view of a castle. We had followed the map into Warwick as best we could. We rounded a corner, looking for someone who could give us directions. In front of us, a group of police trainees were practicing radar-gunning, pointing the devices in every direction. We could have asked them, but there was no need. Behind them rose a massive, many-sided tower, etched with arrow slits and small windows. From each side of the tower, curtain walls extended. At the top of both walls and tower were crenellations, squares of stone alternating with open spaces, not decorative as you might think, but providing concealment, as well as opportunities to fire down on the enemy. It was a sight that might have deterred many an attacking force in the castle's long history.

B | **Directions** Write a paragraph on one of the following topics. Develop a strong topic sentence, and use at least three linking words or phrases. For help, refer to the WRITE Now features on pages 123 and 154.

- Explain how to do something you know how to do well.

- Describe an incident from work, school, or your personal life.

- Compare two movies or TV shows.

- Describe a place.

- Identify a problem you solved, and explain how you did it.

_____

_____

_____

_____

_____

_____

_____

_____

_____

 **Give your completed application to your instructor for evaluation.**

74 | Comprehensive Review

Directions Underline the correct word in parentheses. Score one point for each correct answer.

Your Score

1. There (is, are) many different (strategys, strategies) for making decisions.   1. _____

2. Logan has always (went, gone) to friends and family members (who, whom) he knows have good judgment for advice.   2. _____

3. One of his ideas (is, are) to make a list of the pros and cons.   3. _____

4. Cindy (trys, tries) to think about the *opportunity cost*—what she would give up by choosing one option over the (other's, others).   4. _____

5. To make a good decision, you (should, would) get as much information as you need or as time permits.   5. _____

6. Even if a decision (doesn't, don't) require a firm deadline, set one.   6. _____

7. Jasmine (was, were) saying that not making a decision is itself a decision, and that adage is true.   7. _____

8. You need to (accept, except, expect) the fact that you will not always make the right decisions.   8. _____

9. There (might, could) be things you couldn't have foreseen or didn't know.   9. _____

10. If you find methods that work for you and practice (it, them) over time, your decisions are more likely to be good ones.   10. _____

11. Please (bring, take) the diagrams when you come to my office.   11. _____

12. The panel (has, have) recommended adding another production line.   12. _____

13. Neither of the managers (favor, favors) the new program.   13. _____

14. The best home care assistant we have is (her, she).   14. _____

15. They (changed, have changed) the design three times since then.   15. _____

16. Do you think the ad will catch (people's, peoples') interest?   16. _____

17. Are all the project (memos, memoes) in this folder?   17. _____

18. The equipment dates back to the (1990s, 1990's).   18. _____

19. The samples and the proposal (is, are) ready to send.   19. _____

20. Either the directors or the chief executive officer (is, are) wrong.   20. _____

21. Our antivirus software is very good; it (catchs, catches) every virus that comes along.   21. _____

22. (Shall, Will) we schedule another benefits seminar for the fall?   22. _____

23. By next Tuesday, they (will tabulate, will have tabulated) the survey data.   23. _____

24. Corian Brothers has (showed, shown) some interest in purchasing the property.   24. _____

25. Randy has (lead, led) the company's fund-raising efforts for victims of domestic violence.   25. _____

Your Total Score _____ /28

Comprehensive Review

PROOF IT!

Directions Proofread the keyed copy of the agenda against the rough draft. Mark any changes that are needed on the keyed copy on the right using the proofreaders' marks on page 317. For help, see the Proofreading Tip on page 156. Turn in this page to your instructor.

Board of Trustees

May 14, 20--, 6 p.m.

Kelper House

6:00 - 6:05	Call to Order.................Shawna McCall
6:05 - 6:15	Approval of Minutes from Previous Meeting.........Emmett Wells
6:15 - 6:45	Action Item: Should we rise faculty salaries?........Sigourney Hays
6:45 - 7:15	Guest Speaker: Garrett Housman, Ph.D. Housman Consulting "Excepting the Challenges of Twenty-First Century Education"
6:45 - 7:15	Update: ISAACs Review.............Simone Carr
7:45 - 8:00	Update: Alumni 10k Race.........Sravanithi Narayan
8:00 - 8:30	New Business: Proposed Members ....Sigourney Hays
8:30 - 8:55	Old Business: Homecoming update.................Cruz Llandes
8:55 - 9:00	Adjournment.................Shawna McCall

Board of Trustees

May 4, 20--, 6 p.m.

Kepler House

6:00 - 6:05	Call to Order ....Shanna McCall
6:05 - 6:15	Approval of Minutes from Previous Meeting...........Emmett Wells
6:15 - 6:45	Action Item: Should we rise faculty salaries?.........Sigourney Hays
6:45 - 7:15	Guest Speaker: Garrett Housman, Ph.D. Housman Consulting "Accepting the Challenges of Twenty-First Century Education"
7:15 - 7:45	Update: ISAACs Review ....Simon Carr
7:45 - 8:00	Update: Alumni 10K Race ....Sravanthi Narayan
8:00 - 8:30	New Business: Proposed New Members ....Sigourney Hays
8:30 - 8:55	Old Business: Homecoming Update ....Cruz Llandes
8:55 - 9:00	Adjournment ....Shanna McCall

Posttest

Directions Underline the correct word in parentheses.

1. We (might, could) get Nina Gage to do it for us, if she's available.

2. Gillian, (lay, laid) the rough draft next to the final copy.

3. Just (sit, set) all the boxes on the front desk for now, please.

4. (Shall, Will) I get a few more bids before we choose a contractor?

5. The court reporter (sits, sets) at that table over there.

6. (May, Can) I take your order?

7. What if we (leave, let) it wait until next week?

8. Andrzej is going to (teach, learn) us some Polish words and phrases.

9. I'll (bring, take) these files right back to you.

10. Do you think interest rates will (raise, rise) over the next year?

11. He (should, would) cancel the contract, if he thought we could get our money back.

12. Hunter (accepted, excepted, expected) the invitation, so all the accountants will attend.

13. Nurea (may, can) key 90 words per minute.

14. The proposed site (lies, lays) on the northeast corner of Front Street.

15. When Damien (lead, led) the team, he (might, could) get better results than anyone.

16. We (will, shall) make our rounds in a few minutes.

17. Aurora (rises, raises) the issue every time we meet.

18. Did you (bring, take) anyone with you when you went to Chicago?

19. I (should, would) be glad to serve on the task force.

20. (Should, Would) you (borrow, lend) me a pen?

unit 7
Adjectives and Adverbs

Pretest

A | **Directions** Underline the adjectives once and the nouns or pronouns they modify twice.

1. Jesse bought that orange ball for his nephew.

2. My aunts attended a last-minute surprise party for me.

3. She was excited about her promotion.

B | **Directions** Write the comparative and superlative degrees of each adjective and adverb.

Positive	Comparative	Superlative
Example cheerful	*more cheerful*	*most cheerful*
1. early	_____	_____
2. politely	_____	_____
3. much	_____	_____

C | **Directions** Underline the adverbs. Above the adverb, write *v* if it modifies a verb, *adj* if it modifies an adjective, and *adv* if it modifies another adverb.

1. Tristan carefully planned her vacation.

2. Inez complained about the extremely loud work environment.

3. Marshall proceeded very cautiously through the intersection.

WORKPLACE FOCUS

E-mail Basics and Etiquette

E-mail is used to communicate within as well as outside an organization. E-mail messages are typically concise and less formal than a letter. Still, it is important for them to be grammatically correct and to contain no spelling errors because they represent you and your organization. E-mail is not always the best medium for a message. If body language and voice tones are important, or if the message could have a strong emotional impact on the receiver, communicate face-to-face instead.

- Write a concise, descriptive subject line.
- Cover only one topic in each message.
- Write short sentences and paragraphs.

- Use a conversational writing style.
- Do not use emoticons.
- Be careful what you write. E-mail is not private.

Adjectives

Adjectives modify (describe or limit) nouns or pronouns. They are the picture words that make sentences more interesting. Adjectives answer these questions about the nouns or pronouns they modify: *what kind, how many,* or *which one.*

> Liberty likes <u>expensive</u> clothes. (***What kind*** of clothes? ***Expensive*** ones.)
>
> We saw <u>two</u> dolphins. (***How many*** dolphins? ***Two.***)
>
> <u>That</u> laptop sells for $800. (***Which*** laptop? ***That*** one.)

Adjectives may be words, phrases, or clauses. (See pages 213–216 and 219 for discussions of adjective phrases and clauses.) More than one adjective may describe a noun or pronoun.

Adjectives should be placed close to the nouns or pronouns they modify. Usually they precede the words they modify. In some instances, they appear after the words.

> I am planning an <u>overseas</u> trip.
>> <u>overseas</u>—adjective—describes the noun *trip*

> He is <u>enthusiastic</u> about the assignment.
>> <u>enthusiastic</u>—predicate adjective—describes the pronoun *He* (See pages 93–94 for a review of predicate adjectives.)

> She makes her lectures <u>interesting.</u>
>> <u>interesting</u>—adjective—describes the noun *lectures*

> Jessie took the car, <u>new</u> and <u>shiny</u>, for a test drive.
>> <u>new</u>, <u>shiny</u>—adjectives—describe the noun *car*

Descriptive and Limiting Adjectives

All adjectives can be divided into two types: descriptive and limiting. **Descriptive adjectives** describe, or provide a better picture or more details, about the nouns or pronouns they modify.

<u>young</u> man	<u>restless</u> crowd	<u>long</u> hours
<u>Muslim</u> cleric	<u>confident</u> salesperson	<u>soft</u> blankets
<u>loud</u> noise	<u>good</u> soup	<u>burning</u> building
<u>blue</u> skirt	<u>glass</u> bowl	<u>ice cream</u> sundae
<u>crooked</u> streets	<u>tired</u> workers	<u>long-term</u> plans

Limiting adjectives limit the scope of the nouns or pronouns.

<u>a</u> hurricane	<u>three</u> bedrolls	<u>that</u> man
<u>an</u> invitation	<u>Kirk's</u> house	<u>some</u> people
<u>the</u> bridge	<u>my</u> job	<u>which</u> cell phone

TRY IT!

Directions Underline each adjective. Check your answers on page 320 or with your instructor before continuing with your assignment.

1. Several members of the audience asked thoughtful questions.

2. My antique dishes broke during a recent earthquake.

3. Manufacturing jobs in eight states are going overseas.

4. Utsav developed simple, practical ways to teach digital photography.

When two modifiers precede a noun, how can you tell whether they should be separated by a comma? Mentally insert the word *and* between the modifiers. If the insertion makes sense, a comma is needed.

It was a <u>cool</u> <u>sunny</u> day in the mountains.

> (Mentally insert the word *and* between *cool* and *sunny*. Does the insertion make sense? If so, a comma is needed: *It was a cool, sunny day in the mountains.*)

The <u>old</u> <u>country</u> road follows the river.

> (Mentally insert the word *and* between *old* and *country*. Does the insertion make sense? If not, do not insert a comma.)

The <u>most</u> <u>serious</u> student was Ahmed.

> (Mentally insert the word *and* between *most* and *serious*. Does the insertion make sense? If not, do not insert a comma.)

Proper Adjectives

When an adjective is derived from a proper noun, it is a proper adjective and begins with a capital letter. A proper adjective may also be a proper noun that is used as a modifier. (See page 33 for a review of proper nouns.)

Several <u>Russian</u> students are enrolled in the <u>French</u> literature class.
> <u>Russian</u>—proper adjective—derived from the proper noun *Russia*
> <u>French</u>—proper adjective—derived from the proper noun *France*

<u>October</u> sales for our <u>Cleveland</u> factory are below projections.
> <u>October</u>—proper adjective—proper noun used as a modifier
> <u>Cleveland</u>—proper adjective—proper noun used as a modifier

We visited a <u>Civil War</u> battlefield.
> <u>Civil War</u>—proper adjective—proper noun used as a modifier

Articles

Articles (*a*, *an*, and *the*) are adjectives. *The* is a **definite article**, and *a* and *an* are **indefinite articles**. *Definite* means a certain person, place, thing, concept, quality, or activity, and *indefinite* means no particular person, place, thing, concept, quality, or activity.

> <u>An</u> administrative professional answered <u>the</u> phone.
>> <u>An</u>—indefinite article—no particular administrative professional
>> <u>the</u>—definite article—a particular phone

> <u>The</u> athlete was <u>an</u> excellent student and <u>a</u> passionate competitor.
>> <u>The</u>—definite article—a particular athlete
>> <u>an</u>—indefinite article—no particular student
>> <u>a</u>—indefinite article—no particular competitor

Use *a* before words that start with a consonant, a long-sounding *u* or *u* sound (*a unique opportunity, a European vacation*), or the sound of *w* (*a one-mile run*). Use *an* before words that start with a vowel (*a, e, i, o,* and short-sounding *u*) or words that sound as if they start with a vowel (*an honest person, an hour-long meeting*).

> Computer skills are <u>a</u> basic requirement for many jobs.
> Antonio discussed the benefits of <u>a</u> universal life insurance policy.
> American Sign Language is <u>an</u> intense course.
> Quyen took <u>an</u> English proficiency test.
> Shad left the military with <u>an</u> honorable discharge.

✓ RULES that work

The sound, not the spelling, of a word determines whether *a* or *an* will be used. For example, when the letter *u* has the sound of a *y*, it is treated as a consonant and *a* is used (*a unanimous vote, a united front*) and when the letter *h* has the sound of a vowel, *an* is used (*an honorary degree, an herbal remedy*).

TRY IT!

Directions Underline the proper adjectives once, the definite articles twice, and the indefinite articles three times. Check your answers on page 320 or with your instructor before continuing with your assignment.

1. I donated a certificate for a free Swedish massage for the fund-raiser.

2. Gibson will serve as an honorary chair of the gala.

3. We studied a recent Supreme Court decision in our government class.

4. The financial planner recommended an aggressive portfolio consisting of European stocks and bonds.

Pronouns Used as Adjectives

Possessive pronouns are used as adjectives when they precede and modify nouns. They are *my*, *his*, *her*, *its*, *our*, *their*, and *your*.

His scholarship to Brown University was announced at their school assembly.

> His—possessive adjective—modifies the noun *scholarship*
>
> their—possessive adjective—modifies the noun *assembly*

My mother and her sister stopped at our boutique last week.

> My—possessive adjective—modifies the noun *mother*
>
> her—possessive adjective—modifies the noun *sister*
>
> our—possessive adjective—modifies the noun *boutique*

Interrogative pronouns such as *whose*, *which*, and *what* may be used as adjectives to modify a noun.

Which suit would you wear to an interview?

> Which—interrogative adjective—modifies the noun *suit*

Whose car are we taking to the movies?

> Whose—interrogative adjective—modifies the noun *car*

Indefinite pronouns may also be used as adjectives. (See pages 70–71 for lists of indefinite pronouns.)

Both newspapers reported a drop in circulation.

> Both—indefinite adjective—modifies the noun *newspapers*

Each department was given a technology budget.

> Each—indefinite adjective—modifies the noun *department*

This, *that*, *these*, and *those* are pronouns that may be used as adjectives. These **demonstrative adjectives** not only modify nouns but also specify or call attention to them. *This* and *that* are singular and modify singular nouns. *These* and *those* are plural and modify plural nouns. *This* and *these* usually refer to something nearby. *That* and *those* usually refer to something farther away.

That smoke detector beeps constantly.

> That—demonstrative adjective—singular—modifies the singular noun *smoke detector*

These movie tickets are for you.

> These—demonstrative adjective—plural—modifies the plural noun *tickets*

TRY IT!

Directions Underline the possessive adjectives once, the demonstrative adjectives twice, and the indefinite pronouns used as adjectives three times. Circle the interrogative adjectives. Check your answers on page 320 or with your instructor before continuing with your assignment.

1. This car was a graduation gift from my parents.

2. All clothing collected by your class will be donated to the homeless shelter.

3. Which classes should Farzad take in the fall?

4. Our summer internship program will place those students in jobs at the YMCA.

Nouns and Participles Used as Adjectives

Nouns and participles may be used as adjectives to modify nouns or pronouns.

There is a glare filter on Preston's monitor.

> glare—noun used as an adjective—modifies the noun *filter*
>
> Preston's—possessive noun used as an adjective—modifies the noun *monitor*

He owns some Depression glassware.

> Depression—noun used as an adjective—modifies the noun *glassware*

You can sign up for private swimming lessons at the country club.

> swimming—participle used as an adjective—modifies the noun *lessons*

Assisted suicide is a controversial topic.

> Assisted—participle used as an adjective—modifies the noun *suicide*

Compound Adjectives

Two or more words may be joined together to act as a single modifier of a noun or pronoun. These compound adjectives are often shortened forms of phrases or clauses.

Phrase or Clause	**Compound Adjective**
a bill that was due in the past	a past-due bill
a procedure performed step by step	a step-by-step procedure
a fax machine that runs at high speed	a high-speed fax machine

If such modifiers precede a noun, they are usually hyphenated. (The hyphens hold together the elements of the modifier, enabling you to read it as a unit.) If they follow a noun, they are hyphenated only if they function as compound adjectives and if they are in a shortened or an otherwise altered form (the hyphens are needed so you can read the words easily as a unit).

financial goals for the short term
short-term financial goals
These financial goals are short-term.

> for the short term—prepositional phrase—*term* is the object of the preposition *for*—not hyphenated

> short-term—compound adjective modifying the noun *goals*—shortened form—hyphenated

a fact that is well known
a well-known fact

> that is well known—adjective clause—*known* is part of the verb form *is known*—not hyphenated

> well-known—compound adjective modifying the noun *fact*—shortened form—hyphenated

Familiar compound nouns serving as adjectives do not require hyphens because they are easily understood as a unit (*high school students, post office box*). Proper names serving as adjectives are not hyphenated (*a Wall Street report, a Maroon Five song*).

WRITE NOW

Coherence and Unbiased Language

A document contains independent bits of information. Unless those bits of information flow smoothly and logically and the relationship between them is clear, the reader may not understand the message as you intended it. Coherence results when the different parts of a message are presented and arranged in such a way as to make the ideas clear. The following steps will improve the coherence of your writing:

- Create tie-in sentences that lead the reader from one idea to the next, making the connection obvious.

- Repeat key words to show the link between pieces of information.

- Use linking words and phrases (see page 154) to connect ideas.

Good writing also uses unbiased language. Avoid words that reflect unfavorably on any group of individuals (men or women, people of different cultures, people with disabilities, etc.).

Instead of	Use
mailman	mail carrier
If an employee's work is not satisfactory, give him a warning.	Any employee who does unsatisfactory work will be given a warning.

TRY IT!

Directions Underline the nouns or participles used as adjectives once and the compound adjectives twice. Check your answers on page 320 or with your instructor before continuing with your assignment.

1. Hybrid cars use both a gasoline-powered engine and an electric motor.

2. Which was the fastest-selling hybrid last year?

3. Car dealers are seeing an increased demand for fuel-efficient vehicles.

4. Aditya asked for an up-to-date inventory list.

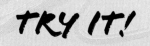
APPLICATION ▶ **Complete Applications 75–76, pages 175–176, at this time.**

75 | Adjective Identification

A | **Directions** Underline each adjective. Score one point for each correct identification.

1. Our keynote speaker stressed that water conservation needs to be a priority for all American households.

2. Two important factors in conservation are quantity and quality.

3. High-quality reclaimed water is being produced every day in this country.

4. A common definition of reclaimed water is wastewater that has been purified to such a high degree that it meets federal and state standards for drinking water.

5. A low-flow showerhead in the bathroom will save a significant amount of water.

6. Mikhail plants native and drought-tolerant plants in his yard; these plants use less water.

7. Do laundry when you have a full load of clothes.

8. Establish a rain garden in low-lying areas to filter water that would otherwise run off, collecting and spreading pollutants and contributing to erosion.

9. Let your conservation efforts be an example for future Americans.

10. Which recommendations for saving water will you adopt?

1. _____

2. _____

3. _____

4. _____

5. _____

6. _____

7. _____

8. _____

9. _____

10. _____

Your Total Score _____ /40
If your score was 30 or less, review Section 20, pages 169–174, before continuing.

B | **Directions** Underline each adjective. Write *IP* for *indefinite pronoun used as adjective*, *PA* for *possessive adjective*, *N* for *noun*, *DA* for *demonstrative adjective*, or *art* for *article* above the adjective. Score one point for each correct adjective and one point for each correct type.

1. Some states rely on other states for their water.

2. Graywater is any water used in a person's home, except from toilets.

3. This water can often be reused for other purposes.

4. Place a pail in the shower to catch the water while it is warming up; use this water for your plants.

5. Sari suggested a few tips to her classmates on how to conserve water.

6. Use the garbage disposal less, and start composting.

7. Put mulch or wood chips, not grass clippings, around plants to help the soil hold water.

1. _____

2. _____

3. _____

4. _____

5. _____

6. _____

7. _____

Your Total Score _____ /42
If your score was 32 or less, review pages 171–173 before continuing.

76 | Adjective Practice

A | **Directions** Underline each adjective. Write *prop* for *proper adjective*, *int* for *interrogative adjective*, *part* for *participle*, *CA* for *compound adjective*, or *art* for *article* above the adjective. Score one point for each correct adjective and one point for each correct type.

Your Score

1. How many voting-age citizens are registered to vote?   1. _____

2. Which town always votes first in the primaries?   2. _____

3. Mery is voting in the Ohio Democratic primary.   3. _____

4. Whose candidacy is favored in the Midwestern states?   4. _____

5. The state-level races are often exciting.   5. _____

6. What rules will govern the Friday debate?   6. _____

7. The proposed debate would be in a town hall format.   7. _____

8. High school students are urged to learn about the issues and to get involved.   8. _____

9. The speeches to Hispanic and Latino organizations will be followed by question-and-answer sessions.   9. _____

10. Nestor prides himself on being an informed voter and making well-thought-out decisions.   10. _____

Your Total Score _____ /56
If your score was 42 or less, review pages 170–173 before continuing.

B | **Directions** Underline the adjectives once and the nouns or pronouns they modify twice. Score one point for each correctly identified adjective and one point for each correctly identified noun or pronoun that is modified.

1. Presidential elections are held every four years.   1. _____
2. The American president is not elected directly by the general population.   2. _____
3. Straw polls are conducted periodically during a race.   3. _____
4. Huong was chosen as a delegate to the national convention in Chicago.   4. _____
5. He feels honored to have been selected.   5. _____
6. Up-to-the-minute reports are broadcast on television the day of an election.   6. _____
7. Each state has a minimum of three electoral votes.   7. _____
8. Polling locations may use paper or electronic ballots.   8. _____

Your Total Score _____ /40
If your score was 30 or less, review Section 20, pages 169–174, before continuing.

An **adverb** modifies a verb, an adjective, or another adverb. It makes the verb, adjective, or adverb clearer or more specific. Adverbs answer questions like *when, where, how,* and *to what extent.*

Shawanda <u>quickly</u> closed the safe.

> <u>quickly</u>—adverb modifying the verb *closed*

He seems <u>so</u> happy.

> <u>so</u>—adverb modifying the adjective *happy*

Timothy responded <u>too</u> slowly to my request.

> <u>too</u>—adverb modifying the adverb *slowly*

Adverbs of Time

Adverbs of time answer the question *when. Now, then, soon, often, seldom, rarely,* and *finally* are adverbs of time.

We <u>rarely</u> hold our sales meeting in the winter.

> <u>rarely</u>—adverb of time—answers the question *when*—modifies the verb *hold*

Howard <u>often</u> flies to corporate headquarters for meetings.

> <u>often</u>—adverb of time—answers the question *when*—modifies the verb *flies*

Adverbs of Place

Adverbs of place answer the question *where.* Two common adverbs of place are *here* and *there.* Often *there* is used at the beginning of a sentence and is mistakenly identified as the subject.

The students stay <u>here</u> for their art class.

> <u>here</u>—adverb of place—answers the question *where*—modifies the verb *stay*

After English class, the students rush <u>down</u> to the cafeteria.

> <u>down</u>—adverb of place—answers the question *where*—modifies the verb *rush*

Adverbs of Manner

Adverbs of manner answer the question *how.* These adverbs usually end in *ly* (*creatively, efficiently*). Note, however, that *friendly, lively, lonely, lovely,* and *ugly* are adjectives, not adverbs.

Speak <u>clearly</u> and <u>slowly</u> when answering questions.

> <u>clearly</u>, <u>slowly</u>—adverbs of manner—answer the question *how*—modify the verb *Speak*

The managers <u>enthusiastically</u> endorsed the proposal.

> <u>enthusiastically</u>—adverb of manner—answers the question *how*—modifies the verb *endorsed*

Adverbs of manner may also communicate affirmation or negation. *Yes* is an example of an adverb that affirms something within a sentence. Words such as *not*, *never*, *barely*, *scarcely*, and *hardly* are adverbs of manner that express negative thoughts.

> She <u>barely</u> made her airport connection in Dallas.

> > <u>barely</u>—adverb of manner—answers the question *how*—conveys negative thoughts about the verb *made*

> Do <u>not</u> allow anyone access to the personnel files.

> > <u>not</u>—adverb of manner—answers the question *how*—expresses negative thoughts about the verb *Do allow*

Use only one negative expression in a sentence to convey an idea. A double negative is created when two negatives are used in the same sentence. A double negative actually gives the sentence a positive meaning.

> **Incorrect** I have <u>not</u> received <u>no</u> phone calls from my broker.
>
> **Correct** I have received <u>no</u> phone calls from my broker.
>
> I have <u>not</u> received any phone calls from my broker.

Adverbs of Degree

Adverbs of degree answer the question *to what extent*. The most common are *too*, *really*, *so*, *quite*, and *very*. Such adverbs often modify adjectives.

> The car I purchased is <u>very</u> expensive and <u>really</u> powerful.

> > <u>very</u>—adverb of degree—answers the question *to what extent*—modifies the adjective *expensive*

> > <u>really</u>—adverb of degree—answers the question *to what extent*—modifies the adjective *powerful*

Interrogative Adverbs

How, *when*, *why*, and *where* are interrogative adverbs. They introduce questions.

> <u>Where</u> are you going for spring break?

> > <u>Where</u>—interrogative adverb—introduces a question—modifies the verb *are going*

> <u>When</u> will we have the final budget figures?

> > <u>When</u>—interrogative adverb—introduces a question—modifies the verb *will have*

Frequently Used Adverbs

The following are some frequently used adverbs:

always	however	never	often	sometimes	there	what
finally	indeed	not	probably	soon	too	when
here	later	now	seldom	still	very	where

Placement of Adverbs

Adverbs should be placed close to the words they modify. The following examples show how the placement of an adverb can change the meaning of the sentence:

> Josef <u>only</u> wrote the proposal for an in-house day care center.

> > (Josef only wrote the proposal; he did not do the research or present the proposal.)

Josef wrote the proposal for an in-house day care center <u>only</u>.

(Josef wrote the proposal for the day care center only; he did not write proposals for anything else.)

<u>Only</u> Josef wrote the proposal for an in-house day care center.

(Josef is the only person who wrote the proposal. In this sentence, *only* is an adjective.)

 **Proofreading TIPS**   Here are some tips to proofread documents with numbers:

- Recheck all figures against the original source document.

- For long numbers, verify the number of digits; then compare them in groups of three.

- Read down columns in a table, even if you're supposed to read across to use the information. Columns are sometimes easier to proofread than rows because any extra digits are more obvious.

- Use a calculator to verify calculations in the original document.

- Check totals in the document you prepared.

- Watch for transposed numbers ($150 becoming $105). If you are using software that automatically calculates and your total is off by a number divisible by 9, you have transposed two numbers.

- Have someone read the numbers to you from the original source as you read your prepared copy.

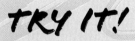 **TRY IT!**

Directions Underline the adverbs. Check your answers on page 320 or with your instructor before continuing with your assignment.

1. Your account manager left on vacation yesterday.

2. I have very high expectations for myself.

3. The Outstanding Employee Award is usually presented on the first of each month.

4. Finally, someone completely deserving of the award won it!

5. Jody immediately reported the confidentiality breach.

APPLICATION ▶   **Complete Applications 77–78, pages 180–181, at this time.**

77 | Adverb Identification and Double Negatives

A | **Directions** Underline each adverb. Above the adverb, write *P* if it is an adverb of *place*, *M* for an adverb of *manner*, *T* for an adverb of *time*, *D* for an adverb of *degree*, and *I* for an *interrogative* adverb. Score one point for each correct adverb and one point for each correct type.

Your Score

1. Ms. Swift asked me to wait here until the interviewer was ready.   1. _____

2. Always take your resume to the interview.   2. _____

3. Listen carefully to the entire question, and then answer it completely and thoughtfully.   3. _____

4. Graham was asked one question that was totally unexpected.   4. _____

5. Owen thoroughly researched the company before preparing his application letter.   5. _____

6. The benefits package Jaxson Inc. offered me was really outstanding.   6. _____

7. Some of the job-related questions Ms. Sussex asked were very specific.   7. _____

8. Holden meticulously completed his online application form.   8. _____

9. The interview appraisal form was optional but often used.   9. _____

10. The current interview form will be honestly assessed.   10. _____

11. Do not give a copy of the new appraisal form to Zachary until it has been approved.   11. _____

12. Go up one flight of stairs and turn left; the receptionist will advise Mr. Bussman that you have arrived for your interview.   12. _____

13. Carole sensibly arrived for her interview 20 minutes early.   13. _____

Your Total Score _____/36
If your score was 27 or less, review Section 21, pages 177–179, before continuing.

B | **Directions** Rewrite the sentences to eliminate the double negatives. Score one point for each correct sentence.

1. She couldn't hardly wait to use her new computer. _____

_____

2. I haven't got no money for lunch. _____ _____

3. We haven't heard nothing about a hostile takeover of our company. _____

_____

Your Total Score _____/3
If your score was 2 or less, review the discussion of double negatives on page 178 before continuing.

78 | Adverb Practice

A | **Directions** Underline the adverbs once and the words they modify twice. Score one point for each correct adverb and one point for each correct verb, adjective, or adverb modified. (A verb consisting of more than one word counts for one point.)

Your Score

1. She efficiently entered the new clients into the database.

1. _____

2. Tasha knowingly misled a customer about the bank fees for a loan.

2. _____

3. Ms. Bailey solved an unusually difficult problem.

3. _____

4. Jorge submitted an unbelievably creative video.

4. _____

5. How can we reach you for the conference call?

5. _____

6. Ramona walked outside for some fresh air.

6. _____

7. The government generally sets the annual maximum contribution for a Roth IRA.

7. _____

8. Tornado warnings were issued yesterday.

8. _____

9. The training session was rather boring.

9. _____

10. The webcast started late.

10. _____

11. Do not grant access to persons without a name badge.

11. _____

12. When will you schedule the conflict resolution workshop?

12. _____

B | **Directions** Write a short sentence using each adverb. Score one point for each correct sentence.

1. rarely _____

2. strongly _____

3. very _____

4. originally _____

5. too _____

6. nervously _____

7. quite _____

8. not, financially _____

9. educationally _____

10. usually _____

Your Total Score _____/34

If your score was 26 or less, review Section 21, pages 177–179, before continuing.

Degrees of Comparison of Adjectives

The positive, comparative, and superlative are the three degrees of comparison for adjectives. The positive degree is used when the person, place, thing, concept, quality, or activity modified is not being compared with another. An adjective does not change its form in the positive degree. The comparative degree is used when comparing two persons, places, things, concepts, qualities, or activities. In most cases, add *er* to an adjective to form the comparative. The superlative degree is used when comparing three or more persons, places, things, concepts, qualities, or activities. In most cases, add *est* to an adjective to form the superlative. If the adjective ends in *e*, add just *r* for the comparative and *st* for the superlative.

Joaquin is a <u>strong</u> man.

> <u>strong</u>—talking of only one person—positive degree

Jordy is <u>stronger</u> than Joaquin.

> <u>stronger</u>—comparison between two people—comparative degree

Brett is the <u>strongest</u> man on the wrestling team.

> <u>strongest</u>—comparison of more than two people—superlative degree

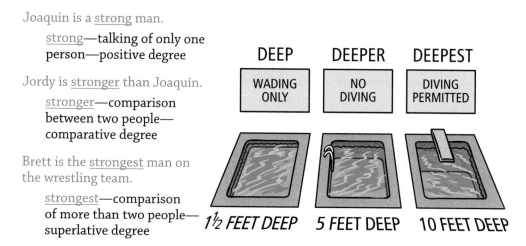

To form the comparative and superlative degrees of adjectives that end in *y* preceded by a consonant (*dry, happy*), change the *y* to *i* before adding *er* or *est*. For one-syllable adjectives that end in a single consonant preceded by a single vowel (*big, mad*), double the last consonant before adding *er* or *est*.

The Minneapolis store is <u>bigger</u> than the Denver store.

> <u>bigger</u>—comparison between two things—comparative degree

Of all our stores, the Atlanta store is the <u>biggest</u>.

> <u>biggest</u>—comparison of more than two things—superlative degree

Most two-syllable adjectives and all adjectives of more than two syllables form their degrees by adding the adverb *more* (or *less*) for the comparative degree and the adverb *most* (or *least*) for the superlative degree.

A guideline for determining the proper form of a comparative adjective is to ask yourself whether it would sound awkward if you added *er* or *est* to it. An example is *careful*. *More, most, less,* and *least* are used for such words.

Paolo is <u>more creative</u> than Kelsey.

> <u>more creative</u>—comparison between two people—comparative degree

Brooks is the <u>most creative</u> person in my art class.

> <u>most creative</u>—comparison of more than two people—superlative degree

Exceptions Some adjectives are different in all three forms. Study these adjectives so that you remember them. You probably already know most of them, as they are often used in speech and writing.

Positive	Comparative	Superlative
bad	worse	worst
far	farther or further	farthest or furthest
good or well	better	best
little	less, lesser, littler	least, littlest
much or many	more	most

Fina is a <u>bad</u> driver.

> <u>bad</u>—talking of only one person—positive degree

Marguerite is the <u>worse</u> driver of the two.

> <u>worse</u>—comparison between two people—comparative degree

My grandmother is the <u>worst</u> driver I have ever seen.

> <u>worst</u>—comparison of more than two people—superlative degree

Absolute adjectives are adjectives that cannot logically be compared. The positive degree is the only degree for an absolute adjective. For example, to say that a square table can be more square is illogical. Here are some examples of absolute adjectives:

complete	empty	horizontal	true
correct	endless	perfect	unique
dead	final	straight	wrong

Another common mistake in using adjectives is to make double comparisons. Do not use *more* and the *er* ending together or *most* and the *est* ending together.

Incorrect	Correct
more nicer	nicer
more pretty	prettier
most highest	highest

APPLICATION **Complete Applications 79–80, pages 185–186, at this time.**

Degrees of Comparison of Adverbs

Like adjectives, adverbs have three degrees of comparison: positive, comparative, and superlative.

Caroline talks <u>fast</u>.

> <u>fast</u>—describing how only one action is performed—positive degree

Caroline talks <u>faster</u> than Marvin.

> <u>faster</u>—comparison of how two actions are performed—comparative degree

Of all my friends, Caroline talks the <u>fastest</u>.

> <u>fastest</u>—comparison of how three or more actions are performed—superlative degree

The rules for forming the comparative and superlative degrees of adverbs are nearly the same as those for adjectives. For one-syllable adverbs, add *er* or *est* to the adverb.

hard   harder   hardest

For most two-syllable adverbs and all adverbs of more than two syllables, add *more* or *less* (or *most* or *least*) before the adverb. One exception is *early* (*earlier, earliest*).

seldom   more (or less) seldom   most (or least) seldom
quietly   more (or less) quietly   most (or least) quietly

You can sometimes determine the correct form of a comparative adverb by asking yourself whether it would sound awkward if you added *er* or *est* to it (*quicklier*).

Exceptions There are a few adverbs whose spellings change completely from one degree to the next.

Positive	Comparative	Superlative
badly	worse	worst
far	farther or further	farthest or furthest
little	less	least
much	more	most
well	better	best

Two of the same mistakes that are sometimes made in using adjectives are also made in using adverbs. Some adverbs, like some adjectives, cannot be compared. A few examples are *completely, correctly, perfectly, uniquely,* and *universally.* In addition, adverbs are sometimes mistakenly used in double comparisons (*more better*).

TRY IT!

Directions Complete each sentence by writing in the blank at the right the correct form of the adjective or adverb in parentheses. Check your answers on page 320 or with your instructor before continuing with your assignment.

Example   Hayoto ran a (fast) race than Umeki.   *faster* _____

1. This is the (long) I have gone without texting my friends.   1. _____

2. Marcus is (busy).   2. _____

3. Annabel scored (high) on the chemistry exam than I did.   3. _____

4. I did (well) than she on the English test, though.   4. _____

5. Which sport demands the (much) of athletes?   5. _____

6. Rosalie has the (little) seniority of anyone in the department. 6. _____

7. Which weight lifter is (strong): Alexander or Ashunte?   7. _____

8. Of all the managers, Alana speaks the (thoughtfully).   8. _____

APPLICATION ▶   **Complete Applications 81–85, pages 187–189 and 191–192, at this time.**

79 | Degrees of Comparison for Adjectives

A | Directions
Identify the degree of comparison for the underlined word or words. Write *P* for *positive*, *C* for *comparative*, and *S* for *superlative* in the blank at the right. Score one point for each correct answer.

Answers

Example   The train station is <u>closer</u> to our office than the airport.   **___C___**

1. Your website is <u>more organized</u> than Gabriel's.   1. _____

2. The marketing plan he submitted was the <u>most detailed</u> I have seen in years.   2. _____

3. This is the <u>worst</u> turnout we have ever had at the job fair.   3. _____

4. Anu's personality is <u>more subdued</u> than Sally's is.   4. _____

5. Marissa is a <u>strong</u> candidate for the open position.   5. _____

6. Haley was <u>less articulate</u> than Jameson in the interview.   6. _____

7. Maxwell is the <u>most recent</u> hire in our department.   7. _____

8. Of all the accountants, Elliot is the <u>least talkative</u>.   8. _____

9. The conference expenses this year were <u>higher</u> than last year.   9. _____

10. They advocated for a <u>quick</u> settlement.   10. _____

11. Mr. Peters is the <u>most conservative</u> member on the board.   11. _____

12. The design she submitted was <u>attractive</u>.   12. _____

13. Which of the two printers is <u>more reliable</u>?   13. _____

B | Directions
Write the comparative and superlative degrees of each adjective. Score one point for each correct answer.

Positive	Comparative	Superlative
1. reputable	_____	_____
2. friendly	_____	_____
3. bad	_____	_____
4. expensive	_____	_____
5. much	_____	_____
6. difficult	_____	_____
7. effective	_____	_____
8. responsible	_____	_____
9. wide	_____	_____
10. good	_____	_____
11. busy	_____	_____
12. great	_____	_____

Your Total Score _____ /37

If your score was 28 or less, review "Degrees of Comparison of Adjectives," pages 182–183, before continuing.

80 | Degrees of Comparison for Adjectives

A | Directions
Complete each sentence by writing in the blank at the right the correct form of the adjective in parentheses. Score one point for each correct answer.

Answers

Example   You are the (fast) keyboarder in our department.   *fastest* _____

1. The photographs are an (essential) component of the project.   1. _____

2. Of all the committee members, Jacque is the (knowledgeable).   2. _____

3. A (lively) discussion followed the budget presentation.   3. _____

4. Evelyn is (conscientious) about her work than Roger.   4. _____

5. Rodney's report had (few) inaccuracies than Taylor's.   5. _____

6. Plan A for our computer training is (economical) than Plan B.   6. _____

7. Anna's presentation was the (professional) we heard today.   7. _____

8. Choosing that vendor was not the (wise) decision I have made.   8. _____

9. That was the (unusual) method of leading a session I have ever seen.   9. _____

10. Hannah's plan was (feasible) than James's plan.   10. _____

11. Jehan's job application package was (complete).   11. _____

12. The new features make this machine (efficient) than its predecessor.   12. _____

B | Directions
Underline the correct choice in parentheses. Score one point for each correct answer.

Your Score

1. This assignment is (importanter, more important) than that one.   1. _____

2. Our new employment contract is (confusinger, more confusing) than our previous contract.   2. _____

3. The (greatest, most greatest) compliment you can give your co-workers is that you respect their work.   3. _____

4. This product is (unique, the most unique) in addressing environmental concerns.   4. _____

5. Documents printed on a laser printer have (sharper, more sharper) resolution than those printed on an inkjet printer.   5. _____

6. Aaliyah is the (perfect, most perfect) recruiter.   6. _____

7. Janette is (patienter, more patient) than our last supervisor.   7. _____

8. Which set of results is (correct, more correct)?   8. _____

9. Our projected profit margin for this year is (better, more better) than our profit margin for last year.   9. _____

10. Put the three (heavier, heaviest) boxes on the bottom of the pallet.   10. _____

Your Total Score _____ /22

If your score was 17 or less, review "Degrees of Comparison of Adjectives," pages 182–183, before continuing.

81 | Degrees of Comparison for Adverbs

A | **Directions** Write the comparative and superlative degrees of each adverb. Score one point for each correct answer.

Positive	Comparative	Superlative
1. often	_____	_____
2. recently	_____	_____
3. clearly	_____	_____
4. soon	_____	_____
5. harshly	_____	_____
6. early	_____	_____
7. badly	_____	_____
8. reasonably	_____	_____
9. conscientiously	_____	_____
10. loud	_____	_____
11. effectively	_____	_____
12. earnestly	_____	_____

B | **Directions** Underline the correct choice in parentheses. Score one point for each correct answer.

Your Score

1. When she's training, Ella runs (farther, more farther) than anyone else.   1. _____

2. Tong (accidentally, most accidentally) distributed the virus.   2. _____

3. Of all the participants, the president spoke (more briefly, the most briefly).   3. _____

4. We need to talk (quietly, more quietly); they can still hear us.   4. _____

5. I've seen a lot of summer movies, and I liked that one (less, the least).   5. _____

6. Did the Senate or the House act (quicklier, more quickly)?   6. _____

7. The sales manager is worried about the problem, but Ms. Wylie takes it
   (seriously, more seriously).   7. _____

8. Our sales force worked (harder, more hard) than ever last year.   8. _____

9. Which is labeled (more clearly, the most clearly): that cleaner or ours?   9. _____

10. The new rules will apply (universally, more universally) in all our divisions.   10. _____

Your Total Score _____ /34

If your score was 26 or less, review "Degrees of Comparison of Adverbs," pages 183–184, before continuing.

82 | Unit Review

Directions Identify the adjectives and adverbs. Underline the adjectives once and the adverbs twice. Score one point for each correct identification.

Your Score

1. Pearls are the only gemstones that grow inside a living organism.   1. _____

2. Few natural pearls are harvested for jewelry because cultured pearls can be produced more cheaply.   2. _____

3. Pearls hardly ever result from the natural intrusion of a grain of sand into a mollusk.   3. _____

4. Highly trained technicians surgically implant a spherical nucleus of mussel shell into an oyster to start growing a cultured pearl.   4. _____

5. The creation of a cultured pearl can take several years.   5. _____

6. Mollusks continually secrete nacre, a material that lines the insides of their shells.   6. _____

7. This smooth lining is often called the pearly layer.   7. _____

8. Occasionally an irritant becomes embedded between the shell and the mantle (the organ that produces the material of which the shell is made).   8. _____

9. The mantle cells cover the irritant with layers of nacre.   9. _____

10. Nacre is mostly limestone, and it is very strong.   10. _____

11. The shape of a pearl depends primarily on the position of the irritant in the shell as the pearl develops.   11. _____

12. A saltwater oyster usually contains only one pearl.   12. _____

13. Pearls are generally harvested in the winter.   13. _____

14. Nacre is an iridescent material; another name for it is mother-of-pearl.   14. _____

15. Iowa was the center of the mother-of-pearl button trade until World War II.   15. _____

16. Natural pearls are becoming more difficult to find now.   16. _____

17. Many mussel species are endangered or threatened.   17. _____

18. In the 1800s, Japanese pearl divers manually pulled oysters from the ocean floor and individually checked them for pearls.   18. _____

19. Irregularly shaped pearls are more common in nature.   19. _____

20. Perfect pearls are extremely rare.   20. _____

21. A pearl is an organic gem.   21. _____

22. Organic gemstones are not as durable as gemstones from minerals.   22. _____

Your Total Score _____ /100

If your score was 75 or less, review Sections 20 and 21, pages 169–174 and 177–179, before continuing.

83 | Unit Review

A | **Directions** Write the comparative and superlative degrees of each adjective and adverb. Score one point for each correct answer.

Positive	Comparative	Superlative
1. light	_____	_____
2. stressful	_____	_____
3. crafty	_____	_____
4. loudly	_____	_____
5. attractive	_____	_____
6. assertively	_____	_____
7. painful	_____	_____
8. cautious	_____	_____
9. seriously	_____	_____
10. rapidly	_____	_____
11. warm	_____	_____
12. busy	_____	_____
13. plain	_____	_____
14. reputable	_____	_____
15. smoothly	_____	_____

B | **Directions** Write a sentence using the appropriate degree of comparison for each word. Score one point for each correct sentence.

1. polite (comparative degree) _____

_____

2. polite (superlative degree) _____

_____

3. politely (comparative degree) _____

_____

4. politely (superlative degree) _____

_____

Your Total Score _____/34
If your score was 26 or less, review Section 22, pages 182–184, before continuing.

© Blend Images/Jupiter Images

Paralegals assist lawyers in performing their work. One of the most important responsibilities of paralegals is to help lawyers prepare for hearings, trials, closings, and corporate meetings. Paralegals may do investigative work so that all relevant information about a case is uncovered and readily accessible. Helping to draft legal documents, organizing and analyzing case files and information, supervising other employees, and maintaining financial records are all tasks that a paralegal may be asked to perform. The specific tasks will depend on the size of the office, the experience of the paralegal, and his or her area of specialization.

Although the scope of work may vary among law firms, there are some skills every paralegal should possess for success. Communication skills, both written and oral, are critical. In addition, paralegals must have strong organizational, multitasking, and time management skills. Sound research skills and a good knowledge of legal terminology are required. Paralegals also need to demonstrate ethical behavior, the ability to maintain confidentiality, and the desire to stay current in their field by taking continuing legal education courses. Competence on computers is important because legal articles, legal texts, and past cases are increasingly stored in electronic databases and on CD-ROMs.

The job outlook for paralegals is very good. Demand is expected to increase as the growing population requires more legal services in areas such as intellectual property, health care, and elder issues.

Directions Identify the adjectives and adverbs. Underline the adjectives once and the adverbs twice. Score one point for each correct identification.

Your Score

1. Paralegals routinely perform many of the same duties that lawyers do.   1. _____

2. Jeanette is using the main conference room for witness interviews in a personal-injury lawsuit.   2. _____

3. Gil often calls the crime lab to get the results of DNA tests for upcoming cases.   3. _____

4. Valerie carefully organized all the papers that Mr. Herzan will need for court.   4. _____

5. Joy primarily researches settlements and passes any relevant discoveries to her supervisor.   5. _____

6. That is our law library; paralegals may do research there or at their own workstations, using one of the online legal databases to which we subscribe.   6. _____

7. Park's research skills are much better than mine.   7. _____

8. I am seriously considering a job transfer to the probate area of the firm.   8. _____

9. Sonya's specialties are international trade and corporate finance, and she speaks three languages fluently.   9. _____

10. She will definitely send her resume to the highly regarded Sidley and Austin LLC.   10. _____

11. Terra is very confident about the quality of the deposition summary she prepared.   11. _____

Your Total Score _____ /54

If your score was 41 or less, review Sections 20 and 21, pages 169–174 and 177–179, before continuing.

84 | Writing Improvement

Directions Write a short paragraph (four to five sentences) in response to each question. Use adjectives and adverbs in your answers. Your responses should be clear, concise, and coherent.

1. Describe the skills and personal characteristics you would bring to a job.

Topic sentence I have a number of skills and personal characteristics that would make me a productive and effective employee. (Write explanatory sentences to describe each skill and characteristic identified.)

_____

_____

_____

_____

_____

_____

2. What courses have you taken that would prepare you for a job?

Topic sentence I have taken several courses that have given me a good foundation for what I will be doing in the workplace. (Explain the relevancy of what you learned in each course and how you will apply it on the job.)

_____

_____

_____

_____

_____

_____

3. Which courses did you like best? Why?

Topic sentence My favorite courses were . . . (Identify each course individually, and explain why you liked the course.)

_____

_____

_____

_____

_____

_____

 **Give your completed application to your instructor for evaluation.**

85 | Comprehensive Review

Directions Match each item in Column A with the underlined item it describes in Column B. Write the identifying letter from Column A in the blank provided at the right. Score one point for each correct answer.

Column A	Column B	Answers
a. adverb of manner	1. Victoire is <u>shorter</u> than Elyse.	1. _____
b. adverb of time	2. Most of my friends like <u>Mexican</u> food.	2. _____
c. collective noun	3. <u>Two</u> students will be awarded the Hayes scholarship.	3. _____
d. comparative degree of adjective	4. When answering the telephone, speak <u>clearly</u>.	4. _____
e. compound adjective	5. Please take me <u>there</u> tomorrow afternoon.	5. _____
f. demonstrative pronoun	6. <u>We under the oak tree</u>.	6. _____
g. future-tense verb	7. Mr. Hendricksen <u>will write</u> a letter of recommendation for me.	7. _____
h. helping verb	8. Alexandra <u>overslept</u> this morning.	8. _____
i. incomplete sentence	9. The audience gave Mr. Hershey a <u>standing</u> ovation.	9. _____
j. article	10. I am hoping to find a <u>low-cost</u> airline ticket so I can visit my grandmother.	10. _____
k. interrogative sentence	11. The <u>legislature</u> adjourns for summer recess in August.	11. _____
l. limiting adjective	12. <u>We</u> were not prepared for class.	12. _____
m. noun used as an adjective	13. The check <u>that</u> was deposited yesterday was my bonus.	13. _____
n. past-tense verb	14. <u>This</u> is the course he wants to take.	14. _____
o. personal pronoun	15. Harris ordered two <u>boxes</u> of paper for the office.	15. _____
p. plural noun	16. We <u>often</u> hold our sales meetings by videoconference.	16. _____
q. proper adjective	17. Monique purchased <u>a</u> graphing calculator.	17. _____
r. relative pronoun	18. Estella <u>will</u> create a portfolio of her work to show prospective employers.	18. _____
s. adverb of place	19. A <u>court</u> hearing was scheduled for next week.	19. _____
t. participle used as an adjective	20. <u>What time does the library close on Saturday?</u>	20. _____

Your Total Score _____ /20

PROOF IT!

Directions Proofread the e-mail attachment, using the Proofreading Tips on page 179. Mark any changes that are needed using the proofreaders' marks on page 317. Then key the document, making all necessary corrections. Proofread your work, and make any corrections that are needed. Turn in both this page and your finished document to your instructor.

EMB Pharmaceuticals Sales to Date

The following chart shows the sales figures for the past six months for the pharmaceutical

representatives in your district.

Goals were set more earlier in the year for all personnel for the first six-month period of 2010. If a

representatives' sales was more than $750,000, he or she is eligible for a 2.5 percent bonus on actual

sales. If actual sales exceeded $1,000,000 for this period, the representative is eligible for a 4 percent

bonus. If actual sales were below $750,000, no bonus will be paid. Bonuses checks will be sent out

in approximately six weeks. Please review this figures and verify they are correct. E-mail me any

corrections by Friday, May 7.

DISTRICT 3 SALES
January 1–June 30, 2010

Employee ID	Name	Territory	Actual Sales	Bonus
865901	Ayres, Barbara	633	$1,084,368.79	$43,374.57
724309	Calderon, Tito	792	$723,649.83	$0.00
907435	Kinney, Leo	186	$765,988.75	$19,149.72
382654	Youssef, Bree	487	$792,473.64	$19,811.84
543893	Zimmer, Wyatt	024	$917,400.62	$22,935.02
Total Bonuses				$105,271.51

Posttest

A | **Directions** Underline the adjectives once and the nouns or pronouns they modify twice.

1. Benjamin climbed the four tallest peaks in Colorado.

2. My younger sister is training in that lifeguard program.

3. Grant is excited about his selection for an internship.

4. He is enthusiastic, energetic, and bright.

B | **Directions** Write the comparative and superlative degrees of each adjective.

Positive	Comparative	Superlative
Example hot	*hotter*	*hottest*
1. attractive		
2. good		
3. successful		
4. soft		

C | **Directions** Underline the adverbs. Above the adverb, write *v* if it modifies a verb, *adj* if it modifies an adjective, and *adv* if it modifies another adverb.

1. A good singer breathes deeply.

2. She handled that situation very well.

3. Lita submitted her request too late.

4. We were completely satisfied with the work done by the contractor.

D | **Directions** Write the comparative and superlative degrees of each adverb.

Positive	Comparative	Superlative
Example easily	*more easily*	*most easily*
1. actively		
2. little		
3. frequently		
4. badly		

unit 8
Prepositions and Conjunctions

Pretest

A | Directions
Circle the prepositions and underline the prepositional phrases. In the blank at the right, write *adj* for an adjective phrase or *adv* for an adverbial phrase.

Example   The rent check (from) *Eugenia* was returned.   **_adj_**

1. Imogen drove to the movies.   1. _____

2. Please return the library books that are on my desk.   2. _____

3. We sat beside the luncheon speaker.   3. _____

4. Phuoc ran the half marathon with me.   4. _____

5. The sprinter in the blue running suit won the race.   5. _____

6. His attitude toward studying is not good.   6. _____

B | Directions
Underline the conjunctions once and the items they connect twice. In the blanks at the right, identify the conjunctions as coordinating, subordinating, or correlative.

Example   *Jack called while you were out*.   **_subordinating_**

1. Kaitlyn and Reto completed their degrees at the University of California at Los Angeles.   1. _____

2. Danica won the race because she timed her pit stops perfectly.   2. _____

3. Josiah can have either popcorn or candy at the movies.   3. _____

4. Lisa can have a snack when she gets home from school.   4. _____

WORKPLACE FOCUS

Business Etiquette and Protocol

Business etiquette refers to manners that are acceptable in business. These manners may be based on customs, cultures, or situations. Think of business etiquette as a way of making others feel at ease and, at the same time, eliminating barriers to conducting business.

Business settings change constantly, and there are accepted guidelines for each business setting. You may want to research what etiquette or protocols are acceptable before participating in a particular business situation.

The most important rules of business etiquette are as follows:

- **Apply the golden rule.** Treat others as you want to be treated, regardless of their position in the organization. Treat people with respect and courtesy, recognize their achievements, and appreciate their efforts. Use the following five words: *please, thank you,* and *well done.*

- **Develop strong people skills.** Your effectiveness on the job is a direct result of your people skills. Take the time to show interest in and for colleagues and business associates. Address individuals by name, and recall one point of information about the individual to show your interest.

- **Be professional in your actions and appearance.** Dress appropriately for the business environment and/or specific business situation.

Section 23 Prepositions

Hold your book *in* your right hand. Now place your left hand *over* the book, *beneath* the book, *toward* the book, *on* the book, and *below* the book. The italicized words show the relationship between your hand and the book. These words are called prepositions. A **preposition** is a word that shows the relationship of a noun or pronoun to some other part of the sentence.

The professor <u>with</u> a sharp wit is my English instructor.

> with—preposition—shows relationship between *wit* and *professor*

The corporate headquarters is <u>in</u> Chicago.

> in—preposition—shows relationship between *Chicago* and *headquarters*

Mr. Rainey brought the test books <u>for</u> them.

> for—preposition—shows relationship between *them* and *brought*

Avoid the use of unnecessary prepositions.

> Kara does not know where her purse is <u>at</u>. (Omit *at*.)
> Kara does not know where her purse is.

> The gymnast fell off <u>of</u> the balance beam. (Omit *of*.)
> The gymnast fell off the balance beam.

> Where has Emilio taken the generator <u>to</u>? (Omit *to*.)
> Where has Emilio taken the generator?

Avoid using *of* after *all* or *both* unless it is needed for clarity.

> Both <u>of the</u> swimmers broke the old record. (Omit *of the*.)
> Both swimmers broke the old record.

> All <u>of us</u> were surprised by the news. (*Of us* is needed for clarity. It tells which group of people *All* refers to.)

RULES that work

Every preposition has a noun or pronoun as an object. Remember that if a pronoun follows a preposition, it must be in the objective case (*me, him, her, us, them*). Be careful of compound objects when the pronoun is the second object mentioned.

The bus left without Xavier and <u>me</u>.

> (me—pronoun—object of the preposition *without*—objective case)

Everyone except Skylar and <u>him</u> is going to the party.

> (him—pronoun—object of the preposition *except*—objective case)

(See page 60 for a review of pronouns as objects of prepositions.)

Frequently Used Prepositions

about	around	between	in	out	under
above	at	by	into	over	until
across	before	down	like	past	up
after	behind	during	near	since	upon
against	below	except	of	through	with
along	beneath	for	off	to	within
among	beside	from	on	toward(s)	without

Uses of the Prepositional Phrase

A phrase is a group of related words that does not contain a subject and a verb in combination. A prepositional phrase consists of a preposition, a noun or pronoun that is the object of the preposition, and any modifiers that fall in between. If the prepositional phrase modifies a noun or pronoun, it is an adjective phrase. If it modifies a verb, an adjective, or an adverb, it is an adverbial phrase. (A more detailed explanation of phrases is given on pages 213–216. Commonly misused prepositions are discussed on pages 281–282 and 285, and some mistakes in preposition use are covered on pages 291–292.)

> The nurse <u>with the empathetic manner</u> is the best.
>
>> <u>with the empathetic manner</u>—adjective phrase—modifies the noun *nurse*
>
> We drove <u>through a heavy rainstorm</u>.
>
>> <u>through a heavy rainstorm</u>—adverbial phrase—modifies the verb *drove*

TRY IT!

Directions Circle the prepositions and underline the prepositional phrases. In the blank at the right, write *adj* for an adjective phrase or *adv* for an adverbial phrase. Check your answers on page 320 or with your instructor before continuing with your assignment.

Example   Grant walked (to) *the train station*.   <u>__adv__</u>

1. Summer will be joining us at the restaurant.   1. _____

2. The judge's decision is expected within the hour.   2. _____

3. The jury filed into the courtroom.   3. _____

4. My class schedule for the fall term has been finalized.   4. _____

5. Charlotte rehearsed with the band.   5. _____

6. The man in the black convertible ran a red light.   6. _____

7. Several friends from my dorm are studying together.   7. _____

8. My brothers bought Final Four tournament tickets through an online vendor.   8. _____

APPLICATION **Complete Applications 86–87, pages 199–200, at this time.**

86 | Identifying Prepositions and Prepositional Phrases

A | **Directions** Circle the prepositions and underline the prepositional phrases. Score one point for each correct preposition and one point for each correct prepositional phrase.

Example Code talkers have impacted the outcome (of) battles (for) nearly 100 years.

Your Score

1. Are you familiar with the windtalkers?   1. _____

2. The Navajo code talkers were employed by U.S. military intelligence.   2. _____

3. They participated in every Marine-led assault in the Pacific from 1942 to 1945.   3. _____

4. The code, based on the complex Navajo language, was never broken.   4. _____

5. The windtalkers transmitted their coded messages over military radios and phones.   5. _____

6. The original windtalkers completed basic training at Camp Elliot in California.   6. _____

7. They developed a dictionary and code words and memorized them during training.   7. _____

8. Six code talkers transmitted and received nearly 1,000 messages at the battle of Iwo Jima.   8. _____

9. The messages at Iwo Jima were handled within a 48-hour period.   9. _____

10. The windtalkers chose Navajo words for military terms they didn't have in their language; for example, *submarine* became *iron fish*.   10. _____

11. Speaking an undecipherable code behind enemy lines provided a decisive intelligence advantage.   11. _____

12. The code was also used during the Korean and Vietnam wars.   12. _____

B | **Directions** Underline the prepositional phrase in each sentence. In the blank at the right, write *adj* for an adjective phrase or *adv* for an adverbial phrase. Score one point for each correct prepositional phrase and one point for each correct use.

Answers

1. The house down the road has been sold.   1. _____

2. The exhibit hall is located between the Grand Ballroom and the Chicago Ballroom.   2. _____

3. The newspaper was slid under my hotel door.   3. _____

4. Mr. Roane parked across the street.   4. _____

5. I stayed calm until the awards presentation.   5. _____

6. The surround sound speaker beside the stage was not working.   6. _____

7. The contest judges worked through their lunch hour.   7. _____

8. The students were presenting without notes.   8. _____

9. The restaurant around the corner has the best burgers.   9. _____

10. The families of the participants arrived early and remained late.   10. _____

Your Total Score _____ /60
If your score was 45 or less, review Section 23, pages 197–198, before continuing.

Name _____ Date _____ Score _____

87 | Prepositional Phrases and the Objective Case

A | **Directions** Write a sentence using each prepositional phrase. Score one point for each correct sentence.

Example with the innovative idea ***The man with the innovative idea for recycling spoke first.***___

1. after a two-part examination _____

_____

2. before noon _____

_____

3. during the summer months _____

_____

4. through the national park _____

_____

5. toward the south _____

_____

6. along the highway _____

_____

7. except you _____

_____

8. after the speech _____

_____

9. against the wall _____

_____

10. among the papers _____

_____

B | **Directions** Underline the correct pronoun in parentheses. Remember that the objective case is used after prepositions. Score one point for each correct answer.

Your Score

1. With Paul Yamashire and (she, her), we learned about being prepared for an emergency.   1. _____

2. I spent time with Erin, Matt, and (they, them) on class projects.   2. _____

3. Did Arlene finish the test before Chris and (I, me)?   3. _____

4. From (who, whom) did you get the most help?   4. _____

5. Tobias was assisted by Davood and (he, him) in preparing for the presentation.   5. _____

Your Total Score _____ /15
If your score was 11 or less, review Section 23, pages 197–198, before continuing.

Conjunctions

Conjunctions join words, phrases (groups of related words that do not contain a subject and verb in combination), or clauses (groups of related words that contain a subject and a verb). Conjunctions are classified as coordinating, subordinating, or correlative. (See pages 213–216 and 219–221 for a detailed treatment of phrases and clauses.)

Coordinating Conjunctions

Coordinating conjunctions join sentence parts of equal rank. Clauses of a compound sentence are connected by coordinating conjunctions. (For a discussion of compound sentences, see the WRITE Now feature on page 220.) Frequently used coordinating conjunctions are *and*, *but*, *or*, *nor*, and *yet*.

> Work <u>and</u> leisure are necessary for a well-balanced life.
>
>> <u>and</u>—coordinating conjunction—joins two words to form the compound subject *Work and leisure*
>
> Students take online courses for logistical considerations <u>or</u> for scheduling flexibility.
>
>> <u>or</u>—coordinating conjunction—connects the two phrases *for logistical considerations* and *for scheduling flexibility*
>
> A few teachers are sometimes rude, <u>but</u> most instructors are considerate.
>
>> <u>but</u>—coordinating conjunction—joins the two clauses *A few teachers are sometimes rude* and *most instructors are considerate*

Subordinating Conjunctions

Subordinating conjunctions introduce and connect subordinate (dependent) clauses to the main clause. (See pages 219–221 for a detailed treatment of subordinate clauses.) These are some frequently used subordinating conjunctions:

after	as soon as	except	once	that	when
although	as though	if	since	though	where
as	because	in order that	so that	unless	wherever
as if	before	inasmuch as	than	until	while
as long as	even though				

> Our health often suffers <u>before</u> we decide to change our lifestyle.
>
>> <u>before</u>—subordinating conjunction—introduces and connects the subordinate clause *before we decide to change our lifestyle* to the main clause *Our health often suffers*
>
> <u>As</u> you present to the board, maintain eye contact with them.
>
>> <u>As</u>—subordinating conjunction—introduces and connects the subordinate clause *As you present to the board* to the main clause *maintain eye contact with them*

Correlative Conjunctions

Correlative conjunctions are conjunctions used in pairs. Like coordinating conjunctions, they connect equal sentence parts: words to words, phrases to phrases, and clauses to clauses. The main correlative conjunctions are *both–and*, *either–or*, *neither–nor*, *not only–but (also)*, and *whether–or*. The use of *also* in *not only–but (also)* is optional.

You may be judged <u>either</u> by your words <u>or</u> by your actions.

> <u>either</u>, <u>or</u>—correlative conjunctions—connect the phrases *by your words* and *by your actions*

Dana proofread her resume <u>both</u> quickly <u>and</u> accurately.

> <u>both</u>, <u>and</u>—correlative conjunctions—connect the words *quickly* and *accurately*

WRITE NOW!

Parallelism

Parallelism helps give writing equality and balance. In using parallelism, you simply write all similar parts of a sentence the same way. Here are a few tips:

- Make sure items connected by coordinating or correlative conjunctions are grammatically the same.

  Nan likes <u>golf</u>, <u>concerts</u>, and <u>to go shopping</u>.
  > noun, noun, infinitive phrase—not parallel

  Nan likes <u>golf</u>, <u>concerts</u>, and <u>shopping</u>.

  Nan likes <u>to play golf</u>, <u>to attend concerts</u>, and <u>to go shopping</u>.

- When you use a correlative conjunction, make sure you use its correct partner.
- Watch the placement of verbs in sentences with correlative conjunctions.

  She not only <u>bought a CD player</u> but also <u>a stereo rack</u>.
  > a verb appears after one conjunction but not the other—not parallel

  She <u>bought</u> not only <u>a CD player</u> but also <u>a stereo rack</u>.
  > a verb appears before both conjunctions—parallel

  She not only <u>bought a CD player</u> but also <u>ordered a stereo rack</u>.
  > verbs appear after both conjunctions—parallel

TRY IT!

Directions Underline the conjunctions. In the blanks at the right, identify them as coordinating, subordinating, or correlative. Check your answers on page 320 or with your instructor before continuing with your assignment.

1. Layla will be running and jumping at the track meet.

   1. _____

2. Yosemite is not only a photographer's dream but also a hiker's paradise.

   2. _____

3. Although gas prices are high, we will probably take a road trip this summer.

   3. _____

 **APPLICATION**   **Complete Applications 88–92, pages 203–205 and 207–208, at this time.**

88 | Identifying Conjunctions

Directions Underline the conjunctions. In the blanks at the right, identify them as coordinating, subordinating, or correlative. Score one point for each correct conjunction and one point for each correct type.

Answers

1. My new job is not only challenging but also satisfying.

2. Burton mentors new employees and students participating in job-shadow programs.

3. Try to relax when you are meeting someone for the first time.

4. Whether in person or on the phone, always serve your customers professionally.

5. As soon as we started using the ergonomic keyboards, we noticed an improvement.

6. She had to answer some difficult questions, yet she stayed poised.

7. Both aptitudes and interests should be major factors in job selection.

8. Ms. Metcalf has a lot of responsibilities in her job, but she always makes time to talk with her employees.

9. He doesn't manage his time wisely, nor does he keep people informed.

10. Employees should know where they can seek help against discrimination.

11. I must prepare a written itinerary before I leave on my trip.

12. Neither Lee nor Audrey had any idea how much responsibility came with her new job.

13. Lorraine or Mitchell will speak to the local Business Professionals of America chapter tomorrow on the importance of networking.

14. I will buy a new computer tonight unless they are out of stock.

15. Janet asked me to wait until she returns from her meeting.

16. Colby will be working with either the Denver representative or the Salt Lake City representative on Monday.

17. The software that we ordered will be delivered tomorrow.

18. You'll have to call because the website is down.

19. Once Vivian had straightened out the seating arrangements, everything went smoothly.

20. Would you please e-mail me the figures so that I can finish my report?

1. _____

2. _____

3. _____

4. _____

5. _____

6. _____

7. _____

8. _____

9. _____

10. _____

11. _____

12. _____

13. _____

14. _____

15. _____

16. _____

17. _____

18. _____

19. _____

20. _____

Your Total Score _____ /45
If your score was 34 or less, review Section 24, pages 201–202, before continuing.

89 | Identifying Conjunctions

A | **Directions** Underline the coordinating and correlative conjunctions once and the items they connect twice. Score one point for each correct conjunction and one point for each correct connecting item.

> **Example** *Either **Laurie** or **I*** will attend the small business seminar. (This sentence would count for 4 points.)

Your Score

1. The bike-sharing program saves money, promotes fitness, and helps the environment. 1. _____
2. The automated telephone system is frustrating to use both for employees and for customers. 2. _____
3. Sales fell again last quarter, but our losses were smaller. 3. _____
4. Teleconferencing is not only economical but also green. 4. _____
5. Whether we do it by phone or we do it by e-mail, the account team needs to be told at once. 5. _____
6. Neither the board nor the chief executive officer has authorized the expenditures. 6. _____
7. Pietro never set foot outside Italy before last year, yet he speaks English flawlessly. 7. _____
8. They ship by overnight mail or for three-day delivery. 8. _____
9. We are not laying off employees, nor has that been suggested for the future. 9. _____

B | **Directions** Write a sentence using the words provided and the type of conjunction in parentheses. Score one point for each correct sentence.

1. cell phone (subordinating)_____

_____

2. healthy foods (coordinating)_____

_____

3. to the left, to the right (correlative)_____

_____

4. last week (subordinating)_____

_____

5. concessions (subordinating)_____

_____

6. to the mall (coordinating)_____

_____

7. Kunal, Madeleine (correlative)_____

_____

8. on vacation (subordinating)_____

_____

9. movie (subordinating)_____

_____

Your Total Score _____ /41

If your score was 31 or less, review Section 24, pages 201–202, before continuing.

90 | Unit Review

A | **Directions** Underline the prepositional phrase in each sentence. In the blank at the right, write *adj* for an adjective phrase or *adv* for an adverbial phrase. Score one point for each correct prepositional phrase and one point for each correct use.

Answers

1. Everyone except Terence has submitted the forms.   1. _____
2. In 1928, Alexander Fleming discovered penicillin.   2. _____
3. Rhonda stayed for the panel discussion.   3. _____
4. There are significant differences between the websites.   4. _____
5. Donations through last Friday exceeded our goal.   5. _____
6. By Wednesday, the volunteers had finished assembling the packages.   6. _____
7. The newspaper editor spoke at the fund-raising dinner.   7. _____
8. The picnic was held along the riverbank.   8. _____
9. The candy from the piñata spilled everywhere.   9. _____
10. The team ran up the mountain.   10. _____
11. As a nurse, I work 12-hours shifts during the week.   11. _____
12. I admire those doctors with a great bedside manner.   12. _____
13. The instructor answered questions after the lecture.   13. _____

Your Total Score _____ /26
If your score was 20 or less, review Section 23, pages 197–198, before continuing.

B | **Directions** Underline the conjunctions. In the blanks at the right, identify them as coordinating, subordinating, or correlative. Score one point for each correct conjunction and one point for each correct type.

1. My claim was denied because my insurance company determined I was at fault.   1. _____
2. Visibility was affected by fog and rain.   2. _____
3. Jamie got not only the other driver's insurance information but also her personal contact information.   3. _____
4. There were two witnesses, but they did not want to get involved.   4. _____
5. I submitted my claim a week ago, yet no one has contacted me about repairs.   5. _____
6. Although the damage looks minimal, the repair estimate was $750.   6. _____
7. Neither Rameez's Auto Repair nor Kaper Body Shop had the part in stock.   7. _____
8. Agustin has lowered his deductible since the accident.   8. _____
9. Both the other driver and I filed a police report.   9. _____

Your Total Score _____ /21
If your score was 16 or less, review Section 24, pages 201–202, before continuing.

Culinary arts is a fast-growing and multifaceted field with many career paths. The degree or occupational title that an individual holds may determine in which part of the industry he or she is qualified to work. Common areas are restaurants, hotels and resorts, catering and institutional establishments, and private households.

There are different levels of jobs within the culinary arts field. Of course, jobs farther up the career ladder require more responsibility. For example, food preparation workers perform routine tasks; cooks and chefs do the actual cooking; and executive chefs and head cooks, in addition to designing dishes and preparing them, also supervise employees, order supplies, and estimate food requirements. The responsibilities vary depending on where the employment is.

Culinary arts professionals must be efficient and quick. They must also work well as part of a team. Creativity, personal cleanliness, and good hand-eye coordination are essential. Workers must be able to communicate clearly with colleagues, supervisors, suppliers, and customers. Knowledge of a foreign language can be an asset.

The job outlook in culinary arts is strong and growing. On-the-job training is common for entry-level positions; employers usually prefer postsecondary training for jobs beyond entry level. Because work schedules are flexible, many people are attracted to the field for part-time employment. Advancement opportunities depend on experience, training, and personal abilities.

A | Directions Underline the prepositional phrase in each sentence. In the blank at the right, write *adj* for an adjective phrase or *adv* for an adverbial phrase. Score one point for each correct prepositional phrase and one point for each correct use.

Answers

1. The newly hired chef earned his degree from a Las Vegas culinary school.   1. _____

2. The banquet was prepared for 400 diners.   2. _____

3. Mr. Wong answered questions about the new Occupational Safety and Health Administration requirements.   3. _____

Your Total Score _____ /6
If your score was 4 or less, review Section 23, pages 197–198, before continuing.

B | Directions Underline the conjunctions. In the blanks at the right, identify them as coordinating, subordinating, or correlative. Score one point for each correct conjunction and one point for each correct type.

1. Tenzing demonstrated teamwork skills and culinary expertise.   1. _____

2. You need to have your own knives when you are a chef.   2. _____

3. Both LouAnn and Reyelle have planned the wedding reception menu.   3. _____

Your Total Score _____ /7
If your score was 5 or less, review Section 24, pages 201–202, before continuing.

91 | Writing Improvement

A | **Directions** If the sentence is parallel in construction, write *P*. If it is not, rewrite it to be parallel.

Example The lecture was both a boring one and too long. ***The lecture was both boring and too long.***

1. It is not a time for emotion but clear thinking. _____
_____

2. Writing in a journal is both relaxing and stimulates my mind. _____
_____

3. This morning I cleaned the house, baked a cake, and volunteered at the YMCA. _____
_____

4. Please write your evaluation of the course carefully, truthfully, and with conciseness. _____
_____

5. After quitting my part-time job, I had less stress, more flexibility in my schedule, and spent more time on my classes. _____
_____

6. Nicolette not only wrote a short story but also a poem. _____
_____

B | **Directions** Communication and hard work are very important in every area of work and school. Choose one of the following questions, and write four to seven sentences for it. Use at least five prepositional phrases and conjunctions. Try to be clear and concise in your sentences.

- Many people writing about training say that you get out of school only what you put into it. What do they mean by that?
- How do you think you can utilize your communication skills in any job?

_____
_____
_____
_____
_____
_____
_____
_____
_____

 **Give your completed application to your instructor for evaluation.**

92 | Comprehensive Review

Directions Match each item in Column A with the underlined item it describes in Column B. Write the identifying letter from Column A in the blank at the right. Score one point for each correct answer.

Column A	Column B	Answers
a. adjective phrase	1. <u>When</u> will we receive our final grades?	1. _____
b. adverb of degree	2. I worked <u>until</u> closing time.	2. _____
c. adverb of place	3. <u>If</u> you set the security of your firewall too high, you may have trouble accessing your online class.	3. _____
d. adverbial phrase	4. I <u>had taken</u> an economics course before I transferred to this school.	4. _____
e. comparative degree of adverb	5. We ran <u>around the track</u>.	5. _____
f. misused verb	6. <u>Whom</u> do you wish to nominate for the position?	6. _____
g. coordinating conjunction	7. <u>Neither</u> students <u>nor</u> faculty were issued their parking permits before school started.	7. _____
h. correlative conjunctions	8. The time <u>between the connecting flights</u> was short.	8. _____
i. interrogative adverb	9. The <u>most expensive</u> suit is not necessarily the one I would choose.	9. _____
j. interrogative pronoun	10. Jessup's paid internship will continue into the <u>summer</u>.	10. _____
k. linking verb	11. Shimada's presentation <u>more closely</u> followed the guidelines we were given.	11. _____
l. past-perfect-tense verb	12. Kiyan's directions <u>are</u> always detailed and accurate.	12. _____
m. plural possessive noun	13. The <u>team's</u> performance was excellent.	13. _____
n. possessive pronoun	14. Please <u>except</u> this gift with our thanks.	14. _____
o. preposition	15. Lewis's key would not open <u>his</u> locker.	15. _____
p. object of preposition	16. This <u>scholarship pays</u> your tuition and book costs.	16. _____
q. passive-voice verb	17. My textbooks for this class were <u>very</u> expensive.	17. _____
r. singular possessive noun	18. Hurricane evacuees will stay <u>here</u> until it is safe to return to their homes.	18. _____
s. subject-verb agreement	19. The <u>boxes'</u> contents were broken.	19. _____
t. subordinating conjunction	20. Her idea for attracting new customers was great, <u>but</u> it was not financially feasible.	20. _____
u. superlative degree of adjective	21. The mayor <u>was invited</u> to speak before the assembly.	21. _____

Your Total Score _____ /21

PROOF IT!

Directions Review the WRITE Now feature on page 202 and the Proofreading Tips on page 120. Then proofread the slides. Mark any changes that are needed, using the proofreaders' marks on page 317. Key each slide, making all necessary corrections, using word processing or presentation software. Proofread your work, and make any corrections that are needed. Turn in both this page and your finished slide copy to your instructor.

LISTENING

- Listen activly.

- Take note on major points.

- Ask appropriate questions.

- Key in on nonverbal cues.

TECHNOLOGICAL COMMUNICATION

- Gather information by phone.

- Input and formatting documents with software.

- Use e-mail to gather and desiminate information.

- Conduct research using electronic resources.

Written communication

- Use correct grammer, useage, and mechanics.

- Outline or plan message before writing.

- Use references (electronic and printed).

- Analyze and respond to problems both individually and collaboratively

- Writing clear and concisely

- Incorporate graphics or visuals where appropriate.

Posttest

A | **Directions** Circle the prepositions and underline the prepositional phrases. In the blank at the right, write *adj* for an adjective phrase or *adv* for an adverbial phrase.

Example I put the check (in) the mail.   **_adv_**

1. Wanda studied during her lunch break.   1. _____

2. Alia worked in the downtown office.   2. _____

3. I voted against the ballot issue.   3. _____

4. Bao attended private school through tenth grade.   4. _____

5. The bus with the broken stop-sign arm is late.   5. _____

6. The team from Westview won the championship game.   6. _____

B | **Directions** Underline the conjunctions once and the items they connect twice. In the blanks at the right, identify the conjunctions as coordinating, subordinating, or correlative.

Example _Sally acted_ as if _nothing was wrong_.   **_subordinating_**

1. Mantero worked on his paper until it was finished.   1. _____

2. Some people are always late, but most people are on time.   2. _____

3. Chips and salsa is my favorite snack.   3. _____

4. Neither computers nor calculators are available in the
   conference room.   4. _____

unit 9
Phrases and Clauses

Objectives

1. To recognize and use prepositional, infinitive, and participial phrases
2. To recognize and use independent and dependent (subordinate) clauses
3. To recognize and write effective and grammatically correct compound sentences

Sections

Pretest

A | **Directions** Underline the phrase in each sentence. In the blank at the right, write *prep* for a prepositional phrase, *inf* for an infinitive phrase, or *part* for a participial phrase.

1. Evan paid to see the webcast.

1. _____

2. Smelling the smoke, we evacuated the building.

2. _____

3. We will be taking inventory for the next two days.

3. _____

B | **Directions** Underline the independent clauses once and the dependent clauses twice. In the blank at the right, write *adj* if the dependent clause is an adjective clause or *adv* if it is an adverbial clause.

Example *Ms. Crakes, **whose opinion I value**, gave me some advice.*   *adj*

1. Until the cost of gas drops, I will be riding the bus.

1. _____

2. When the weather is good, we eat our lunch outdoors.

2. _____

3. My colleagues who walk with me at lunch have become good friends.

3. _____

C | **Directions** Underline the noun clause in each sentence.

1. Whoever organized the relief effort was well informed about the victims' needs.

2. It is a known fact that exercise is good for you.

3. Jamison was amazed by how much I could eat.

Business Ethics

Business ethics is a set of guidelines for dealing with people and with situations that arise in the business environment. These guidelines address how a business should interact with the world at large, as well as in one-on-one dealings with individuals. About 90 percent of Fortune 500 companies have a code of ethics (sometimes called a code of conduct) to help guide their employees' behavior. The word *ethics* is derived from the Greek word meaning character. Being ethical means doing what is right.

Successful businesses are built on relationships with clients and colleagues. Effective interpersonal relationships with these parties are built on trust, honesty, and fairness. You will face ethical questions at work every day. If you do not act ethically, you may cause irreparable damage not only to your own reputation but to the reputation of your employer as well. That damage may come with a high cost in time, money, and effort to repair the relationship.

Ethical behavior in your job (and personal life) deals with values—yours, your organization's, and perhaps your profession's. It may also deal with legal issues. If you are not sure whether an action is ethical, consider the following: (1) Is it legal? (2) Does it agree with your values, the values of your profession, and the values of your organization? (3) If you know it is wrong, don't do it. (4) If you don't know, find out.

A phrase is a group of related words used as a noun, an adjective, or an adverb. It does not contain a subject and a verb in combination. Most phrases consist of a preposition plus a noun or pronoun (and modifiers). (See page 198 for a list of prepositions.) Three important types of phrases are prepositional phrases, infinitive phrases, and participial phrases.

Prepositional Phrases

Prepositional phrases are used as adjectives to modify nouns or pronouns (adjective phrases) or as adverbs to modify verbs, adjectives, or other adverbs (adverbial phrases). (See page 198 for a review of prepositional phrases.)

Bethany read the report <u>during her flight</u>.

> <u>during her flight</u>—prepositional (adverbial) phrase. It contains the preposition *during*, the noun *flight*, and the modifier *her*. The phrase modifies the verb *read*.

Tien drove <u>to the Grand Canyon</u>.

> <u>to the Grand Canyon</u>—prepositional (adverbial) phrase. It contains the preposition *to*, the noun *Grand Canyon*, and the modifier *the*. The phrase modifies the verb *drove*.

The alley <u>behind my house</u> is blocked.

> <u>behind my house</u>—prepositional (adjective) phrase. It contains the preposition *behind*, the noun *house*, and the modifier *my*. The phrase modifies the noun *alley*.

Petitions <u>against term limits</u> were circulated.

> <u>against term limits</u>—prepositional (adjective) phrase. It contains the preposition *against*, the noun *limits*, and the modifier *term*. The phrase modifies the noun *Petitions*.

Cal Ripken, Jr., <u>of the Baltimore Orioles</u> was a great ballplayer <u>with superb abilities</u>.

> <u>of the Baltimore Orioles</u>—prepositional (adjective) phrase. It contains the preposition *of*, the noun *Baltimore Orioles*, and the modifier *the*. The phrase modifies the noun *Cal Ripken, Jr.*

> <u>with superb abilities</u>—prepositional (adjective) phrase. It contains the preposition *with*, the noun *abilities*, and the modifier *superb*. The phrase modifies the noun *ballplayer*.

The papers blew <u>across the room</u> and <u>into the foyer</u>.

> <u>across the room</u>—prepositional (adverbial) phrase. It contains the preposition *across*, the noun *room*, and the modifier *the*. The phrase modifies the verb *blew*.

> <u>into the foyer</u>—prepositional (adverbial) phrase. It contains the preposition *into*, the noun *foyer*, and the modifier *the*. The phrase modifies the verb *blew*.

Directions Underline the prepositional phrase in each sentence. In the blank at the right, write *adj* for an adjective phrase or *adv* for an adverbial phrase. Check your answers on page 320 or with your instructor before continuing with your assignment.

1. The race was routed through the state park.　　　　　1. _____

2. The ceremony ended before four o'clock.　　　　　　2. _____

3. The antivirus program on my computer is updating.　　3. _____

4. Whose laptop is that in the conference room?　　　　4. _____

5. The woman with the leather briefcase is the speaker.　　5. _____

Infinitive Phrases

After the prepositional phrase, the infinitive phrase is used most often. An **infinitive phrase** consists of an **infinitive** (the main form of the verb, usually preceded by *to*) and any objects or modifiers.

> Rose wants <u>to rent an apartment</u>.
>
> > <u>to rent an apartment</u>—infinitive phrase. It contains the infinitive *to rent*, its object *apartment*, and the modifier *an*.

Infinitive phrases may have an object, or they may include an adverb modifier.

> She needs <u>to finish the report</u>.
>
> > <u>to finish the report</u>—infinitive phrase. It contains the infinitive *to finish*, its object *report*, and the modifier *the*.
>
> I will try <u>to write legibly</u>.
>
> > <u>to write legibly</u>—infinitive phrase. It contains the infinitive *to write* and the modifier *legibly*.

Most infinitive phrases are used as nouns, either as the subject or as the direct object of the sentence. (See page 59 for a review of direct objects.)

> <u>To climb the mountain</u> will take five hours.
>
> > <u>To climb the mountain</u>—infinitive phrase. It contains the infinitive *To climb*, its object *mountain*, and the modifier *the*. The phrase is used as a noun (subject).
>
> <u>To see the movie</u> costs $9.
>
> > <u>To see the movie</u>—infinitive phrase. It contains the infinitive *To see*, its object *movie*, and the modifier *the*. The phrase is used as a noun (subject).
>
> Vincente hoped <u>to attend his family reunion</u>.
>
> > <u>to attend his family reunion</u>—infinitive phrase. It contains the infinitive *to attend*, its object *reunion*, and the modifiers *his* and *family*. The phrase is used as a noun (direct object of the verb *hoped*).
>
> Ileana learned <u>to drive defensively</u>.
>
> > <u>to drive defensively</u>—infinitive phrase. It contains the infinitive *to drive* and the modifier *defensively*. The phrase is used as a noun (direct object of the verb *learned*).

Infinitive phrases may be used as adverbs to modify verbs, adjectives, or other adverbs. They answer questions like *where*, *why*, *how (in what way)*, and *to what extent*.

> Tyler insulated his attic to save energy.
>> to save energy—infinitive phrase used as an adverb—modifies the verb *insulated*—answers the question *why*

> The kit was easy to assemble.
>> to assemble—infinitive phrase used as an adverb—modifies the adjective *easy*—answers the question *how (in what way)*

Infinitive phrases may also be used as adjectives to modify nouns or pronouns. They answer questions like *what kind* and *which one*.

> Are you making a presentation to introduce the project?
>> to introduce the project—infinitive phrase used as an adjective—modifies the noun *presentation*—answers the question *what kind*

> The decision to promote Sal was made yesterday.
>> to promote Sal—infinitive phrase used as an adjective—modifies the noun *decision*—answers the question *which one*

Note that infinitive phrases sometimes contain other types of phrases.

> To qualify for the Olympics was Sasha's dream.
>> To qualify for the Olympics—infinitive phrase. It contains the infinitive *To qualify* and the modifier *for the Olympics*, a prepositional phrase.

TRY IT!

Directions Underline the infinitive phrase in each sentence. In the blank at the right, write *n* if the phrase is used as a noun, *adj* if it is used as an adjective, or *adv* if it is used as an adverb. Check your answers on page 321 or with your instructor before continuing with your assignment.

1. Roy's attempt to run a marathon was successful.   1. _____

2. Roy runs to relax.   2. _____

3. Roy hoped to finish early.   3. _____

4. The meeting to discuss the strategy will be held on Monday.   4. _____

5. Natasha spoke loudly to be heard.   5. _____

6. To ride my horse is my favorite exercise.   6. _____

7. He went to meet the new regional manager.   7. _____

8. When do you plan to declare your major?   8. _____

9. Dorothine has some stories to tell us.   9. _____

10. Would you like to visit Florence and Venice?   10. _____

11. The surgery to reset Abe's broken wrist was successful.   11. _____

12. Kelly offered to make my wedding cake.   12. _____

Participial Phrases

A **participial phrase** begins with the present participle (verb form ending in *ing—seeing, loving*) or the past participle (verb form usually ending in *ed*, *t*, or *en—covered, kept, forgotten*). (Irregular past participles may be found in the tables on pages 133–134.) The participle and the rest of the phrase act as an adjective to modify a noun or pronoun. A participial phrase does not have a subject.

Auditing our records, Lyndon found several errors.

> Auditing our records—participial phrase. The present participle is formed by adding *ing* to the verb *audit*. The phrase modifies the noun *Lyndon*.

Providing good service, the company became well known.

> Providing good service—participial phrase. The present participle is formed by dropping the *e* and adding *ing* to the verb *provide*. The phrase modifies the noun *company*.

The concert announced this morning is already sold out.

> announced this morning—participial phrase. The past participle is formed by adding *d* to the verb *announce*. The phrase modifies the noun *concert*.

Built 300 years ago, the house has many interesting architectural features.

> Built 300 years ago—participial phrase formed with the irregular past participle of the verb *build*. The phrase modifies the noun *house*.

Like infinitive phrases, participial phrases sometimes contain other kinds of phrases.

Returning to the restaurant, Ana met her friends for dessert.

> Returning to the restaurant—participial phrase. It contains the modifier *to the restaurant*, a prepositional phrase.

TRY IT!

Directions Underline the participial phrase in each sentence once and the noun or pronoun it modifies twice. Check your answers on page 321 or with your instructor before continuing with your assignment.

1. Running in the rain, Liam became soaked.

2. LaWanda, seeing the lightning, remained in the house.

3. The woman driving the red convertible is my supervisor.

4. Verona found several articles supporting her viewpoint.

5. The president moved slowly down the line, greeting each guest.

6. Speaking quietly but persuasively, he soon gained everyone's confidence.

7. Given the conditions, the equipment performed very well.

8. The candidate refused to concede, demanding a recount.

APPLICATION **Complete Applications 93–94, pages 217–218, at this time.**

93 | Prepositional and Participial Phrases

A | **Directions** Underline the prepositional phrase in each sentence. In the blank at the right, write *adj* for an adjective phrase or *adv* for an adverbial phrase. All these sentences are popular sayings from Benjamin Franklin's writings. Score one point for each correct prepositional phrase and one point for each correct type.

Answers

1. The doors of wisdom are never shut.

2. The cat in gloves catches no mice.

3. Fish and house guests stink after three days.

4. Applause waits on success.

5. An investment in knowledge always pays the best interest.

6. There are no gains without pains.

7. Trouble springs fast from idleness.

8. The battle for independence has just begun.

9. A quiet conscience sleeps in thunder.

10. Even peace may be purchased at too high a price.

1. _____
2. _____
3. _____
4. _____
5. _____
6. _____
7. _____
8. _____
9. _____
10. _____

Your Total Score _____ /20
If your score was 15 or less, review "Prepositional Phrases," page 213, before continuing.

B | **Directions** Underline the participial phrase in each sentence. Score one point for each correct phrase.

Your Score

1. Submitting her term paper, Vondale felt relieved.

2. Teng and Joi, preparing for a test, studied together.

3. Recognizing an opportunity, Alonzo spoke with the owner.

4. The employees riding in the car pool enjoyed the trip.

5. Arriving at the human resources office, the new employees read about their benefits.

6. Covered by health insurance, Bobbie felt protected.

7. Lee, rushing to catch the train, slipped and fell on the sidewalk.

8. Beginning at midnight, his shift ended at 8 a.m.

9. Kept until ten in the evening, Malik slept late the next morning.

10. Rhianna, paying particular attention to details, created her resume.

1. _____
2. _____
3. _____
4. _____
5. _____
6. _____
7. _____
8. _____
9. _____
10. _____

Your Total Score _____ /10
If your score was 7 or less, review "Participial Phrases," page 216, before continuing.

94 | Infinitive Phrases

Directions Underline the infinitive phrase in each sentence. In the blank at the right, write *n* if the phrase is used as a noun, *adj* if it is used as an adjective, or *adv* if it is used as an adverb. Score one point for each correct infinitive phrase and one point for each correct use.

Answers

1. To get a job is Melonee's first priority.   1. _____

2. The company expects to hire 20 new employees this year.   2. _____

3. Kyle works hard to appear confident.   3. _____

4. To be a lifelong learner is Stacy's objective.   4. _____

5. My supervisor was selected to handle the interviews.   5. _____

6. The screening committee did the work thoughtfully to ensure accuracy.   6. _____

7. To find skilled individuals is necessary for success in business.   7. _____

8. The interviewer, Mrs. Ellis, wanted to reassure the applicants.   8. _____

9. Marcy's desire to make a good impression was apparent.   9. _____

10. To keep focused is important.   10. _____

11. It pays to get a good night's sleep before an interview.   11. _____

12. To make your resume more effective, use action words.   12. _____

13. After the interview, Clay stopped to say hello.   13. _____

14. Dotty learned to appreciate the importance of preparation.   14. _____

15. All incidents of sexual harassment need to be reported.   15. _____

16. My employer has taken steps to prevent sexual harassment.   16. _____

17. Jude learned quickly to identify different types.   17. _____

18. Is it illegal to retaliate against a whistleblower?   18. _____

19. There are different routes for employees to file complaints.   19. _____

20. Yearly meetings are held to review existing policies.   20. _____

21. To handle harassment issues effectively, Casey conducts training on the subject. 21. _____

22. To fill out reports immediately results in a more timely resolution.   22. _____

23. My company will pay to train employees in cardiopulmonary resuscitation (CPR). 23. _____

24. To know CPR is invaluable.   24. _____

25. Eldrich's selection to attend diversity training was surprising.   25. _____

Your Total Score _____ /50

If your score was 38 or less, review "Infinitive Phrases," pages 214–215, before continuing.

Section **26** Clauses

A **clause** is a part of a sentence that contains a complete subject and a complete **predicate** (what the subject says or does or what is done to it). The two types of clauses are independent clauses and dependent clauses.

Independent Clauses

An **independent clause** expresses a complete thought and has a subject and a verb. It is the main thought of the sentence and can stand alone correctly as a simple sentence without anything attached to it.

> <u>A rainy spring caused major flooding</u>, which delayed the planting of crops.
>> <u>A rainy spring caused major flooding</u>—independent clause. It is the main idea of the sentence and can be used alone as a simple sentence.
>
> <u>All residents were evacuated</u> before the river crested.
>> <u>All residents were evacuated</u>—independent clause. It is the main idea of the sentence and can be used alone as a simple sentence.
>
> When Thad and Kathleen returned to their home, <u>they were shocked by the extent of the damage</u>.
>> <u>they were shocked by the extent of the damage</u>—independent clause. It is the main idea of the sentence and can be used alone as a simple sentence.

Dependent Clauses

The **dependent** (or **subordinate**) **clause** depends upon the independent (main) clause for understanding. A dependent clause when standing alone is not a complete sentence. Just as a person needs food in order to live and a plant needs water in order to grow, a dependent clause needs an independent clause to express a complete thought.
Dependent clauses may be used as adjectives, adverbs, or nouns.

Dependent Clauses as Adjectives

Dependent clauses used as adjectives (describing nouns or pronouns) are usually introduced by relative pronouns (*who, whom, whose, that, which*) and sometimes by adverbs like *when, where,* or *why.* (See page 75 for a review of relative pronouns.)

> President Carter, <u>who won the Nobel Peace Prize</u>, was born in Plains, Georgia.
>> <u>who won the Nobel Peace Prize</u>—dependent clause introduced by the relative pronoun *who*. It modifies the noun *President Carter* and is an adjective clause.
>
> The fireworks display, <u>which was scheduled after the concert</u>, was unbelievable.
>> <u>which was scheduled after the concert</u>—dependent clause introduced by the relative pronoun *which*. It modifies the noun *display* and is an adjective clause.
>
> The house <u>where I grew up</u> looks just the same.
>> <u>where I grew up</u>—dependent clause introduced by the adverb *where*. It modifies the noun *house* and is an adjective clause.

Dependent Clauses as Adverbs

Dependent clauses used as adverbs are introduced by subordinating conjunctions. They usually modify verbs, but sometimes adjectives or other adverbs, by answering a question like *how, where, when, why, to what extent,* or *under what conditions.* (See page 201 for a list of subordinating conjunctions.)

Since the school offers paralegal training, Megan applied for admission.

> Since the school offers paralegal training—dependent clause introduced by the subordinating conjunction *Since*. It modifies the verb *applied* and is an adverbial clause.

They waited until the tide came in.

> until the tide came in—dependent clause introduced by the subordinating conjunction *until*. It modifies the verb *waited* and is an adverbial clause.

The starting salary was lower than he had thought.

> than he had thought—dependent clause introduced by the subordinating conjunction *than*. It modifies the adjective *lower* and is an adverbial clause.

WRITE NOW!

The Compound Sentence

A compound sentence contains two or more independent clauses. These clauses may be connected by a coordinating conjunction (such as *and, but, or, nor,* or *yet*), a conjunctive adverb (an adverb that connects and relates main clauses, such as *moreover, nevertheless,* or *consequently*), or a connecting phrase (such as *as a result* or *for example*). A compound sentence does not always contain a coordinating conjunction, conjunctive adverb, or connecting phrase. In these cases, the two independent clauses are separated by a semicolon.

In a compound sentence, each independent clause expresses a complete thought and can stand alone as a simple sentence. A compound sentence has no dependent clauses.

> The wind was strong yesterday, but it didn't do any property damage.
>
> > Each independent clause expresses a complete thought and can stand alone as a simple sentence. Since the clauses are equal in rank, they are joined by the coordinating conjunction *but*. A comma usually precedes the coordinating conjunction.

> Mischelle was not scheduled to work; nevertheless, she came in at once.
>
> > The independent clauses are joined by the conjunctive adverb *nevertheless*. A semicolon precedes the conjunctive adverb, and a comma follows it.

> Barry's car had a flat tire; as a result, we missed the opening session of the conference.
>
> > The independent clauses are joined by the connecting phrase *as a result*. A semicolon precedes the connecting phrase, and a comma follows it.

> My parents' anniversary is next month; we are sending them on a cruise to Alaska.
>
> > The independent clauses have no connecting word or phrase and are separated by a semicolon.

Dependent Clauses as Nouns

Dependent clauses used as nouns (subjects, objects, or predicate nouns) are noun clauses. Most noun clauses are used as subjects or direct objects. Occasionally they are used as indirect objects or objects of prepositions. Look for the verb first, and then determine how the clause is used.

Most noun clauses are introduced by a word like *that*, *how*, *why*, *what*, *whatever*, *whoever*, or *whether*, followed by a group of words that are used as a single noun.

How Rosa Parks played a part in our history is well known.

> How Rosa Parks played a part in our history—dependent clause used as a noun. It is the subject of the verb *is*.

A less-known fact is that she and her husband worked quietly for civil rights all their lives.

> that she and her husband worked quietly for civil rights all their lives—dependent clause used as a noun. It is a predicate noun because it follows a linking verb and refers to the subject *fact*.

Kirby realizes what great contributions naturalized citizens have made to the United States.

> what great contributions naturalized citizens have made to the United States—dependent clause used as a noun. It is the direct object of the verb *realizes*.

He will give whoever asks him a number of examples.

> whoever asks him—dependent clause used as a noun. It is the indirect object of the verb *will give*.

My classmates were amazed by what I had accomplished.

> what I had accomplished—dependent clause used as a noun. It is the object of the preposition *by*.

(See pages 59–60 for a review of direct and indirect objects and pages 93–94 for a review of predicate nouns.)

TRY IT!

Directions Underline the dependent clause in each sentence. In the blank at the right, write *adj* for an adjective clause, *adv* for an adverbial clause, and *n* for a noun clause. Check your answers on page 321 or with your instructor before continuing with your assignment.

1. Please fill out this form so that we can contact you.   1. _____
2. Yang Wie knew that the negotiations would take time.   2. _____
3. As soon as Elise is ready, we will leave for the airport.   3. _____
4. Braden works harder than the others do.   4. _____
5. Everyone who took part in the workshop benefited from it.   5. _____
6. How well we perform our tasks will be monitored.   6. _____
7. Is that the cemetery where John Hancock, Samuel Adams, and Paul Revere are buried?   7. _____
8. Many of us were stunned by what he had accomplished.   8. _____

 **APPLICATION** **Complete Applications 95–100, pages 222–225 and 227–228, at this time.**

95 | Independent, Dependent, Adjective, and Adverb Clauses

A | **Directions** Underline the independent clauses once and the dependent clauses twice. Score one point for each correct independent clause and one point for each correct dependent clause.

Your Score

1. Unless I am mistaken, ten Americans have been honored with the Nobel Prize in Literature.   1. _____

2. John Steinbeck, who received the prize in 1962, wrote extensively about the human condition.   2. _____

3. The book that I liked best was *The Grapes of Wrath*.   3. _____

4. The Monterey Bay area, where Steinbeck grew up, was the setting for many of his works of fiction.   4. _____

5. The Trask and Hamilton families, whose lives are central to the story in *East of Eden*, were fictional residents of rural California from 1862 to 1918.   5. _____

6. The theme of the novel, which Steinbeck considered his greatest work, is the struggle between good and evil.   6. _____

7. While he is known as a novelist, Steinbeck was also a journalist.   7. _____

8. *The Acts of King Arthur and His Noble Knights* was published after he died.   8. _____

Your Total Score _____ /16
If your score was 12 or less, review Section 26, pages 219–221, before continuing.

B | **Directions** Underline the dependent clause in each sentence. In the blank at the right, write *adj* for an adjective clause and *adv* for an adverbial clause. Score one point for each correct dependent clause and one point for each correct use.

Answers

1. Until Sinclair Lewis received the award in 1930, no American had won the Nobel Prize in Literature.   1. _____

2. Eugene O'Neill, who was awarded the prize in 1936, wrote many plays.   2. _____

3. Pearl Buck was the first American woman whose works earned her that honor.   3. _____

4. One technique that distinguishes William Faulkner's writing is stream of consciousness.   4. _____

5. When Ernest Hemingway wrote *A Farewell to Arms*, he drew upon his experiences as an ambulance driver in World War I.   5. _____

6. Terri is reading Saul Bellow's novel *Herzog*, while I am reading *Henderson the Rain King*.   6. _____

7. Isaac Bashevis Singer wrote in Yiddish, which he said has "a quiet humor . . . and a gratitude for every day of life, every crumb of success, each encounter of love."   7. _____

8. Czeslaw Milosz, a poet whom Brady admires, was the 1980 winner.   8. _____

9. Toni Morrison's selection deserves special notice because she was the first African-American woman to win the prize.   9. _____

Your Total Score _____ /18
If your score was 14 or less, review pages 219–220 before continuing.

96 | Noun, Adjective, and Adverb Clauses

A | **Directions** Underline the noun clause in each sentence. Score one point for each correct noun clause.

Your Score

1. Whatever Neil Simon wrote was a success.   1. _____

2. The critic explained that writing was a difficult task.   2. _____

3. Our teacher will give whoever sees *Brighton Beach Memoirs* extra credit.   3. _____

4. Why Mark Twain is still popular is not a mystery to scholars.   4. _____

5. Some experts think that *The Adventures of Huckleberry Finn* was his best novel.   5. _____

6. My friend was amazed by how relevant and timeless Twain's observations are.   6. _____

7. What William Shakespeare wrote has enriched our language and pleasure.   7. _____

8. Many scholars believe that Shakespeare was the greatest writer.   8. _____

9. Her question is whether political events of the day figure in Shakespeare's plays.   9. _____

10. Whatever tickets were available for the play were quickly sold.   10. _____

Your Total Score _____ /10

If your score was 7 or less, review "Dependent Clauses as Nouns," page 221, before continuing.

B | **Directions** Underline the dependent clause in each sentence. In the blank at the right, write *adj* for an adjective clause, *adv* for an adverbial clause, or *n* for a noun clause. Score one point for each correct dependent clause and one point for each correct use.

Answers

1. The influence of Walt Disney on cartoons and animation is greater than I knew.   1. _____

2. Hank Ketcham, who created the *Dennis the Menace* comic strip, was an animator.   2. _____

3. He worked on animated films such as *Bambi*, *Fantasia*, and *Pinocchio* when he was employed by The Walt Disney Studios.   3. _____

4. While he was in the Navy, Ketcham produced cartoons for posters, training materials, and promotions of war bond sales.   4. _____

5. When Ketcham's wife described their misbehaving son as a menace, the comic strip was born.   5. _____

6. Not everyone knows that characters in the comic strip are based on real people.   6. _____

7. Animated films that support family values have long been a popular form of entertainment.   7. _____

8. Ernst described how Pixar Animation Studios started with award-winning animated short films, commercials, and logos.   8. _____

9. The first movie coproduced by Disney and Pixar that won critical acclaim was *Toy Story*.   9. _____

10. Whoever has seen any Pixar animated films understands their wide appeal.   10. _____

Your Total Score _____ /20

If your score was 15 or less, review "Dependent Clauses," pages 219–221, before continuing.

97 | Unit Review

A | **Directions** Underline the phrase in each sentence. In the blank at the right, write *prep* for a prepositional phrase, *inf* for an infinitive phrase, or *part* for a participial phrase. Score one point for each correct phrase and one point for each correct type.

Answers

1. The Franklin stove helped to warm homes efficiently.   1. _____

2. Ben Franklin needed glasses for reading and distance viewing.   2. _____

3. To see both near and far, he invented bifocal glasses.   3. _____

4. Franklin invented a musical instrument called the armonica.   4. _____

5. The famous lightning rod protected buildings and ships from lightning strikes.   5. _____

6. His "extendable arm" could grasp books on high shelves.   6. _____

7. Enjoying the water, Franklin invented swim fins.   7. _____

8. To swim more quickly was his goal.   8. _____

9. The devices invented by Franklin improved everyday life.   9. _____

Your Total Score _____ /18
If your score was 14 or less, review Section 25, pages 213–216, before continuing.

B | **Directions** Underline the independent clauses once and the dependent clauses twice. In the blank at the right, write *adj* if the dependent clause is an adjective clause or *adv* if it is an adverbial clause. Score one point for each correct clause and one point for each correct use.

1. Benjamin Franklin, whose father was a soap maker, played an important role in
   our nation's history.   1. _____

2. Individuals who see the benefits of volunteerism are civic-minded like Franklin.   2. _____

3. He established efficient delivery routes when he served as postmaster general.   3. _____

4. He invented an odometer that counted carriage wheel rotations.   4. _____

5. Franklin was the only founding father to sign all five documents that established
   American independence.   5. _____

6. In colonial America, not everyone could afford books, which were expensive.   6. _____

7. So that he and others could have books to read, Franklin founded the first public library. 7. _____

8. Franklin and other printers, who were known as the Leather Apron Club, started
   a lending library.   8. _____

9. After he moved to Philadelphia, Franklin bought a newspaper and made it a success.   9. _____

10. When he retired from business, Franklin concentrated on his science experiments
    and inventions.   10. _____

11. Although Franklin had no formal education after age ten, he received honorary
    degrees from Harvard University and Yale University.   11. _____

Your Total Score _____ /33
If your score was 25 or less, review pages 219–220, before continuing.

Name _____ Date _____ Score _____

98 | Unit Review

A | Directions Underline the phrase in each sentence. In the blank at the right, write *prep* for a prepositional phrase, *inf* for an infinitive phrase, or *part* for a participial phrase. Score one point for each correct phrase and one point for each correct type.

Answers

1. Did the other members of the group have any comments?   1. _____

2. Proofreading the figures, Pam and Barb found several errors.   2. _____

3. Parviz is saving his money to buy a motorcycle.   3. _____

4. Mr. Sims spoke first, outlining the new proposal.   4. _____

5. She has dinner reservations, so she hopes to finish early.   5. _____

6. Without Abby's help, we would never have made the deadline.   6. _____

7. To become a veterinarian has always been Harlow's goal.   7. _____

8. Kole submitted his findings to the committee.   8. _____

9. The person arranging the conference is very competent.   9. _____

10. The package sent yesterday included all the items.   10. _____

Your Total Score _____ /20
If your score was 15 or less, review Section 25, pages 213–216, before continuing.

B | Directions Underline the dependent clause in each sentence. In the blank at the right, write *adj* for an adjective clause, *adv* for an adverbial clause, or *n* for a noun clause. Score one point for each correct dependent clause and one point for each correct use.

1. Stephanie told me that she is working the night shift.   1. _____

2. If Odessa stops by later, please give her these files.   2. _____

3. My question is how we can encourage more employees to participate in our 401(k) plan.   3. _____

4. We can't hire temporary help because we don't have the funds.   4. _____

5. What the parties wanted was a quick settlement.   5. _____

6. Cecilia Forrester, who heads the Denver office, will be the new regional manager.   6. _____

7. There are many occasions with customers when you should just listen.   7. _____

8. Ray understands the terms of the contract better than I do.   8. _____

9. Parking passes are available for whoever needs them.   9. _____

10. The solution that we propose considers all the stakeholders.   10. _____

Your Total Score _____ /20
If your score was 15 or less, review Section 26, pages 219–221, before continuing.

Photodisc/Getty Images

A virtual assistant (VA) is an entrepreneur who contracts with businesses to provide administrative, technical, and/or creative services. Virtual assistants maintain their own work environment (they are not at the clients' work site); this explains the word *virtual* in the job title. A successful VA develops long-term, collaborative relationships with an organization rather than seeking to provide occasional administrative services. Relationships take time to develop because the VA is not on-site and must rely on his or her communication skills, website, and marketing efforts to engage a prospective client.

Virtual assistants must have strong soft skills in organization, initiative, responsibility, flexibility, vision, problem solving, and decision making if they are to be successful. Communication skills are probably among the most important skills for a VA because most communication is done electronically using technology such as e-mail, telephone, and videoconferencing. Virtual assistants create a large amount of written communication. Most VAs have at least five years of upper-level administrative experience, a high level of technological competence, a strong work ethic, and a commitment to building a successful business. A professional certification is available.

Because being a virtual assistant is a business as well as a career, a business plan and a marketing plan need to be developed and implemented, and a work environment must be established. It is not unusual for VAs to have both domestic and international clients.

Virtual assistants are and will continue to be in demand because businesses are constantly streamlining; contracting with a VA can be very cost-effective. Employers do not have to pay for office space, equipment, training, or employment benefits. In the United States, medical and legal practitioners, realtors, and corporate trainers are among the most prominent users of VAs.

Directions Underline the independent clauses once and the dependent clauses twice. In the blank at the right, write *adj* if the dependent clause is an adjective clause or *adv* if it is an adverbial clause. Score one point for each correct clause and one point for each correct use.

Answers

1. Candace marketed her VA business to real estate professionals because she had worked in real estate for 20 years.

1. _____

2. The International Virtual Assistants Association, which is the professional organization for VAs, offers a certification program.

2. _____

3. The services that Serafina provides are listed on the website.

3. _____

4. She bills a client when the job is completed.

4. _____

5. Since I decided to take courses in the virtual assistant program, I have learned more about my strengths.

5. _____

6. My largest client, who is in France, communicates with me electronically.

6. _____

Your Total Score _____ /18
If your score was 14 or less, review Section 26, pages 219–220, before continuing.

99 | Writing Improvement

A | **Directions** Construct complete sentences by adding independent clauses to the dependent clauses. The independent clause may be used anyplace in the sentence. Try to make your sentences interesting.

1. as you evaluate the software _____

_____

2. that participation is declining _____

_____

3. although tuition and fees are increasing _____

_____

B | **Directions** Construct complete sentences by adding dependent clauses to the independent clauses. The dependent clause may be used anyplace in the sentence. Try to make your sentences interesting.

1. Carolyn proofread her resume eight times _____

_____

2. Nonh was a student government officer _____

_____

3. Friday meetings were canceled _____

_____

C | **Directions** Write a paragraph on one of the following topics. Include a topic sentence, put your sentences in a logical sequence, and make them clear and concise. Develop sentences that are amusing, serious, or informational. Underline and identify at least three phrases and three clauses in your paragraph.

- Suppose you could have any job anywhere in the world for two years. What would you choose, and where?
- Describe something you enjoy doing.
- If you could take an all-expense-paid vacation anyplace in the world for a month, where would you go?
- What is your favorite television commercial? Why?

_____

_____

_____

_____

_____

_____

_____

 **Give your completed application to your instructor for evaluation.**

100 | Comprehensive Review

Directions Match each item in Column A with the item it describes in Column B. Write the identifying letter from Column A in the blank at the right. Score one point for each correct answer.

Column A	Column B	Answers
a. participial phrase	1. not, too, very	1. _____
b. infinitive phrase used as a subject	2. The movie <u>that we saw</u> was very good.	2. _____
c. adverbs	3. <u>Why he called</u> is a mystery to me.	3. _____
d. dependent clause used as an adverb	4. <u>Searching the Internet</u>, Honore found a bookcase for her apartment.	4. _____
e. dependent clause used as an adjective	5. smarter, more beautiful	5. _____
f. prepositional phrase used as an adjective	6. The tips were divided <u>between Yuan and Keo</u>.	6. _____
g. comparative degree of adjectives	7. <u>While we waited</u>, the bus came.	7. _____
h. noun clause used as a subject	8. Keisha backed into the car <u>in the handicapped parking space</u>.	8. _____
i. infinitive phrase used as a direct object	9. <u>To write well</u> is a great advantage.	9. _____
j. prepositional phrase used as an adverb	10. Darrell wanted <u>to get a job</u>.	10. _____

Column A	Column B	Answers
a. subordinate conjunctions	1. throw, teach, speak	1. _____
b. dependent clause used as an adjective	2. If Rex passes his CPA exam, <u>he will receive a raise</u>.	2. _____
c. irregular verbs	3. which, who, what	3. _____
d. infinitive phrase used as an adjective	4. enjoy, call, walk	4. _____
e. independent clause	5. Sam made a phone call <u>after we had finished our meeting</u>.	5. _____
f. regular verbs	6. after, because, if, that, until	6. _____
g. dependent clause used as an adverb	7. The person <u>to call</u> is Mrs. Watts.	7. _____
h. noun clause used as a subject	8. <u>That Wahid did the right thing</u> was noticed by the supervisor.	8. _____
i. interrogative pronouns	9. The presenter <u>who spoke on ethics</u> works for James & Sons.	9. _____
j. prepositions	10. between, by, near, with	10. _____

Your Total Score _____ /20

PROOF IT!

Directions Proofread the announcement. Mark any changes that are needed using the proofreaders' marks on page 317. Then key the announcement, making all necessary corrections. Make the two paragraphs of instructions easier to read by changing them into bulleted lists. Proofread your work, and make any corrections that are needed. Turn in both this page and your finished document to your instructor.

Fire Safety Tips for Travelers*

Please review the safety tips below to ensure you are safe if there is a fire in the hotel or motel where you are staying.

After Check-in

Study the evacuation plan posted in your room. If a plan is not posted, request one. Locate at least two exit near your room. Count the number of doors between your room and each exit. Because if you are unable to see in a fire, you can feel your way to the closest exit. Find the fire alarms on your floor.

In Case of Fire

If the fire is in your room, get out quicker. Close the door, activate the alarm, and notify the front desk. Use the stairs, not the elevater. If the fire is not in your room, leaf only if it is safe to do so. Take your room key with you in case fire blocks your escape and you need to return to the room. To check the hallway for fire, touch the door with the back of your hand. If the door is cool, crouch and open the door slowly. Be ready to close it quickly if there is flames on the other side. Crawl to the nearest exit; the most freshest air is near the floor. If your door is hot, do not open it. Instead, sit rolled-up, wet towels or sheets at the base of the door to keep out smoke. Turn of fans and air conditioners. Call the fire department to give your location. Single from your window.

*These guidelines are suggested by FireSafety.gov, a government resource for information on residential fire safety and prevention.

Posttest

A | **Directions** Underline the phrase in each sentence. In the blank at the right, write *prep* for a prepositional phrase, *inf* for an infinitive phrase, or *part* for a participial phrase.

1. My checkbook fell behind the desk.   1. _____

2. I wrote my sister an e-mail describing the events.   2. _____

3. To have my own apartment would be fantastic.   3. _____

4. Henry worked quickly to finish the project.   4. _____

5. Preparing quality meals, the company developed a great reputation.   5. _____

6. The clerk gave me a receipt for the returned items.   6. _____

7. The house with the blue shutters is mine.   7. _____

B | **Directions** Underline the independent clauses once and the dependent clauses twice. In the blank at the right, write *adj* if the dependent clause is an adjective clause or *adv* if it is an adverbial clause.

Example   <u>*Because I did not study for my exam*</u>, <u>I did poorly</u>.   *adv*

1. After I register, I need to buy supplies.   1. _____

2. The taco shop, which is on the corner, offers inexpensive lunches.   2. _____

3. The band members who are in my physics class are good students.   3. _____

4. She returned the sweater because it did not fit.   4. _____

C | **Directions** Underline the noun clause in each sentence.

1. Whatever you want to do is fine with me.

2. Francisco told me that my contribution was appreciated.

3. Robin was surprised by how many people attended the rally.

4. How Salinda deals with her fear of thunderstorms and lightning was shared with us.

unit 10
Punctuation

Objectives

1. To recognize and use periods, question marks, exclamation points, and commas
2. To recognize and use other common punctuation marks
3. To avoid comma splices

Sections

Pretest

Directions Add the necessary punctuation marks and underscore.

1. We won a house

2. It started as a small wedding but weve invited 400 people

3. Have you read the novel Empire of the Sun by J G Ballard

4. The movie which starred Christian Bale came out in 1987

5. Jo is a security guard she works from 9 30 p m to 7 30 a m

6. Ms Smiths article is called Coping with Change

7. The hours are good besides I can use the extra money

8. The offices are in Brussels Belgium and Aalborg Denmark

9. The race took us over some rough hilly terrain

10. Golda Meir was born on May 3 1898 in Kiev Russia

WORKPLACE FOCUS

Ergonomics

Ergonomics is the design of products and processes with a focus on safety, comfort, and efficiency. Using good posture and keyboarding techniques while working at a computer and lifting a patient the correct way are two examples. Ergonomic techniques, guidelines, and equipment are developed by experts as the best means of keeping people from being injured at work.

The chances of suffering a work-related injury are greater than many people imagine. In a recent year, some 3.9 million U.S. workers were injured on the job. Sprains, strains, and other musculoskeletal disorders accounted for nearly one in three injuries and illnesses causing days missed from work. Carpal tunnel syndrome (pressure on the median nerve that can produce pain, weakness, or numbness in the hand or wrist) caused a median 27 missed days, and repetitive motion injuries resulted in some of the longest absences. An added concern is that some workplace injuries can recur and become more severe, even permanently disabling.

What can you do to minimize the chance that you will be injured at work?

- Spend whatever time is required to learn to do tasks and use equipment correctly.

- Even though it may sometimes be inconvenient, practice what you've learned.

- Follow all written and posted instructions that have been provided for your safety.

- See your doctor at the first sign that you may have a work-related injury. Don't wait for it to get worse.

Period, Question Mark, and Exclamation Point

Punctuation in writing indicates pauses, gestures, and desired changes of expression. Punctuation keeps words from running together so the meaning is clear.

Period .

End Punctuation

A **period** at the end of a sentence serves the same purpose as a stop sign. It brings you to a halt. The period marks the end of a **declarative sentence** (a statement of fact) or an **imperative sentence** (a command or request for someone to do something). Every sentence that is a statement should end with a period.

> He sells most of his photos online.   (declarative sentence)
> Please schedule a meeting for next Monday.   (imperative sentence)

Periods are used in many **abbreviations** (shortened forms of words or groups of words), but most abbreviations are not commonly used in formal writing. Some abbreviations (described in the following paragraphs) are always acceptable.

Initials and Titles

Use a period after an initial and after the courtesy titles *Mr.*, *Mrs.*, and *Ms.*

> The keynote speaker is <u>Ms</u>. <u>A</u>. <u>G</u>. Scott. (Note there should be a space between a first and a middle initial.)

Most professional titles are spelled out. An exception is *Dr.*

> <u>Dr</u>. Johnson volunteers for Doctors Without Borders.

A professional title can be abbreviated if the person's full name is used.

> <u>Lt</u>. Bryan Sackenheim has returned from a six-month Western Pacific deployment.

Degrees and Professional Designations

Use periods in academic degrees that follow a person's name.

> Dilip Shah, <u>R.N.</u>, has joined the staff of Metro Hospital.

A degree such as *M.D.*, *J.D.*, *Ph.D.*, or *D.D.S.* is a doctoral degree. Do not use *Dr.* and a doctoral degree together.

> **Incorrect** <u>Dr</u>. Vincent Getchell, <u>M.D.</u>, will serve as an expert witness.
> **Correct**   <u>Dr</u>. Vincent Getchell **or** Vincent Getchell, <u>M.D.</u>

Within the health care field, medical degrees are often written without periods. Professional designations such as *CPA* (*certified public accountant*) are written without periods when used alone but with periods when used with academic degrees.

> Federico Morales, <u>CLU</u>, will speak on investment planning.

> Cheryl Gates, <u>M.B.A.</u>, <u>C.P.A.</u>, announces the opening of her full-service tax and accounting firm in downtown Lansing.

Time and State Names

Use periods with *a.m.* and *p.m.* to designate time. Use the United States Postal Service state abbreviations (two capital letters, no periods) in letter addresses.

> Did Herschel take the 9:30 a.m. flight?   Newark, NJ

Company Names

Abbreviations are sometimes part of a company's official name. Abbreviations people commonly use for some organizations' names have become official names.

> Pier 1 Imports, Inc.   UPS

Other Abbreviations

Sometimes using an abbreviation makes sense. If you are writing a paper about the National Oceanic and Atmospheric Administration, for example, it will be easier for your reader if you use the abbreviation NOAA. Spell out the term the first time you use it, with the abbreviation in parentheses. After that, use the abbreviation.

> You can download tax forms from the Internal Revenue Service (IRS) website.

Other abbreviations, while not appropriate for school or business writing, may be used in forms, tables, and charts. They also may be used in less formal writing. The rule for abbreviations is this: when in doubt, spell them out. The chart on page 235 lists common abbreviations.

Question Mark ?

A **question mark**, like a period, is used as a full stop in punctuation. A question mark is used after an **interrogative sentence**. These sentences ask direct questions.

> Where is the subway station?   Did he start his clinical internship?

Exclamation Point !

An **exclamation point** is used after words, phrases, or sentences to express sudden emotion (joy, fear, pain, happiness, anger) and forceful commands. Use exclamation points sparingly in your writing. Reserve them to express truly strong feeling.

> I can't believe it!   Congratulations!   Help!   Ouch!   Watch out!

TRY IT!

A | **Directions** Add the necessary period (.), question mark (?), or exclamation point (!).

1. Next summer, we will visit my sister   2. Wow   3. When are you leaving

B | **Directions** In the first column, add periods where they are needed. In the second column, write the meaning of each abbreviation. Check your answers on page 321 or with your instructor before continuing with your assignment.

1. G C Cameron, CLU   3. GB _____

2. Ms Maeve Gansenburg   4. FYI _____

APPLICATION ▶ **Complete Applications 101–102, pages 239–240, at this time.**

Common Abbreviations

Days

Sun.	Mon.	Tues.	Wed.	Thurs.	Fri.	Sat.

Months

Jan. Feb. Mar. Apr. Aug. Sept. Oct. Nov. Dec. *May, June,* and *July* are not abbreviated.

Units of Measure

oz	ounce(s)	in	inch(es)	l	liter(s)
lb	pound(s)	ft	foot (feet)	kg	kilogram(s)
qt	quart(s)	yd	yard(s)	cm	centimeter(s)
gal	gallon(s)	mi	mile(s)	m	meter(s)
		mph	miles per hour	km	kilometer(s)

Computer Terms

PC	personal computer	MHz	megahertz	FTP	file transfer protocol
FAQ	frequently asked questions	ISP	Internet service provider	PDF	portable document format
GB	gigabyte	LAN	local area network	RAM	random-access memory
KB	kilobyte	WAN	wide area network	ROM	read-only memory
MB	megabyte				

Miscellaneous

acct.	account	EEO	equal employment opportunity	No.(s)	Number(s)
amt.	amount			pd.	paid
approx.	approximately	e.g.	for example	PIN	personal identification number
attn.	attention	e.o.m., EOM	end of month	P.O.	Post Office (adj.)
ASAP	as soon as possible	etc.	*et cetera*	qty.	quantity
Ave.	Avenue	fax	facsimile	R&D	research and development
bal.	balance	FYI	for your information	recd.	received
bc	blind copy	hr	hour(s)	reg.	registered, regular
Blvd.	Boulevard	Inc.	Incorporated	ROI	return on investment
c	copy	intl.	international	RSVP	please reply
CEO	chief executive officer	Jr.	Junior	Sr.	Senior
chg.	charge	Ltd.	Limited	St.	Street
c.o.d., COD	cash on delivery	mdse.	merchandise	U.S.	United States (adj.)
Corp.	Corporation	mfg.	manufacturing	vol.	volume
dept.	department	mgt.	management	vs.	versus
doz.	dozen	mo	month(s)	yr	year(s)
ea.	each	NA, N/A	not applicable	YTD	year to date

The comma is similar to a traffic warning sign. When you want to make a turn while you are driving, you signal and then turn. In writing, if you want to change your thoughts, insert some other ideas, or identify parts, you use the comma. Often, the sound of the spoken sentence with a pause and change of voice pitch will serve as a guide in the placement of commas in writing.

Commas clarify the meaning of your sentences. They show you where one word or group of words ends and the next word or group of words begins.

Series

Commas separate three or more items in a series. Notice how these sentences read without commas, and then see how they sound with commas.

Wrong	Carlo Nellie and Genevieve went skiing.
Right	Carlo, Nellie, and Genevieve went skiing.

Wrong	Our ski package includes lodging lift tickets and equipment rental.
Right	Our ski package includes lodging, lift tickets, and equipment rental.

Introductory Words, Phrases, and Clauses

Introductory words and phrases are separated from the rest of the sentence by a comma. (An exception is *then*.)

Unfortunately, neither of us will be able to attend the conference.
In a Category 5 hurricane, wind speeds exceed 155 miles per hour.

A comma is also used after a dependent clause that precedes a main clause at the beginning of a sentence. The comma sets off the independent (main) clause.

While Keelan was in Salt Lake City, he visited the Clark Planetarium.

The slight pause indicated by the comma prevents reading words together. If it is omitted or misplaced, the sentence may be confusing, or its meaning may change.

Inside the house was in complete disarray.
Inside, the house was in complete disarray.

When I called Garrett Drew picked up the phone.
When I called Garrett, Drew picked up the phone.
When I called, Garrett Drew picked up the phone.

Nonessential Elements

Use commas to set off nonessential elements—words, phrases, and clauses that could be left out of a sentence without affecting its structure (it would still be a sentence) or meaning. In speaking, you would pause before and after these words, phrases, and clauses.

The biggest surprise, <u>however</u>, was the drop in online sales.

Ms. Cloud, <u>my manager</u>, is being transferred.

The county, <u>expecting a big turnout</u>, has arranged for extended polling hours.

Machu Picchu, <u>which is in Peru</u>, is a World Heritage Site.

Sachi is majoring in psychology, <u>while Brady has chosen elementary education</u>.

Essential elements are words, phrases, and clauses that are necessary to the meaning of the sentence. In speaking, you would not pause before or after them. Do not set off essential elements with commas.

They're waiting <u>until next year</u> to change the policy.

Shawne told us <u>that he sells digital ads</u>.

Independent Clauses

A comma is used before a coordinating conjunction such as *and, but, or, nor,* or *yet* when it links independent (main) clauses. The comma may be omitted if the two clauses are short or closely related in subject matter: *He failed the test and he didn't care.*

Mitch made a vegetable stew with polenta, and Fatima brought apple cobbler.

Are you selling your house, or did you decide to wait?

Independent Adjectives Before a Noun

You have already learned that independent adjectives before a noun should be separated by a comma. (See page 170 for a review.)

It was a <u>cool</u>, windy day.

Can you get <u>lush</u>, green grass if you use an organic fertilizer?

Quotations

Quotations (direct speech) are set off by commas from the rest of the sentence. (See pages 247–248 for more information on punctuation with quotation marks.)

"Success is more permanent when you achieve it without destroying your <u>principles</u>," said Walter Cronkite.

"A <u>professor</u>," wrote W. H. <u>Auden</u>, "is one who talks in someone else's sleep." (Note that *is* does not have a capital letter.)

"Just because a man lacks the use of his eyes doesn't mean he lacks <u>vision</u>," remarked Stevie Wonder.

Do not use commas when the quotation fits smoothly into the sentence.

Dave Barry wrote that doing your own car repairs is "an easy way to save money and possibly maim yourself for life."

Dates, Addresses, and Letters

The comma is used to set off the second and all following items in complete dates and in addresses.

Layne's grandmother was born on <u>June 28</u>, <u>1942</u>, in Scotland.

My new address is <u>101 Park Boulevard</u>, <u>Virginia Beach</u>, Virginia.

No comma is needed when the date has only two parts or uses the word *of*.

My sister graduated from college in <u>June 2008</u>.

The wedding will take place on the <u>ninth of September</u>.

In a letter, a comma is used after the complimentary close if a colon has been used after the salutation.

Dear Mrs. West: Sincerely <u>yours</u>,

States and Countries

Use commas to set off the name of a state or country that follows the name of a city.

Dwight grew up in <u>Baltimore</u>, Maryland.

Jordi was transferred from <u>Oslo</u>, <u>Norway</u>, to <u>Bern</u>, Switzerland.

Numbers

For numbers greater than zero, use a comma to separate the digits into groups of three. Do not use a comma in parts of a number that are less than zero (decimals) and years.

36,108 residents $2,456,000   5,028,358,721 chips

But 1,569.0184543   the year 1934

WRITE NOW!

Comma Splice

A common mistake is to use only a comma to connect two independent clauses in a compound sentence. This is known as a comma splice.

Franklin ate dinner, then he went to the movies.

Don't buy a sedan, buy a hatchback.

Here are four ways to correct a comma splice:

- Add a coordinating conjunction, such as *and*, *but*, *or*, *nor*, or *yet*.
  Franklin ate dinner, <u>and</u> then he went to the movies.
- Add a conjunctive adverb (page 220). Note the punctuation.
  Don't buy a sedan; <u>instead</u>, buy a hatchback.
- Use just a semicolon.
  Franklin ate <u>dinner</u>; then he went to a movie.
- Make two separate sentences.
  Don't buy a <u>sedan</u>. Buy a hatchback.

APPLICATION Complete Applications 103–106, pages 241–244, at this time.

101 | End Punctuation

Directions Add the necessary periods (.), question marks (?), or exclamation points (!). Score one point for each correct mark.

Your Score

1. Please meet me this afternoon at the British Museum   1. _____

2. Would you like to spend a few hours seeing the Parthenon sculptures   2. _____

3. About half the surviving sculptures are there   3. _____

4. The Parthenon is in Athens, Greece   4. _____

5. It was built nearly 2,500 years ago as a temple to the goddess Athena   5. _____

6. The temple is an excellent example of the Doric style, which emphasizes simplicity
   and strength   6. _____

7. Can you see examples of that style in buildings today   7. _____

8. Is it true the Parthenon was later a church, a mosque, and a storehouse for gunpowder   8. _____

9. Tell me about Phidias, who was responsible for the sculpture   9. _____

10. He was a famous sculptor, as well as an architect and a painter   10. _____

11. Most sculptures in the museum's collection are from outside the building—the pediments,
    metopes, and frieze   11. _____

12. The frieze shows a procession on the way to make an offering to Athena   12. _____

13. Which pediment depicts the contest between Athena and Poseidon   13. _____

14. The metopes show scenes of battle, some from history and some from mythology   14. _____

15. What is a metope   15. _____

16. It is a square, carved panel   16. _____

17. The sculptures are so lifelike   17. _____

18. They are in incredible condition   18. _____

19. Look at the flowing robes and the facial expressions   19. _____

20. See how well the sculptors captured physical movement and emotion   20. _____

21. The Parthenon sculptures are some of the best surviving sculptures of ancient Greece
    and some of the finest of all time   21. _____

22. Who acquired the sculptures from Athens   22. _____

23. It was Lord Elgin, British ambassador to the Ottoman Empire   23. _____

24. Was Athens part of the Ottoman Empire at that time   24. _____

25. What did the Parthenon symbolize for the Athenians   25. _____

Your Total Score _____ /25
If your score was 19 or less, review pages 233–234 before continuing.

102 | Abbreviation Practice

A | **Directions** Underline the correct abbreviation in parentheses. Score one point for each correct answer.

Your Score

1. Did you read that article by (R. K., R.K, R K, RK) Zilg on using the Internet in your job search?   1. _____

2. Please see (Mrs, Mrs.) Hancock at the reservations desk to pick up an audio tour.   2. _____

3. Pion Nopsuwan, (R.N., RN, R N, R. N.), leads a caregiver support group.   3. _____

4. I took the medicine at 7 (a.m., AM) and again at 1 (p.m., PM).   4. _____

5. Gap (Inc., Inc) is traded on the New York Stock Exchange under the symbol GPS.   5. _____

B | **Directions** In the first answer column, write the proper abbreviation for each item. In the second answer column, write the meaning of each abbreviation. Score one point for each correct answer.

	Answers			Answers
1. certified public accountant	_____		16. PIN	_____
2. kilometer	_____		17. m	_____
3. Friday	_____		18. YTD	_____
4. copy	_____		19. GB	_____
5. Avenue	_____		20. FAQ	_____
6. Limited	_____		21. N/A	_____
7. Numbers	_____		22. Inc.	_____
8. for example	_____		23. fax	_____
9. March	_____		24. vs.	_____
10. *et cetera*	_____		25. mi	_____
11. as soon as possible	_____		26. FYI	_____
12. inch	_____		27. attn.	_____
13. equal employment opportunity	_____		28. mo	_____
14. megahertz	_____		29. oz	_____
15. Post Office	_____		30. acct.	_____

Your Total Score _____ /36
If your score was 27 or less, review pages 233–235 before continuing.

103 | Comma Usage—Series, Independent Adjectives, Dates, States and Countries, and Numbers

Directions Add the necessary commas. Score one point for each comma that is correctly placed.

Your Score

1. Jules Verne was born in Nantes France on February 8 1828.

   1. _____

2. Verne was a prolific author who accurately predicted submarines space travel a moon landing and many other scientific inventions and accomplishments.

   2. _____

3. He did his research by talking to people and reading books newspapers and journals.

   3. _____

4. A few of his many books are *Journey to the Center of the Earth From the Earth to the Moon Twenty Thousand Leagues Under the Sea* and *Around the World in 80 Days*.

   4. _____

5. Phileas Fogg wagers 20000 pounds that he can travel around the world in 80 days.

   5. _____

6. He travels on steamers trains carriages a pilot boat an elephant and a sledge with sails.

   6. _____

7. His stops include Bombay (Mumbai) Calcutta (Kolkata) Hong Kong Shanghai and Yokohama.

   7. _____

8. Fogg presents himself at his club in London on December 21 1872 at 8:45 p.m.

   8. _____

---

9. A reporter named Nellie Bly set out to beat Phileas Fogg's record; she traveled around the world in 72 days 6 hours and 11 minutes.

   9. _____

10. She met Jules Verne and his wife in Amiens France along the way.

   10. _____

11. Bly took just one small piece of hand luggage that contained a few items of clothing needles thread toilet articles a flask a cup pens pencils and an inkstand.

   11. _____

12. She was an intrepid pioneering journalist who wrote about needed social reforms.

   12. _____

13. The first man to sail alone around the world arrived in Newport Rhode Island on June 27 1898 in an 11-meter sloop called *Spray*.

   13. _____

14. He encountered pirates a gale and other dangers on his three-year 46000-mile journey.

   14. _____

15. Four Douglas World Cruiser biplanes left Seattle Washington on April 4 1924 to attempt the first round-the-world flight.

   15. _____

16. Of the planes—*Seattle Boston Chicago* and *New Orleans*—two finished the 175-day trip.

   16. _____

17. In the National Air and Space Museum in Washington D.C. hangs the first plane to fly around the world without stopping or refueling.

   17. _____

18. Dick Rutan and Jeana Yeager flew 24986 miles in nine days and landed on December 23 1986 with just a few gallons of fuel left.

   18. _____

19. The first person to orbit the earth was the dedicated outgoing cosmonaut Yuri Gagarin.

   19. _____

20. His historic flight took place on April 12 1961.

   20. _____

21. Gagarin circled the globe in 108 minutes at a speed of 27400 kilometers per hour.

   21. _____

Your Total Score _____ /59

If your score was 44 or less, review pages 236 and 237–238 before continuing.

104 | Comma Usage—Introductory Items, Nonessential Elements, Independent Clauses, and Quotations

Directions Add the necessary commas. Score one point for each comma that is correctly placed.

Your Score

1. The electoral college a system by which electors rather than voters choose the president and vice president originated with the founding fathers.

1. _____

2. "They wanted a compromise" explained Jared "between election by Congress and election by popular vote."

2. _____

3. For each state the number of electors equals the number of members it has in Congress.

3. _____

4. Since membership in the House of Representatives is based on state population more populous states get more electors.

4. _____

5. "When a candidate wins a state's popular vote" said Jalen "he or she gets all the state's electoral votes."

5. _____

6. "That's true for all but two states and it's true for the District of Columbia which gets three electoral votes" Ricci added.

6. _____

7. To be elected president or vice president a candidate must receive 270 electoral votes.

7. _____

8. Thousands of bills are introduced in the House and Senate each year; only a very small percentage however become laws.

8. _____

9. After a bill has been introduced it is assigned to a committee.

9. _____

10. The committee often gives the bill to a subcommittee which studies it in detail.

10. _____

11. Once a bill has been approved it goes on the calendar for consideration.

11. _____

12. The Rules Committee as its name implies sets rules for how the bill will be handled— whether to limit debate or amendments for example.

12. _____

13. The bill goes to the floor where it is read in its entirety.

13. _____

14. Finally the House or Senate votes on the bill.

14. _____

15. Sirena said "A bill that passes I think moves to the other branch of Congress."

15. _____

16. If the bill is approved there it goes to a conference committee whose members are from the House and Senate.

16. _____

17. "The committee works out any differences between the House and the Senate versions" Tyrique noted.

17. _____

18. The president may sign the bill or he or she may veto it.

18. _____

19. To override a veto two-thirds of the House and two-thirds of the Senate must vote for the bill.

19. _____

Your Total Score _____ /30
If your score was 23 or less, review pages 236–237 before continuing.

105 | Comma Review

Directions Add the necessary commas. Score one point for each comma that is correctly placed.

Your Score

1. The policy will be in effect from January 1 2009 to June 30 2010.

2. Featured in *Fortune* magazine it's one of the country's top 100 employers.

3. The company has offices in Albuquerque New Mexico and Chattanooga Tennessee.

4. Last year the firm spent $1527048 on new equipment.

5. E-mail texting cell phones and the Internet are examples of workplace distractions.

6. Mrs. Alice Compton a restaurant inspector spoke about safe food-handling practices.

7. He's written a practical step-by-step guide to strategic planning.

8. Kendall has a bachelor's degree but Haleigh has more work experience.

9. "What separates the talented individual from the successful one is a lot of hard work" said Stephen King.

10. The bond's yield traded yesterday at 2.2765 percent unless I am mistaken.

11. According to this analysis we're going to see a rate increase of 3.5 percent.

12. "With the advent of the fax machine and e-mail" wrote Marya W. Holcombe "people are now able to embarrass themselves in writing hundreds of times faster than ever before."

13. Gage Power Company is purchasing 375000 smart meters.

14. I'm traveling on business to Kyiv Ukraine and Belgrade Serbia.

15. The files could be in that cabinet on the shelf or in one of those boxes.

16. The fund has performed very poorly yet the company continues to promote it.

17. We need a reliable inexpensive method of backing up files.

18. The mailing address is 102 Fourth Street Saint Paul Minnesota; you can look up the ZIP Code at http://www.usps.com.

19. Ted Feeley who does our taxes is someone we recommend highly.

20. The company announced a plan for growth which will be explained in detail at the annual shareholders' meeting in April.

21. At my company we've started a workplace mentoring program.

22. To be a good team member you should do your share of the work encourage others to participate and look for roles that you can fill ably.

23. I've put money in that account every month since January 2007 so I've saved a substantial amount.

24. Kwaku attends Salem State College where he is majoring in speech communication.

25. Still you can't argue with the fact that he is the best-qualified candidate.

1. _____
2. _____
3. _____
4. _____
5. _____
6. _____
7. _____
8. _____
9. _____
10. _____
11. _____
12. _____
13. _____
14. _____
15. _____
16. _____
17. _____
18. _____
19. _____
20. _____
21. _____
22. _____
23. _____
24. _____
25. _____

Your Total Score _____ /42

If your score was 32 or less, review Section 28, pages 236–238, before continuing.

106 | Comma Review

Directions Add the necessary commas. Score one point for each comma that is correctly placed.

Your Score

1. Representatives from our company attended a conference on January 20 2009 on reducing workplace injuries.

1. _____

2. It was held at the Metro Convention Center 102 Third Street Fayetteville Arkansas.

2. _____

3. The first speaker Dr. Karis Black is a certified professional ergonomist.

3. _____

4. She said that musculoskeletal disorders which constitute a significant percentage of workplace injuries often develop gradually.

4. _____

5. Dr. Black listed three risk factors for these types of injuries: overexerting yourself doing work in awkward or unnatural positions and repeatedly making the same movements.

5. _____

6. Struggling to lift a patient for instance would be an example of overexerting.

6. _____

7. If a work area is improperly arranged or designed employees may constantly have to reach too far or bend in an awkward way.

7. _____

8. Many occupations she noted require repetitive motions.

8. _____

9. Musculoskeletal disorders can often be prevented depending on the choices that employers and employees make.

9. _____

10. In determining how to do a task more safely employee input is crucial.

10. _____

11. When you are working at a computer make sure you use the correct keying position.

11. _____

12. "Your feet should be flat on the floor" Reva said.

12. _____

13. "Sit up straight" Val advised "with your lower back supported."

13. _____

14. Your fingers should be curved and you should place them over the home keys.

14. _____

15. Keep your wrists and forearms low and parallel to the keyboard your arms near your sides and your arms and shoulders relaxed.

15. _____

16. Strike the keys lightly using your fingertips.

16. _____

17. Kelly said "The keyboard should be at the edge of the desk."

17. _____

18. The monitor should be at a comfortable distance while the mouse should be near the keyboard and as close to your body as possible.

18. _____

19. With the top of the screen at or below eye level you are ready to work.

19. _____

20. It's true isn't it that the Centers for Disease Control and Prevention recommends not using a laptop as your primary computer?

20. _____

21. Take short frequent breaks—every 20 to 30 minutes.

21. _____

Your Total Score _____ /32

If your score was 24 or less, review Section 28, pages 236–238, before continuing.

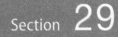

Section **29** # Other Punctuation Marks

Semicolon ;

The semicolon is used to separate independent clauses when they are not joined by a coordinating conjunction. It is used as a "slow down" signal, stronger than a comma but not a complete stop. You can remove a semicolon and put a period in its place, and you will have two complete sentences instead of one.

> The tuition for my multimedia course is $795; the books and software cost $210.
> Osahon will pick us up at 7; the play starts at 8.

The semicolon is used between independent clauses when they are joined by a conjunctive adverb (an adverb that connects and relates main clauses, such as *besides, however, nevertheless, still, then,* and *therefore*). When phrases like *as a result, for example,* or *for instance* connect and relate main clauses, the semicolon is used, too.

> The plane was late departing; however, we arrived on time due to a strong tailwind.
> Traffic was heavy; as a result, I was late for my interview.

Colon :

The colon is used to direct the reader's attention to what comes after it, usually a list. The colon often is used after words like *the following* or *as follows.*

> The following employees have completed 35 years of service: Jamie Dell, Devin Lace, and Ilana Wood.
> Trevor enrolled in three business courses: international business, marketing, and financial accounting.

The colon is always preceded by an independent clause, except when the listed items are on separate lines.

Use the colon between the hour and the minutes in writing times.

> Our customer service center is open from 8 a.m. to 5:30 p.m.

A colon may be used after the salutation in a letter. (A comma must then be used after the complimentary close.)

> Dear Mr. and Mrs. Sutterman: Sincerely,

Dash —

The dash is most often used in place of commas, parentheses, a colon, or a semicolon when special emphasis is desired.

> Bobby Orr—one of the greatest players of all time—started with the Boston Bruins at the age of 18.
> The plan has just one drawback—it doesn't set a cap on expenditures.

The dash is also used when a sentence is interrupted abruptly and a different thought is added.

> That's Susannah's brother—didn't he work for President Clinton?

Parentheses ( )

Parentheses are used to set off additions that are not necessary to the meaning of a sentence. Unlike the dash, parentheses tend to de-emphasize what they set off. Parentheses are used to enclose explanations, references, directions, and numbers and letters of listed items.

Doing some type of exercise daily (<u>swimming, aerobics, or running</u>) has improved her health.

According to your letter of August 15 (<u>copy enclosed</u>), I have fulfilled my distribution requirements.

Please (<u>1</u>) read the proposal carefully, (<u>2</u>) discuss it with your team, and (<u>3</u>) send me an analysis by Monday.

proofreading TIPS

When you proofread, check for consistency in punctuation and usage. Look for items like these:

- If you see an opening quotation mark or parenthesis, is there a closing mark?
- Is a person's or an organization's name spelled the same way throughout?
- Does the same woman have different courtesy titles?
- Are figures numbered in the correct order?
- If page 2 mentions a chart on page 12, is there a chart on page 12?

TRY IT!

Directions Add the necessary semicolons, colons, dashes, and parentheses. Check your answers on page 321 or with your instructor before continuing with your assignment. Use the proofreaders' marks on page 317 if necessary.

1. You can protect your credit in several ways for instance you can order a copy of your credit report.

2. Federal law the Fair Credit Reporting Act allows you to request one free copy of your credit report every 12 months from each of the major consumer reporting companies.

3. Some websites pretend to offer a free report but trick people into buying products or supplying personal information.

4. Look for items like the following mistaken reports of late payments, accounts that aren't yours, accounts you closed, and accounts you never use.

5. If you find an error, 1 explain the error in writing to the consumer reporting company and 2 notify the creditor, also in writing, that you are disputing an item.

6. Asher verifies his report once a year he also checks it before applying for a loan.

APPLICATION ▶ **Complete Application 107, page 249, at this time.**

Apostrophe '

The **apostrophe** shows ownership or possession. (See page 44 for additional examples.)

> My <u>friend's</u> car was stolen from the school parking lot.

The apostrophe is also used in a **contraction**, a shortened form of a word or words. The apostrophe shows the omission of one or more letters.

> <u>It's</u> colder today than it was yesterday.
>> <u>It's</u>—contraction for *It is*. The apostrophe takes the place of the *i* in the word *is*.

> The two sides talked for hours, but they <u>couldn't</u> reach an agreement.
>> <u>couldn't</u>—contraction for *could not*. The apostrophe takes the place of the *o* in the word *not*.

An apostrophe plus *s* is used to form the plural of isolated lowercase letters and the capital letters *A*, *I*, *M*, and *U*.

Quotation Marks " "

Direct Quotations

Quotation marks are used to enclose the exact words of a person (direct quotation).

> Someone once said, "The road to success is dotted with many tempting parking places."
> The Governor called the decision "a quick, decisive move that addresses our immediate needs."

When you interrupt a quoted sentence to identify the speaker, close the first part of the sentence at a logical place, and start the second part with a lowercase letter.

> "If you'd like," said Jehan, "we can take my car and go look for him."

When the break occurs between sentences, end the first part with a period. Begin the new quoted sentence with a quotation mark and a capital letter.

> "Our life is frittered away by detail," wrote Henry David Thoreau. "Simplify, simplify."

Literary and Artistic Works

Use quotation marks to set off titles of parts of works such as chapters of books, newspaper or magazine articles, songs, and individual episodes of television series. Titles of books, magazines, newspapers, albums, movies, television series, works of art, and other complete works should be underlined when written in longhand and italicized or underlined when printed. Do not use italics, underlining, or quotation marks for website titles. (See page 266 for a discussion of capitalization of titles.)

> Did you read the article "Presidential Analysis" in *Newsweek*?
> In history class, we watched "The Cause," the first episode in the Ken Burns series *The Civil War*.

Unusual Words and Expressions

Use quotation marks to enclose words or expressions that are unusual or are used in an unusual way.

> You have a "swipeout" if the magnetic strip on your credit card wears out from too much use.
> That "drive it into the dirt" attitude is wearing on their employees.

Quotation Marks and Other Punctuation

Place periods and commas inside quotation marks.

> Davetta said, "Let's go for a run after work."
> "I'll meet you at Sawyer Point at 4:30," P. J. replied.

Place semicolons and colons outside quotation marks.

> I downloaded "City of New Orleans"; it's one of my favorite songs.

Place question marks or exclamation points *inside* the quotation marks if they are part of the quoted matter and *outside* the quotation marks if they punctuate the entire sentence.

> Rafael asked, "Was it Jonas Salk who developed the polio vaccine?"
> Who was it who said, "The only thing we have to fear is fear itself"?

Indirect Quotations

Do not use quotation marks for an indirect quotation. The statement must be the exact words of a person for quotation marks to be used.

> Adesina said she would take me home after art class.

Hyphen -

The **hyphen** is used in most compound adjectives that precede a noun and in some compound nouns. (See page 173 for a review of compound adjectives and pages 39–40 for a review of compound nouns.)

> It's supposed to be one of the <u>fastest-growing</u> tech companies.
> The new initiative is a <u>by-product</u> of the task force's work.

The hyphen is also used in spelled-out compound numbers, phone numbers, nine-digit ZIP Codes, and simple fractions.

> <u>Sixty-seven</u> employees participated in the walk against breast cancer.
> The survey shows that <u>two-thirds</u> of customers are willing to pay more for green power.

The hyphen is used to divide words between one line and the next. Word processing software does end-of-the-line word division automatically. If an occasion occurs when you need to divide a word and you are not sure where to break it, consult a dictionary.

TRY IT!

Directions Add the necessary apostrophes, quotation marks, and hyphens. Check your answers on page 321 or with your instructor before continuing with your assignment.

1. Margarets car was vandalized last night.

2. You should look for a house in Dover, Ranga suggested.

3. Three fourths of the units have already been sold.

APPLICATION Complete Applications 108–113, pages 250–253 and 255–256, at this time.

107 | Semicolon, Colon, Dash, and Parentheses

A | **Directions** Add the necessary semicolons and colons. Score one point for each semicolon or colon that is correctly placed. Use the proofreaders' marks on page 317 if necessary.

Your Score

1. My friend Mykayla works here she's a surgical technologist.

1. _____

2. Her shift runs from 730 a.m. to 430 p.m.

2. _____

3. Sometimes her job is like a medical show on TV for instance, she passes instruments to the surgeon during an operation.

3. _____

4. She holds retractors and cuts sutures she also helps count sponges and other items.

4. _____

5. Before an operation, Mykayla has the following tasks set up instruments and equipment, arrange sterile drapes and solutions, and make sure the equipment is working properly.

5. _____

6. She has these additional responsibilities transporting the patient, helping to position the patient on the table, and draping the patient.

6. _____

7. Mykayla is part of an operating room team surgeons, surgical technologists, anesthesiologists, and nurses.

7. _____

8. She completed an accredited degree program then she obtained her professional certification.

8. _____

9. Most surgical technologists are employed by hospitals however, they also work in doctors' offices and outpatient care centers.

9. _____

10. Mykayla respects her colleagues and values her work consequently, she has a high degree of job satisfaction.

10. _____

B | **Directions** Add the necessary parentheses and dashes. Remember that dashes tend to emphasize, and parentheses tend to de-emphasize, what they enclose. Score one point for each individual mark (each opening parenthesis, closing parenthesis, and dash) that is correctly placed. Use the proofreaders' marks on page 317 if necessary.

1. He seems pleasant enough but he's never worked in development.

1. _____

2. Seventy-four percent see Table 1 rated our service as "highly satisfactory."

2. _____

3. It's not just our store every business in the mall is losing sales.

3. _____

4. Dr. Bruce Tuckman identified four stages in the development of a successful team: 1 forming, 2 storming, 3 norming, and 4 performing.

4. _____

5. The lunchtime seminar the first in a series focuses on managing stress.

5. _____

6. The commission headed by the vice president and two civil rights leaders issues its report tomorrow.

6. _____

7. The café open weekdays from 11 to 4 offers sandwiches, salads, quiches, soups, smoothies, and teas.

7. _____

8. Oscar Novello I know him from the Denver office is the new program manager.

8. _____

9. I'd like to see that report and we've got a meeting tomorrow, right?

9. _____

10. Representative Micah Kissinger North Dakota spoke against the repeal.

10. _____

Your Total Score _____ /34
If your score was 26 or less, review pages 245–246 before continuing.

108 | Apostrophe, Quotation Marks, Underscore, and Hyphen

Directions Add the necessary apostrophes, quotation marks, underscore, and hyphens. Score one point for each individual mark (each apostrophe, opening quotation mark, closing quotation mark, and hyphen) that is correctly placed and one point for each correctly underscored group of words. Use the proofreaders' marks on page 317 if necessary.

Your Score

1. The offer couldnt have come at a better time, Kelly confided.

1. _____

2. I got As in history, English, and biology.

2. _____

3. In a single year, the company reduced water and energy consumption by one third.

3. _____

4. The article Video Games Start to Shape Classroom Curriculum appeared in The Christian Science Monitor.

4. _____

5. When youre at the Museum of Fine Arts, be sure to see the painting Room in Brooklyn by Edward Hopper.

5. _____

6. Farah said, Ill need to leave at 2:45 for my doctors appointment.

6. _____

7. We read The Search for Marvin Gardens, an essay by John McPhee.

7. _____

8. Clydes proposal is the most attractive Ive seen so far.

8. _____

9. The companys best selling product is its Internet security software.

9. _____

10. We read two novels this semester: 1984 by George Orwell and A Passage to India by E. M. Forster.

10. _____

11. When youve completed the paperwork, please come into my office, said Ms. Fox.

11. _____

12. Once we get our new computers, Moya told me, were going to donate the old ones to an elementary school.

12. _____

13. It wasnt the projected costs that bothered me it was the lack of oversight.

13. _____

14. She bought subscriptions to Consumer Reports and two other magazines.

14. _____

15. We celebrated our twenty fifth anniversary in August.

15. _____

16. Eighty five percent of our employees participate in the wellness program.

16. _____

17. You need to get all the xs on one side of the equation.

17. _____

18. Im not sure who wrote As Time Goes By, but Dooley Wilson sang it in the movie Casablanca.

18. _____

19. Our former boss will be remembered for his cant-do attitude.

19. _____

20. Weve been invited to the groundbreaking ceremony for the new Habitat for Humanity project.

20. _____

21. My sisters spending a semester abroad.

21. _____

22. It is better to sleep on things beforehand than to lie awake about them afterwards, wrote Baltasar Gracián.

22. _____

23. At the conference, the chief executive officer outlined the long term strategy.

23. _____

24. Karls son has a part time job with Honda this summer.

24. _____

25. I emailed you an article called Big Winners for Small Investors from The Motley Fool, a financial website.

25. _____

Your Total Score _____ /53
If your score was 40 or less, review pages 247–248 before continuing.

109 | Punctuation Review

Directions Add the necessary semicolons, colons, parentheses, dashes, apostrophes, quotation marks, underscore, and hyphens. Score one point for each individual mark (each opening quotation mark, closing quotation mark, etc.) that is correctly placed and one point for each correctly underscored group of words. Use the proofreaders' marks on page 317 if necessary.

Your Score

1. In his article Accountability on the Job, Grant Lento emphasizes the importance of being answerable for your actions to your supervisor, fellow employees, and customers.   1. _____

2. Our chamber choir will perform in three cities next month Cleveland, St. Louis, and St. Paul.   2. _____

3. The cheetah the fastest animal on land lives mostly in Africa.   3. _____

4. Arthurs schedule allows him little time for relaxation.   4. _____

5. Celie and I will write the report Nazneen and Uffe will develop the presentation.   5. _____

6. Wheres a good place to get Thai food downtown?   6. _____

7. Irene is one of our hardest working employees, Mina told us.   7. _____

8. The meeting will be held at 230 in Ms. Taylors office.   8. _____

9. Guidelines for compliance with the Health Insurance Portability and Accountability Act HIPAA must be developed.   9. _____

10. To join our online study group, please 1 read the group charter, 2 complete the membership form, and 3 choose a username and password.   10. _____

11. We have many details to consider nevertheless, we need to stay focused on our main goal.   11. _____

12. The production schedule see page 4 calls for delivery 185 days after commencement of the work.   12. _____

13. Todays Washington Post has an article Gauging the Economy thats very good.   13. _____

14. People may doubt what you say, said Louis Cass, but they will believe what you do.   14. _____

15. Karonde asked, Wouldnt you like to attend the benefits seminar?   15. _____

16. West Side Story is at the Playhouse, and its getting great reviews.   16. _____

17. Her train isnt due until 655 watch out for that car!   17. _____

18. Please bring proof of residency a drivers license, utility bill, voter registration card, or bank statement.   18. _____

19. I just finished The Known World, a novel by Edward P. Jones.   19. _____

20. Hes written some good short stories one of my favorites is Adam Robinson Acquires Grandparents and a Little Sister.   20. _____

21. Suppose Company As annual revenues continue gradually to grow.   21. _____

22. Twenty three thousand customers were without power after the storm.   22. _____

23. If we put an extra $50 a month with our mortgage payment, said Segundo, well save about $53,000 in interest.   23. _____

24. More than three fourths of households with broadband connections use the Internet to search for health information, according to The some more E-Patient Population, a report from the Pew Internet & American Life Project.   24. _____

25. Did the speaker really say that we are all human beans?   25. _____

Your Total Score _____ /63

If your score was 47 or less, review Section 29, pages 245–248, before continuing.

110 | Unit Review

Directions Add the necessary punctuation marks and underscore. Score one point for each individual mark (each opening quotation mark, closing quotation mark, etc.) that is correctly placed and one point for each correctly underscored group of words. Use the proofreaders' marks on page 317 if necessary.

Your Score

1. What are some strategies for dealing with angry customers   1. _____

2. To begin with try to be calm getting angry wont help   2. _____

3. Dont argue or be defensive instead listen carefully to what the customer has to say   3. _____

4. Its a good idea to stay quiet and allow the customer to vent off steam   4. _____

5. Use active listening skills like leaning toward the customer nodding and asking questions   5. _____

6. Show empathy with remarks like these I understand and I can see what you re saying   6. _____

7. Apologize even if you didnt make a mistake   7. _____

8. Your goal once you understand the problem is to find a solution to satisfy the customer   8. _____

9. Strive for a solution that is reasonable and fair   9. _____

10. Often customers who feel they ve been dealt with fairly in a dispute become more loyal customers than they were before   10. _____

---

11. Someone s stolen our car Ferhan exclaimed   11. _____

12. Joel Carver J D C PA is a partner with Rivera & Taylor in Billings Montana   12. _____

13. Please make a list of the equipment and services you need said Mr Dunn and bring it directly to me   13. _____

14. Keesh has a small shop downtown but he gets most of his business through his website   14. _____

15. There are clean spacious workout rooms with state of the art equipment   15. _____

16. The article is Talking to Your Doctor and the author is A N Narayan Ph D   16. _____

17. Its one of the top childrens hospitals in the country according to U S News & World Report   17. _____

18. Sloan works for the National Oceanic and Atmospheric Administration NOAA   18. _____

19. The block of rooms will be held until Tuesday May 11 at 6 p m   19. _____

20. LaRae said Ive finished checking the blood samples   20. _____

21. This is the last time absolutely the last time that I will cover for him   21. _____

22. My uncle the one who lives in Denver is taking me to China   22. _____

23. Please 1 pull todays charts for me and 2 review any lab results that have come in   23. _____

24. Figure 14 page 32 shows the 20 fastest growing occupations   24. _____

25. Is the correct total $2840 or $2480 Surendra asked   25. _____

Your Total Score _____ /113

111 | Unit Review

Directions Add the necessary punctuation marks and underscore. Score one point for each individual mark (each opening quotation mark, closing quotation mark, etc.) that is correctly placed and one point for each correctly underscored group of words.

Your Score

1. A comet is a chunk of ice and dirt that orbits the Sun   1. _____
2. As it nears the Sun some of the ice begins to evaporate   2. _____
3. The resulting gas and dust form the comets tail   3. _____
4. A comets tail can be more than 93000000 miles long   4. _____
5. For many years people thought comets were omens of disaster   5. _____
6. When beggars die wrote William Shakespeare there are no comets seen   6. _____
7. He continued The heavens themselves blaze forth the death of princes   7. _____
8. In those lines from the play Julius Caesar Caesars wife Calpurnia warns him of his death   8. _____
9. Most comets come from the Kuiper Belt a band of icy bodies beyond the orbit of Neptune   9. _____
10. Little was known about them until 1950 when Dr Fred L Whipple correctly theorized their composition   10. _____
11. He described some of his discoveries and inventions in Of Comets and Meteors which appeared in the journal Science   11. _____
12. Asteroids are lumps of rock and metal   12. _____
13. Most orbit the Sun in a band the asteroid belt between Mars and Jupiter   13. _____
14. Some scientists think asteroids are the remains of a planet however others believe they never were part of a planet   14. _____
15. Some asteroids are the size of pebbles while others are many miles wide   15. _____
16. Meteroids are asteroids and other space debris that orbit the Sun   16. _____
17. A meteor is the bright streak of light created when a meteoroid burns up as it travels through Earths atmosphere   17. _____
18. Meteors shooting stars and falling stars are all the same thing   18. _____
19. When Earths orbit takes it through bits and pieces shed by a comet some of these particles fall into the atmosphere forming a meteor shower   19. _____
20. A meteoroid that strikes Earth is called a meteorite   20. _____
21. Could a big asteroid hit Earth   21. _____
22. The chances are small but its happened before   22. _____
23. A meteorite crater near Flagstaff Arizona is three fourths of a mile wide and 570 feet deep   23. _____
24. Sixty five million years ago a massive asteroid struck the Yucatan Peninsula   24. _____
25. Many scientists believe that volcanic eruptions and asteroid impacts changed Earths climate wiping out plants dinosaurs and other animals   25. _____

Your Total Score _____ /75

ENGLISH ON THE JOB /
Medical Assistant

Image Source Pink/Jupiter Images

Medical assistants help physicians with the examination and treatment of patients. They also do whatever tasks are necessary to keep the office running smoothly. The Bureau of Labor Statistics has projected that, from 2006 to 2016, medical assistant will be one of the fastest-growing occupations.

There are a variety of clinical duties that medical assistants perform. These include taking medical histories and vital signs, preparing patients for examinations, explaining treatments to patients, and assisting during examinations. Medical assistants may also collect laboratory specimens and perform basic lab tests on-site.

Medical assistants have many administrative tasks, some general and some particular to medical settings. They greet patients, answer phones, schedule appointments, and handle bookkeeping and billing. In addition, they update and file patient records, fill out insurance forms, and arrange hospital admissions and lab services.

Employers look for experience and, increasingly, completion of a one- or two-year medical assistant program and certification. Medical assistants must have good communication skills to deal successfully with patients and must be able to communicate accurately and clearly to prevent any physical harm to them.

Directions Add the necessary punctuation marks. Score one point for each individual mark (each opening quotation mark, closing quotation mark, etc.) that is correctly placed.

Your Score

1. Why dont you consider becoming a medical assistant suggested Kamals guidance counselor

1. _____

2. Youre interested in a career in health care she continued and there are several colleges in the area that offer good programs

2. _____

3. A three semester program at a local community college appealed to him especially because it could lead to an associates degree in technical studies

3. _____

4. The curriculum included classes in psychology biology clinical procedures lab techniques medical terminology medical insurance and office skills

4. _____

5. Two years later Kamal Nader ATS joined the practice of Dr Evelyne Story in Greensboro North Carolina

5. _____

6. Medical assistants can specialize in ophthalmology geriatrics obstetrics and other areas

6. _____

7. State law dictates the clinical duties medical assistants may undertake

7. _____

8. Under a physicians direction they may prepare and administer medications

8. _____

9. They may call in prescriptions to pharmacies they also may authorize drug refills

9. _____

10. Medical assistants need good organizational and computer skills in addition they must be flexible and ready to learn

10. _____

Your Total Score _____ /47

112 | Writing Improvement

Directions Rewrite the sentences, correcting the comma splices. Review the WRITE Now feature on page 238. Choose the method for correcting each comma splice that you think is best.

1. Aaquila went shopping, then she visited her sister. _____
   _____

2. Walter doesn't want to pay for the repairs, he thinks his insurance company should. _____
   _____
   _____

3. You can mow the lawn tomorrow, you don't need to do it today. _____
   _____

4. Erika likes swordfish, she doesn't like salmon. _____
   _____

5. You don't need a new computer, you need to add some RAM. _____
   _____

6. Don't worry about changing the service date, that won't be a problem. _____
   _____

7. It's really cold, you can see your breath. _____
   _____

8. You look tired, let me finish up for you. _____
   _____

9. Mariyah needs to leave in the next few minutes, she'll be late. _____
   _____

10. Let's not eat there, the service is always so slow. _____
    _____

11. Don't spend your money on that game, buy this one. _____
    _____

12. The Moores didn't go camping in New England this year, they went on a fossil dig in Nevada. _____
    _____

 **APPLICATION** **Give your completed application to your instructor for evaluation.**

Name _____ Date _____ Score _____

113 | Comprehensive Review

Directions Underline the error in each sentence. In the blank at the right, write the correction. Score one point for each correctly identified error and one point for each accurate correction.

Answers

Example   It was <u>her</u> who prepared the briefs.   _____*she*_____

1. Did you send those faxs this morning?   1. _____

2. What are our short term goals?   2. _____

3. Roeland sat at the front table with Zoe and I.   3. _____

4. Evonne asked, "What is the deadline for this project"?   4. _____

5. If Mr. Polasko was in charge, we would be doing motivational interviewing.   5. _____

6. The courses in the online catalog includes one on technical writing.   6. _____

7. He says the company are providing memory upgrades for our laptops.   7. _____

8. Mindy don't understand the deductions that were taken from her paycheck.   8. _____

9. I didn't know you was from Boston.   9. _____

10. So far, 3,500 customers responded to our customer satisfaction survey.   10. _____

11. She lead the initiative to develop affordable housing in the downtown area.   11. _____

12. Kirsten excepted a job in Houston because she wanted to be near her family.   12. _____

13. Chrystal is a childrens' librarian at the Terrace Park branch.   13. _____

14. Which temporary service is the best: Tri-City Temps or Vista Employment?   14. _____

15. The handbook is out of date, we need to revise it.   15. _____

16. Its the first time Eloise has done the audit on her own.   16. _____

17. I completed the form and clicked the button marked "Accept".   17. _____

18. I have a lot of message's on my voice mail.   18. _____

19. We ordered: printer paper, toner cartridges, and CD-RW disks.   19. _____

20. Neither of the men wore their safety gear.   20. _____

21. The person who we hire must have completed an accredited medical assisting
    program.   21. _____

22. This cell phone is Gerald's, so that phone must be her's.   22. _____

23. When you get to the airport please give me a call.   23. _____

24. Do we have enough members for a quorum.   24. _____

25. Etsuko just returned from the conference in Denver and she will leave for
    Rio de Janeiro tomorrow.   25. _____

Your Total Score _____/50

PROOF IT!

Directions Proofread the letter. Mark any changes that are needed using the proofreaders' marks on page 317. Watch especially for errors in consistency in punctuation and usage. For help, see the Proofreading Tips on page 246. Key the letter, making all necessary corrections, and proofread your work. Turn in both this page and your finished letter to your instructor.

46 Brill Road

Fairfax, Va. 22036-3849

July 18, 2,010

Dr. Jeffrey Heekin, M.D

Pathmark Hospital

2584 Grant Boulevard

Washington, D.C. 20016-3485

Dear Dr Heekin,

Please consider me as an applicant for the position of medical assistant advertised in today's "Washington Post."

In May, I completed the one year medical assisting program at Willmeth College in Fairfax. In my third semester internship at Roslyn Community Hospital, I practiced many of the skills listed in your ad. I assisted physicians during examinations, took vital signs, obtained blood and tissue specimens, gave injections, and removed sutures. I scheduled and greeted patient, logged them in, and took their medical histories. I speak Spanish fluently and I have been certified by the American Association of Medical Assistants. The enclosed resume details my educational background and work experience.

I look forward to meeting with you to discussed this position. Please call me at (703 555-0138. Thank you for your time and consideration.

Sincerely,

Harry Gardner

Enclosure

Directions Add the necessary punctuation marks and underscore. Use the proofreaders' marks on page 317 if necessary.

1. D J is bringing hummus pita chips and iced tea

2. Jerald leases from Fleet Street Cars because he gets a money back guarantee

3. This is the article I was telling you about Kayaking on the Outer Banks

4. When its 9 30 a m in Manhattan what time is it in Hong Kong

5. We could see North by Northwest at the Classic Film Festival or we could go to Pattys party

6. Please review the current guidelines copy enclosed before our next meeting

7. As a child Doug lived in Oxford Mississippi and Ocala Florida

8. Jagdish pays the rent Stace pays for food and utilities

9. Getting a new bike is tempting still I really like my Peugeot

10. Watch out

11. I read about a California redwood named Hyperion Citlali said

12. It may be the tallest tree in the world nearly 75 feet taller than the Statue of Liberty

13. The March on Washington took place on August 28 1963 and was attended by 250 000 people

14. Mrs Trask asked for volunteers to help with the alumni mailing

15. Alvaro Sanchez D V M has joined the veterinary staff of Gateway Zoo

unit 11
Number Expression and Capitalization

Objectives

1. To identify and apply guidelines for number expression
2. To identify and apply guidelines for capitalization
3. To recognize and write effective and grammatically correct complex sentences

Sections

A | **Directions** Underline the correct number form in parentheses.

1. The booklet offers (25, twenty-five) tips for blogging.

2. Flor received (68%, 68 percent) of the vote for class president.

3. The stadium is located on (12, 12th) Street.

4. (11, Eleven) cars were stolen from our campus last semester.

5. My interview is at (2 o'clock, two o'clock) on (June 8, June 8th).

6. Nearly (200, two hundred) people attended the fashion show.

B | **Directions** Underline each letter that should be capitalized.

1. this issue of *newsweek* contains the article "your financial future."

2. my cousin grace and i will stay in harwich on cape cod.

3. the internal revenue service filing deadline is april 15.

4. she took classes in american literature, speech, and japanese.

WORKPLACE FOCUS

Personal Financial Management

Financial management is a pivotal function in organizations. It is also a critical function in self-management. One of the hardest things about controlling your finances is getting started. The first step to financial independence is developing a budget. A realistic budget is the best weapon for meeting your goals (financial, personal, and professional) and preventing overspending. A budget allows you to see the flow of your money—how much comes in and where it goes. Here are some guidelines that will put you on the path to financial independence:

- Create a realistic budget and stick to it. To do this, determine your total income for a month (what you actually take home), and write down all your expenses.

- Make a list of things you feel you can't live without, and trim your other expenses to accommodate them.

- Resist impulse buying.

- Only charge items if you know you will be able to pay the bill in full when it arrives.

- Do not overspend on housing; increase your housing allowance only as your income increases.

- Avoid joint obligations with people who do not manage money well.

- Find alternatives to spending. There are many free or inexpensive options for most situations or events.

- Check your budget periodically, and readjust your figures and spending habits.

Number Expression

Two questions are always asked about numbers:

(1) When do you write numbers in words?

(2) When do you use figures instead of a number in words?

Keep in mind the following rules about numbers.

Definite Numbers

Definite numbers above ten should be in figures.

> She was admitted to college when she was only 15.

If a sentence contains related numbers any of which is over ten, use figures for all the related numbers.

> I sent 8 text messages Thursday and 17 text messages Friday.
>
> Avnish sold 24 bags of popcorn, 18 hot dogs, and 21 smoothies.

When the numbers in a sentence or paragraph are in different categories, use the style that is appropriate to that category.

> The 18 club members sold seven cases of candy bars in three days.
>
> Please distribute the 30 cases of paper among the seven departments.

Indefinite and Approximate Numbers

Indefinite numbers should be written in words.

> A new highway would cost millions of dollars.
>
> Micaela is in her late sixties.

Approximate numbers above ten should be expressed as figures.

> More than 20 women signed up for the gourmet cooking class.

Numbers at the Beginning of Sentences

A number at the beginning of a sentence should be written in words. This is just like capitalizing the first letter of the first word of a sentence.

> Sixteen students received a perfect score on their final project.
>
> Four videos were on the required viewing list for my political science class.

Percentages, Fractions, and Decimals

When writing a percentage, use figures with the word *percent*. The symbol % is used only in statistical copy. When you write *percent,* make it one word rather than two.

> Nationally, 89 percent of registered voters cast their ballots in the 2004 election.

Spell out isolated simple fractions in words. Write mixed fractions and decimals in figures.

> Only one-third of the surveys had been returned by last Wednesday.
>
> My bread recipe called for 6 1/2 cups of whole-wheat flour.
>
> The instruments have been calibrated within 0.00875 inch of specifications.

It is a good idea to add a zero before decimals that are less than 1 so the decimal point is not overlooked.

Weights, Measures, and Distances

Express weights, measures, and distances in figures.

> The salt for our water softener comes in <u>40-pound</u> bags.
>
> The walk-in closet measured <u>10 feet</u> by <u>6 feet</u>.

Time

To designate time, use a number with *a.m.* or *p.m.* When using *o'clock*, spell out the number. Do not use zeros with on-the-hour times. (An exception is lists and tables that also include times not on the hour.) Use the words *noon* and *midnight* alone, without the number *12*.

> Marty will leave for the meeting at <u>eight o'clock</u>.
>
> The flight leaves at <u>7:20 p.m</u>.
>
> Rey will be working from <u>4 p.m</u>. until <u>midnight</u> this Saturday.

Money

Amounts under $1 are expressed with a figure and the word *cents*. Omit the decimal and zeros to the right of the decimal when expressing whole dollar amounts, even if they appear with mixed dollar amounts.

> She paid <u>99 cents</u> for a granola bar.
>
> You can rent new releases at Hometown Video for <u>$5</u>.

Use figures for amounts under a dollar when used with related amounts over a dollar.

> To mail the three packages, Thien paid <u>$.74</u>, <u>$2.43</u>, and <u>$3.31</u>.

Dates, Addresses, and Ordinal Numbers

A common problem is not knowing when to use *st, th,* or *d* in a date or street address. If the figure (or date) follows the month, you do not use *st, th,* or *d*.

> Khalaf will graduate from college on <u>June 22, 2010</u>.

If, however, the date stands alone or comes before the month, use *st, th,* or *d* with the figure that represents the date.

> I received my income tax refund on the <u>21st</u>.
>
> Our next meeting will be held on the <u>5th of October</u>.

Streets numbered above ten use *st, th,* or *d*.

> I will meet you at 5 p.m. at the corner of <u>32nd Street</u> and <u>14th Avenue</u>.

Streets numbered ten and under are spelled out.

> It is faster to take <u>Third Street</u> to get to Central Park.

Other ordinal numbers that can be written in one or two words are generally expressed in word form.

> She was the <u>second</u> person we interviewed.
>
> This play is set in <u>eighteenth-century</u> England.

Numbers as Numbers

Use figures for numbers referred to as numbers.

> On a scale of <u>1</u> to <u>10</u>, I would rate the remodel as a <u>9</u>.
>
> Hakeem was elected committee chair by a vote of <u>5</u> to <u>3</u>.

TRY IT!

Directions Underline the correct number form in parentheses. Check your answers on page 321 or with your instructor before continuing with your assignment.

1. Suren will leave on the (9, 9th) of August for sports camp.

2. We are expecting approximately (100, one hundred) people to attend the company picnic.

3. Bradley submitted (24, twenty-four) resumes, (10, ten) applications, and (4, four) portfolios to prospective employers during his job search.

4. (3, Three) ergonomic chairs were on sale for ($59.99, 59 dollars and 99 cents) each.

5. Meet me at (7 p.m., seven p.m.) at the corner of (4th, Fourth) Street and (12th, Twelfth) Avenue.

APPLICATION > **Complete Applications 114–115, pages 267–268, at this time.**

WRITE NOW!

The Complex Sentence

A **complex sentence** contains an independent clause and one or more dependent clauses. An independent clause contains a subject and a verb (either or both of which may be compound) and expresses a complete thought. A dependent clause cannot stand alone and needs the independent (main) clause to make its meaning clear. (See pages 219–221 for a review of dependent clauses.)

> Sue Aitchison, <u>who is a veterinarian</u>, attended Iowa State University.
>
> > The underlined dependent clause does not make a complete statement and cannot stand alone. It needs the independent clause to make its meaning clear.
>
> <u>As the lights dimmed</u>, the curtain was raised.
>
> > The underlined dependent clause needs the independent clause to make its meaning clear.
>
> I'm returning this computer <u>because the touch pad is defective</u>.
>
> > The underlined dependent clause needs the independent clause to make its meaning clear.

Section 31 Capitalization

Sentences

Capitalize the first letter of the first word of every sentence. The first letter of every complete sentence (or of a word or phrase that represents a complete sentence) is capitalized.

> <u>M</u>y computer crashed this weekend.
>
> "<u>W</u>hen will the report be ready?" Ms. Lambert asked.
>
> "<u>I</u>n the afternoon," Mr. Lindahl replied.

The Pronoun *I*

Always use the capital *I* for the pronoun *I* anyplace in any sentence.

> Will <u>I</u> be able to access the database from home?

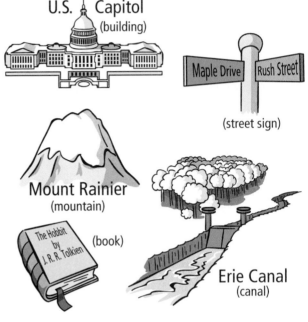

CAPITALIZE PROPER NOUNS.

U.S. Capitol (building)

Maple Drive | Rush Street (street sign)

Mount Rainier (mountain)

The Hobbit by J. R. R. Tolkien (book)

Erie Canal (canal)

Dates and Holidays

Capitalize the days of the week, the months of the year, and holidays.

> <u>Labor Day</u> is the first <u>Monday</u> in <u>September</u>.

Proper Nouns and Adjectives

Capitalize proper nouns, abbreviations of proper nouns, and proper adjectives. (See page 33 for a review of proper nouns, pages 233–235 for a review of abbreviations, and page 170 for a review of proper adjectives.)

> The <u>East Building</u> of the <u>National Gallery of Art</u> was designed by <u>I. M. Pei</u>.
>
> Our class reunion will be held in the <u>Garden Room</u> of the <u>Lake Hotel</u> in <u>Chicago</u>.
>
> We climbed <u>Mount Camerer</u> and went whitewater rafting on the <u>Pigeon River</u>.
>
> With my summer earnings, I bought a used <u>Honda Civic</u>.
>
> We enrolled in MATH 382, <u>Elementary Statistics</u>, at <u>Edgewood Community College</u>.
>
> **But** She has degrees in <u>English</u> and <u>history</u>.
>
> The <u>Federal Bureau of Investigation</u> is headquartered in <u>Washington, D.C.</u>
>
> **But** More than 1.8 million people work for the <u>federal</u> government.
>
> The <u>Gettysburg Address</u> was delivered in 1863.
>
> It honors <u>Union</u> soldiers killed during the <u>Battle of Gettysburg</u> in the <u>Civil War</u>.

Titles

Capitalize **courtesy titles** (*Mr.*, *Mrs.*, *Ms.*, and *Miss*) and all official titles when they precede personal or proper names.

Let's ask <u>Mr</u>. Ramsey to help set up the tents.

Did <u>Professor</u> Karen Owen receive an award for outstanding teaching?

But   My psychology professor, Karen Owen, is an excellent teacher.

Don't tell me <u>Mayor</u> Cochrane was reelected to a second term.

Do not capitalize official titles that follow or are used in place of a person's name.

Ken Price, <u>president</u> of Willmeth College, made his report available.

The <u>mayor</u> held a special town meeting last night.

Do capitalize the titles of high-ranking national, state, and international officials when they follow or are used in place of a personal name.

John G. Roberts, Jr., <u>Chief Justice of the United States</u>, was nominated and confirmed in 2005.

The <u>Governor</u> called out the National Guard.

The <u>Pope</u> has made many trips to foreign countries.

Do not capitalize titles used as a general term of classification or occupational titles.

A United States <u>senator</u> is elected to a six-year term.

Mr. Senft is our biology <u>teacher</u>.

Halicia is the <u>manager</u> for this project.

Capitalize titles that denote family relationships when they are used before a person's name or when they stand alone and refer to a specific person.

Is it <u>Aunt Olga</u> who lives in Claremont, California?

Did you ask <u>Dad</u> if we could go?

Do not capitalize family titles when they are used with a possessive pronoun but no name or when they make a general reference.

My <u>uncle</u> just bought a new car.

The <u>sisters</u> opened a coffee shop.

Academic Degrees and Professional Designations

Capitalize abbreviations for academic degrees and professional designations after a person's name. Do not capitalize general references to degrees.

Hector Silva, <u>M.D.</u>, <u>Ph.D.</u>, is a graduate of Baylor College of Medicine.

LaDonna passed the <u>CPA</u> exam last month.

Tyron received his <u>bachelor of arts</u> degree from Utah State University.

Compass Directions

Capitalize compass directions that refer to particular regions. Do not capitalize general compass points or directions.

Sales in the <u>Southwest</u> have increased 10 percent over last year.

Angela travels frequently to the <u>Middle East</u> on business.

I live in <u>northern</u> New York.

Go <u>east</u> on Del Mar Heights Road.

Literary and Artistic Works

Capitalize the principal words in the titles of literary and artistic works. Such works include books, magazines, movies, long poems, and plays. Parts of complete works (for example, chapters in a book or articles in a magazine) are also capitalized. Articles (*a, an, the*), coordinating conjunctions (*and, but, or, nor, yet*), and prepositions with three or fewer letters are not capitalized unless they appear as the first or last word of the title.

David Guterson wrote the novel *Snow Falling on Cedars*.

Have you ever seen *Gone With the Wind*?

Do not capitalize *the* or *magazine* unless it is officially part of a title.

Katie reads *The New York Times*.

The article "How to Keep Your Job" in *Fortune* magazine is a must-read.

Salutations and Closings

Capitalize the salutation and the first word of the complimentary closing of a letter.

Dear Ms. Tjaden   Sincerely yours

TRY IT!

Directions Underline each letter that should be capitalized. Check your answers on pages 321–322 or with your instructor before continuing with your assignment.

1. selena purchased a sony stereo system at best buy.

2. on thanksgiving, i always watch a football game with my brothers.

3. dr. illyana maxon, chief of surgery, spoke with senator wilton about universal health care.

4. margaret thatcher was the first female prime minister of great britain.

5. reto will receive his bachelor of science degree from the university of florida in june.

6. the *austin gazette* published an editorial by laurie houston, president of the local chapter of the future business leaders of america.

7. america garian, d.d.s., has opened an office in downtown medford.

8. our first assignment in american literature 101 was to read *the grapes of wrath* by john steinbeck.

9. she lives on the west coast—northeast of san diego, in santee.

10. chapter 16 is entitled "the pond in winter."

APPLICATION > **Complete Applications 116–120, pages 269–271 and 273–274, at this time.**

114 | Number Expression

Directions Underline the correct number form in parentheses. Score one point for each correct answer.

Your Score

1. The English Renaissance Festival will run for (6, six) weekends starting October (9, 9th).

1. _____

2. The festival will be held at Pioneer Park, which is located at (6th, Sixth) Avenue and Highview Street.

2. _____

3. Auditions for actors and singers will be held from (8, eight) a.m. to (5, five) p.m. June (7, 7th) through June (11, 11th).

3. _____

4. More than (1,000, one thousand) volunteers will be working at the festival.

4. _____

5. The festival recreates an English festival of the (14th, fourteenth) century.

5. _____

6. Last year, I sold more than (80, eighty) turkey drumsticks in the first (2, two) hours.

6. _____

7. About (2/3, two-thirds) of our club members worked at a booth.

7. _____

8. Admission is ($10, ten dollars) for adults and ($3, three dollars) for children.

8. _____

9. The main stage is (30, thirty) feet by (10, ten) feet and is covered by a canopy.

9. _____

10. The jousting area is (1 1/2, one and a half) miles beyond the main gate.

10. _____

11. Our club members worked at (18, eighteen) stands and served as greeters.

11. _____

12. By a vote of (5, five) to (4, four), my friend Francis won the prize for best costume.

12. _____

13. Pastries were sold for (75¢, 75 cents).

13. _____

14. State law required us to charge an (8%, 8 percent) tax on all sales.

14. _____

15. This year, out-of-state attendance is expected to be in the (1,000s, thousands).

15. _____

16. The (16, sixteen) members of the organizing committee signed contracts with (28, twenty-eight) vendors in the first (3, three) days of booking.

16. _____

17. Local television stations will broadcast live from the site (3, three) times a day; broadcast times are (11, eleven) a.m., (6, six) p.m., and (10, ten) p.m.

17. _____

18. More than (200, two hundred) medieval weapons will be displayed at the festival.

18. _____

19. (4, Four) booths will have activities specifically for children under (5, five).

19. _____

20. Our city's population will grow by (150%, 150 percent) during the festival.

20. _____

Your Total Score _____ /34

If your score was 26 or less, review Section 30, pages 261–263, before continuing.

115 | Number Expression

Directions Underline the correct number form in parentheses. Score one point for each correct answer.

Your Score

1. Presidential elections are held every (4, four) years.

    1. _____

2. To be elected president or vice president of the United States, you must be at least (35, thirty-five) years old, have lived in the United States for at least (14, fourteen) years, and be a natural-born U.S. citizen.

    2. _____

3. Presidents are limited to (2, two) terms by the (22nd, Twenty-Second) Amendment to the Constitution.

    3. _____

4. Impeachment of the president is voted on by the Senate and must be approved by a (2/3, two-thirds) margin.

    4. _____

5. Each state has (2, two) senators, who are elected to a (6-year, six-year) term.

    5. _____

6. Every (2, two) years, (1/3, one-third) of the Senate is up for reelection.

    6. _____

7. The (17th, Seventeenth) Amendment requires senators to be elected by a direct vote of their constituents.

    7. _____

8. There are (435, four hundred thirty-five) members of the House of Representatives.

    8. _____

9. Every (10, ten) years, the U.S. Census Bureau counts the population, which determines the number of congressional seats in a state.

    9. _____

10. (5, Five) members of Congress have no voting rights; they do not represent (1, one) of the (50, fifty) states.

    10. _____

11. The rally for our representative will be held at the Santiago High School stadium, which is located at Willow Glen Road and (8th, Eighth) Avenue.

    11. _____

12. (6, Six) local dignitaries have been asked to extend a welcome at the rally.

    12. _____

13. To feed the attendees, we purchased (275, two hundred seventy-five) pounds of meat to grill, (80, eighty) cases of water, and (50, fifty) watermelons.

    13. _____

14. We have received (100s, hundreds) of e-mails asking how to volunteer.

    14. _____

15. Our candidate will reveal his plan for dealing with the challenges of the (21st, twenty-first) century.

    15. _____

16. Layton will print (500, five hundred) (10-page, ten-page) reports on Representative Sanders's position on various topics for distribution.

    16. _____

17. The rally will start at (4, four) p.m.

    17. _____

18. Speakers should begin assembling in the stadium at (3, three) o'clock.

    18. _____

19. Our last planning session before the rally will be on the (14th, fourteenth) at noon.

    19. _____

20. This year's general election will be on November (3, 3rd).

    20. _____

21. (2, Two) years ago, our representative was reelected with (78%, 78 percent) of the vote.

    21. _____

22. We submitted a petition with approximately (800, eight hundred) signatures to our legislator.

    22. _____

Your Total Score _____ /32
If your score was 24 or less, review Section 30, pages 261–263, before continuing.

116 | Capitalization

Directions Underline each letter that should be capitalized. Score one point for each correctly underlined letter.

Your Score

1. on our trip to washington, d.c., we will arrive by train at union station and then take a cab to the jw marriott hotel, which is only a few blocks from the white house.

   1. _____

2. my trip to the east coast was a birthday gift from dad, mom, and aunt barbara.

   2. _____

3. my teacher worked as a legislative aide while attending georgetown university.

   3. _____

4. we made an appointment to meet with our senator, mark garrick.

   4. _____

5. both the senate and the house of representatives meet in the capitol.

   5. _____

6. in each body, democrats traditionally sit to the presiding officer's right and republicans to the left.

   6. _____

7. the legislative branch is on summer break during august.

   7. _____

8. the franklin delano roosevelt memorial is near the thomas jefferson memorial and the potomac river.

   8. _____

9. some of my favorite sights were the smithsonian institution, the national gallery of art, the united states holocaust memorial museum, the national geographic society, and the vietnam veterans memorial.

   9. _____

10. during our white house tour, we saw a sikorsky helicopter land on the lawn.

   10. _____

11. when you visit washington, d.c., see if you can take a tour of the federal bureau of investigation or the pentagon.

   11. _____

12. massachusetts avenue from dupont circle toward washington national cathedral is known as embassy row.

   12. _____

13. in our hotel room, i took a virtual tour of embassy row on the internet.

   13. _____

14. i bought copies of *the wall street journal*, *the new york times*, *time*, and *national review*.

   14. _____

15. the white house is closed on sundays, mondays, and federal holidays, such as thanksgiving, memorial day, veterans day, and columbus day.

   15. _____

16. there are two presidents and four chief justices of the united states buried at arlington national cemetery.

   16. _____

17. the last night of our vacation, we saw *the phantom of the opera* at the john f. kennedy center for the performing arts.

   17. _____

Your Total Score _____ /128
If your score was 96 or less, review Section 31, pages 264–266, before continuing.

117 | Capitalization

Directions Underline each letter that should be capitalized. Score one point for each correctly underlined letter.

Your Score

1. sally kristen ride was the first american woman in space.

1. _____

2. she was a nationally ranked tennis player, and billie jean king, a professional player and olympic tennis coach, was one of her heroes.

2. _____

3. ride earned a b.a. in english, a b.s. in physics, and a ph.d. in astrophysics from stanford university.

3. _____

4. in 1978, 35 persons were selected for nasa's astronaut training program; one of the six women accepted was sally ride.

4. _____

5. she was involved in the design and testing of the space shuttle's robot arm.

5. _____

6. dr. ride was a member of the commission chosen to investigate the explosion of the space shuttle *challenger* in 1986.

6. _____

7. among her many honors and awards are induction into the u.s. astronaut hall of fame and the nasa space flight medal.

7. _____

8. *exploring our solar system* is a book for children she coauthored with tam o'shaughnessy.

8. _____

9. she is the cofounder, president, and ceo of imaginary lines, inc., a company that encourages middle school students, especially girls, to pursue math and science careers.

9. _____

10. while working at nasa headquarters in washington in the mid-1980s, dr. ride produced a report entitled "leadership and america's future in space."

10. _____

11. charles augustus lindbergh was born in detroit, michigan, on february 4, 1902.

11. _____

12. he left the university of wisconsin during his second year and enrolled in a flight school in lincoln, nebraska.

12. _____

13. lindbergh was a barnstormer, served in the u.s. army, and flew a mail plane between st. louis, missouri, and chicago, illinois.

13. _____

14. he decided to compete for a $25,000 prize for the first nonstop flight between new york, new york, and paris, france.

14. _____

15. the monoplane he helped designed for this flight was named *spirit of st. louis*.

15. _____

16. lindbergh became the first person to fly solo nonstop across the atlantic ocean.

16. _____

17. he was awarded the congressional medal of honor and the distinguished flying cross.

17. _____

18. in 1954, lindbergh received the pulitzer prize for his book *the spirit of st. louis*.

18. _____

19. in his later years, lindbergh devoted his time to preserving the environment and protecting endangered species.

19. _____

20. the aviator's 20-month-old son, charles a. lindbergh, jr., was kidnapped on march 1, 1932.

20. _____

Your Total Score _____ /126

If your score was 95 or less, review Section 31, pages 264–266, before continuing.

118 | Unit Review

Directions Underline the correct number form in parentheses and each letter that should be capitalized. Score one point for each correct number form and for each letter that you correctly underlined.

Your Score

1. the united nations came into existence on october (24, 24th), 1945. 1. _____

2. a main purpose of the united nations is to maintain international peace and security. 2. _____

3. in 2008, (192, one hundred ninety-two) nations were members. 3. _____

4. dag hammarskjöld served as secretary-general of the united nations from 1953 to 1961; he was awarded the nobel peace prize posthumously. 4. _____

5. his many accomplishments included negotiating the release of american soldiers captured by the chinese during the korean war, intervening in the suez canal dispute, and promoting peace missions and nonviolent liberation in africa. 5. _____

6. the amount that each member is requested to contribute to the administrative budget is determined every (3rd, third) year. 6. _____

7. the highest contribution rate was lowered in december 2000 from (25%, 25 percent) to (22%, 22 percent); only the united states, the largest contributor, pays this rate. 7. _____

8. the united nations is located in new york on (1st, First) avenue between (42nd, Forty-Second) street and (48th, Forty-Eighth) street. 8. _____

9. It occupies approximately (17, seventeen) acres in the turtle bay area on the (east, East) side of manhattan. 9. _____

10. the predecessor of the united nations was the league of nations. 10. _____

11. it was established after world war I under the treaty of versailles with the mission of preserving peace and promoting international cooperation in economic and social dealings. 11. _____

12. because it was unable to prevent world war II, the league of nations ceased operations. 12. _____

13. representatives of (50, fifty) countries drew up the united nations charter in 1945. 13. _____

14. united nations tour guides are people from all over the world who share an interest in international issues. 14. _____

15. tour guides may choose to wear dress from their native countries; for example, a guide from india might wear a sari, and a guide from china might wear a cheongsam dress. 15. _____

16. tours are given in more than (15, fifteen) languages by guides representing approximately (20, twenty) countries. 16. _____

17. business at the united nations is conducted in arabic, chinese, english, french, spanish, and russian. 17. _____

18. in 1946, president harry s. truman appointed eleanor roosevelt as a member of the u.s. delegation to the united nations general assembly. 18. _____

19. she headed the united nations human rights commission and played a key role in creating the universal declaration of human rights. 19. _____

20. the security council of the united nations has (5, five) permanent members and (10, ten) members serving (2, two)-year terms. 20. _____

Your Total Score _____ /120

ENGLISH ON THE JOB /
Hospitality Management

Digital Vision/Getty Images

The hospitality industry is one of the largest service industries in our global economy. It encompasses a number of industries, including lodging, food service, casinos, and tourism. The focus in this feature will be on careers in the various lodging establishments and the services they provide to their clients. The scope of jobs and responsibilities in hotels and similar facilities has been expanding over the years because they are no longer just a place to stay, but a destination. Lodging establishments can include resorts, casinos, and hotels that are marketed as sites for conventions, business meetings, and social gatherings.

Hospitality jobs may be found in administrative support, management and operations, and service. Desk clerks and front office operations staff process reservations, check-in, and checkout; handle complaints; and answer general questions. Managerial or operational personnel are responsible for departments within the lodging site, such as restaurants, catering or banquet facilities, purchasing, sales, security, and maintenance. The lodging manager makes decisions that affect the general operation of the establishment and has ultimate responsibility for solving problems. Service employees are the largest group of employees in the industry. Included in this group are housekeeping workers, grounds workers, and food preparation workers and servers.

Postsecondary education is not required for most entry-level positions; however, college training may be helpful for advancement in some occupations. In the service and administrative support areas, soft skills and customer service experience may be more important and appropriate than formal training. In all areas, communication skills and the ability to get along with people are critical. For managerial-level employees, some positions are filled from within. However, managers generally have formal training and job experience.

Because lodging sites are open 24 hours a day, employees frequently work varying shifts. Many employees work part-time, evenings, or weekends because of the flexibility. The field has plenty of jobs for first-time job seekers and people with limited formal training.

Directions Underline the correct number form in parentheses. Underline each letter that should be capitalized. Score one point for each correctly underlined number form and one point for each correctly underlined letter.

Your Score

1. during his (4, four) years of college, hank worked evenings and weekends at the hays hotel.   1. _____

2. the rancho pena resort hosts the troy rotary club for a (12 noon, noon) luncheon on thursdays.   2. _____

3. wait staff in the colonnade room at the hotel average ($35, thirty-five dollars) an hour in tips.   3. _____

4. our catering manager, lilli chung, speaks chinese and vietnamese fluently.   4. _____

5. cabe gray, the general manager, called a meeting for (2, two) p.m. in the constellation ballroom.   5. _____

Your Total Score _____ /28

119 | Writing Improvement

Directions Write a short paragraph (four to five sentences) in response to each possible interview question. Make sure you use complete sentences and correct number expression and capitalization. At least two sentences in each paragraph should be complex sentences. Review the WRITE Now feature on page 263 if you need help.

1. What have the past and present taught you? How can your knowledge and experience be applied to the future?

_____

_____

_____

_____

_____

_____

_____

2. What is your greatest strength? (This is a good opportunity to highlight qualities you feel would demonstrate reliability, initiative, problem-solving skills, flexibility, etc. You may even want to give a specific example of how you used that strength in a job or school setting.)

_____

_____

_____

_____

_____

_____

3. What would your references tell us about you? (Be positive. Before writing, think about the skills or traits that your references admire in a person or an employee.)

_____

_____

_____

_____

_____

_____

_____

 **Submit your completed application to your instructor for evaluation.**

120 | Comprehensive Review

Directions Add the necessary punctuation marks, underline the correct number form or word in parentheses, and underline each letter that should be capitalized. Score one point for each correct answer.

Your Score

1. the (3, three) branches of our government (is, are) the judicial executive and legislative   1. _____

2. the united states supreme court is the highest court in the land   2. _____

3. the building was designed by cass gilbert and was completed in 1935 at a cost of $9640000   3. _____

4. each year the supreme court hears a limited number of cases they usually involve important questions about the constitution or federal law   4. _____

5. when theres a vacancy on the supreme court the president nominates a new justice   5. _____

6. they serve for life callie replied and they must be confirmed by the senate   6. _____

7. thurgood marshall the (1st, first) african-american supreme court justice was appointed by lyndon b johnson   7. _____

8. william o douglas the longest serving justice served (36, thirty-six) years   8. _____

9. sandra day oconnor the first woman on the court was nominated by president ronald reagan in 1981   9. _____

10. on tuesday and wednesday mornings opinions are usually released on thursdays and fridays no public sessions are held   10. _____

_____

_____

11. roxann asked whats the address of the most famous house in the united states   11. _____

12. it is of course 1600 pennsylvania avenue replied kim   12. _____

13. although president washington oversaw the construction of the white house he never lived in it   13. _____

14. the white house has (132, one hundred thirty-two) rooms (35, thirty-five) baths (28, twenty-eight) fireplaces and (3, three) elevators however only (5, five) rooms are open to the public   14. _____

15. the white house has (it's, its) own tennis court jogging track swimming pool movie theater and bowling lane   15. _____

16. john tyler was the president with the (more, most) children he had (15, fifteen)   16. _____

17. franklin d roosevelts fireside chats were (speechs, speeches) given on the radio about national and world events and the governments responses to them   17. _____

18. james garfield could write with either hand and sometimes wrote greek with one hand and latin with the other   18. _____

19. in 1978 president anwar sadat of egypt and prime minister menachem begin of israel signed a peace treaty at the white house   19. _____

Your Total Score _____ /166

PROOF IT!

Directions Proofread the minutes. Mark any changes that are needed using the proofreaders' marks on page 317. Then key the minutes, making all necessary corrections. Proofread your work, and make any corrections that are needed. Turn in both this page and your finished document to your instructor.

Staff Development Committee Meeting

April 25th, 2010

The Staff Development Committee met on April 24th, 2010, at 2 PM in the conference room. Committee members present were Janelle Bullock, Lloyd Casson, Rico Fuentes, and Pianta Crakes.

Business

Management has ask this committee to identify staff development needs for the coming year and to implement training sessions as appropriate. After some discussion, the Group developed a survey that will be distributed to employees asking what types of Training would help him or her be more effective in their jobs. Pianta will prepare the survey and will distribute it by May 15th. After the surveys have been returned, the committee will convene again to prioritize the needs that have been identified and beginning planning the Training.

Adjournment

The next meeting will be hold on May 28th at 2 o'clock PM in the conference room. The meeting was adjourned at 3:30 PM.

Posttest

A | **Directions** Underline the correct number form in parentheses.

1. The class collected (2, two) tons of newspaper to recycle in just (3, three) weeks.

2. At my school, if there are not (18, eighteen) people enrolled in a class, it is canceled.

3. He receives his paychecks on the (15th, fifteenth) and (30th, thirtieth) of each month.

4. I heard that (3/4, three-fourths) of our class did poorly on the exam.

5. More than (50%, 50 percent) of the students have a part-time job.

6. At the parking lot at (8th, Eighth) Avenue and (3rd, Third) Street, it costs only ($8, eight dollars) to park all day.

7. There are (4, four) tests, (2, two) research papers, and (12, twelve) assignments to be submitted for grading in my business communication class.

8. I run (2 1/2, two and a half) miles every day.

B | **Directions** Underline each letter that should be capitalized.

1. dennis yarrow, our real estate agent, found an ideal location for our company on baypoint terrace in arlington near the cruise ship terminal.

2. landscape design 144 is taught by professor flannagan in shima 403.

3. the restaurant rapponga specializes in chinese cuisine.

4. on his trip to the east coast in may, the prime minister of canada will meet with the president.

5. the political thriller *the third option* is by vince flynn.

unit 12
Word Choice

Objectives

1. To recognize misused words in everyday speech and writing
2. To learn the proper usage of frequently misused words
3. To properly use troublesome words and avoid clichés in written communication

Sections

Directions Underline the correct word choice in parentheses.

1. We are using (there, their, they're) condo in Lake Tahoe.

2. (Your, You're) going to love being so close to the ski slopes.

3. We (could have, could of) gone downhill skiing.

4. (Who's, Whose) going to drive to the ski slope?

5. Celeste teaches beginner skiers (good, well).

6. (It's, Its) my first time skiing in two years.

7. I (can hardly, can't hardly) wait to take my first run.

8. The cost of equipment rental is (to, too, two) high!

9. Expert skiers sometimes ski (off of the, off the) marked trails.

10. Squaw Valley is known for (it's, its) expert, lengthy ski runs.

Networking

Networking is the process of developing relationships with people who can provide information about required skills, jobs, and job openings in your chosen career area. It is the top source of job leads today. Therefore, it should play a major role in your job search. Consider including in your network people who know you personally or professionally—friends, relatives, co-workers, classmates, instructors, and business acquaintances. A strong network includes current and former employers, so be sure to stay in contact with them. Membership in a professional or civic organization also provides excellent networking contacts.

Here are a few networking guidelines:

- Build your network before you need it.

- View it as a means of exchanging information and building relationships, not as a source of job leads.

- Be pleasant, respectful, and professional toward every networking contact. Demonstrate qualities that will encourage that person to hire or recommend you.

- Set up informational meetings with persons in your chosen career area. Plan to discuss the job market for your career, the skills you need, and any emerging trends, as well as to ask for names of others in the field with whom you can set up similar meetings.

- Stay in touch with the people in your network.

Word Blunders

Have you ever been misunderstood or embarrassed by using the wrong word to convey your thoughts? These simple mistakes we make in speaking and writing may be called *word blunders*. How many of these word blunders do you avoid?

Who's and *Whose*

Who's is the contraction for *who is*. Remember that a contraction has an apostrophe (') for the omitted letter or letters.

> Who's your accounting instructor?
>> Who's—contraction for *Who is*—*Who is* your accounting instructor?

> Angie Fogel, who's a financial planner, is meeting with me tomorrow.
>> who's—contraction for *who is*—*who is* a financial planner

Whose shows ownership or possession. It is used as a possessive adjective and modifies a noun. *Whose* is the possessive case of *who*.

> Whose cell phone is on the table?
>> Whose—possessive adjective—modifies the noun *cell phone*

> The painter, whose work can be seen at Art in the Park, is opening a gallery.
>> whose—possessive adjective—modifies the noun *work*

It's and *Its*

The most misused pair of words is *it's* and *its*. *It's* is the contraction for *it is*. The apostrophe (') takes the place of the letter *i*, which is omitted. The contraction *it's* acts as the subject and verb of a clause or sentence.

> It's a long flight to London.
>> It's—contraction for *It is*—*It is* a long flight to London.

> It's her best CD yet.
>> It's—contraction for *It is*—*It is* her best CD yet.

Its shows ownership or possession. It is used as a possessive adjective and is followed by a noun. *Its* is the possessive case of *it*.

> The school reports that its graduates do very well.
>> its—possessive adjective—modifies the noun *graduates*

> The company has changed its warranty policy.
>> its—possessive adjective—modifies the noun *policy*

There, *Their*, and *They're*

There is almost always used as an adverb. It is never used to show ownership. As an adverb, it sometimes functions as an **expletive**, or filler, to introduce a sentence (*There is*, *There are*). Be careful in your choice of the verb form in such sentences. *There* is seldom used as a subject and therefore does not determine the singular or plural form of the verb. The subject is usually the noun or pronoun that follows the verb form. If that noun or pronoun is singular, the verb form should be singular. If it is plural, the verb form should be plural. Occasionally, *there* functions as a pronoun or an adjective.

> There are two courses I would like to take.
>> There—adverb—modifies the verb *are*. The plural verb form *are* agrees with the plural subject *courses*.

> I looked there, but I did not find my car key.
>> there—adverb—modifies the verb *looked*

Their denotes ownership or possession. It is used as a possessive adjective and modifies a noun. *Their* is the possessive case of *they*.

> We beat their team.
>> their—possessive adjective—modifies the noun *team*

> Marcia and Cassidy registered for their classes on the Internet.
>> their—possessive adjective—modifies the noun *classes*

They're is the contraction for *they are*. Remember that a contraction has an apostrophe (') for the omitted letter or letters.

> They're the most experienced mechanics.
>> They're—contraction for *They are*—*They are* the most experienced mechanics.

> They're going to the concert at Embarcadero Park on Friday.
>> They're—contraction for *They are*—*They are* going to the concert at Embarcadero Park on Friday.

Your and *You're*

Your is a possessive pronoun that denotes ownership. It is used as a possessive adjective and modifies a noun. *Your* is the possessive case of *you*.

> Your office is being repainted.
>> Your—possessive adjective—modifies the noun *office*

> I saw your mother at the mall.
>> your—possessive adjective—modifies the noun *mother*

You're is the contraction for *you are*. The apostrophe (') represents the letter that is omitted.

> You're going to earn a high grade.
>> You're—contraction for *You are*—*You are* going to earn a high grade.

> You're applying for a scholarship?
>> You're—contraction for *You are*—*You are* applying for a scholarship?

Good and *Well*

Good is almost always an adjective meaning skillful, admirable, or having the right qualities. It describes a noun or pronoun and answers the question *what kind of*.

> Edwin is a good listener.
>> good—adjective—describes the noun *listener*—answers the question *what kind of listener*

My pasta tastes <u>good</u>.

> <u>good</u>—predicate adjective—describes the noun *pasta*—answers the question
> *what kind of pasta*

Well is most often an adverb telling how something is done. It usually modifies a verb and answers the question *how*.

Laptop computers sell <u>well</u>.

> <u>well</u>—adverb—modifies the verb *sell*—answers the question *how*

Well can be used as an adjective to describe someone's health.

She doesn't feel <u>well</u> today.

TRY IT!

Directions Underline the correct word choice in parentheses. Check your answers on page 322 or with your instructor before continuing with your assignment.

1. I understand (your, you're) running for president of Phi Beta Lambda.

2. (Who's, Whose) your favorite teacher?

3. The school announced (it's, its) emergency evacuation plan at the opening assembly.

4. (There, Their, They're) final exam was a take-home essay test.

APPLICATION **Complete Application 121, page 287, at this time.**

In and *Into*

As a preposition, *in* means within a place. The person or thing is already there.

Drew is working <u>in</u> his office.

> <u>in</u>—preposition—Drew is already *in* his office.

Addy and Lane are <u>in</u> the conference room.

> <u>in</u>—preposition—Addy and Lane are already *in* the conference room.

Into is also a preposition, but it means the moving or going from outside to inside.

Elisabeth and Hrishi finally got <u>into</u> the stadium.

> <u>into</u>—preposition—shows movement from outside to inside the stadium

They are going <u>into</u> the sauna now.

> <u>into</u>—preposition—shows movement from outside to inside the sauna

Almost and *Most*

Almost is an adverb meaning nearly.

Amy <u>almost</u> failed the test.

    <u>almost</u>—adverb—means *nearly*

<u>Almost</u> all the pottery was sold in the first hour.

    <u>Almost</u>—adverb—means *nearly*

Most is usually an adjective, an adverb, or a pronoun meaning the greatest in number or quality.

Which athlete holds the record for winning the <u>most</u> gold medals in one Olympics?

    <u>most</u>—adjective—means the greatest in number

His family is the <u>most</u> important thing in his life.

    <u>most</u>—adverb—means the greatest in quality

Beside and *Besides*

Beside means to be next to or at the side of something.

We camped <u>beside</u> the lake.

    <u>beside</u>—next to or at the side of the lake

Ivan sits <u>beside</u> his best friend in American history.

    <u>beside</u>—next to or at the side of his best friend

Besides means in addition to or extra.

<u>Besides</u> the lawn games, Tara brought soft drinks for everyone.

    <u>Besides</u>—in addition to the lawn games

<u>Besides</u> rare stamps, he collects state quarters.

    <u>Besides</u>—in addition to rare stamps

TRY IT!

Directions Underline the correct word choice in parentheses. Check your answers on page 322 or with your instructor before continuing with your assignment.

1. Luigi looked (good, well) in his new suit.

2. Shonda sat (beside, besides) her granddaughter at the banquet.

3. (Almost, Most) all the students complained about the cost of their textbooks.

4. Our car was broken (in, into) while we were at dinner.

APPLICATION > **Complete Application 122, page 288, at this time.**

Fewer and *Less*

Fewer is an adjective that refers to items that can be counted. It modifies a plural noun.

> There are <u>fewer</u> exhibitors at this year's conference.
>> <u>fewer</u>—adjective—means a smaller number

> Our department is giving <u>fewer</u> scholarships than in the past.
>> <u>fewer</u>—adjective—means a smaller number

Less refers to degree or amount. When used as an adjective, it modifies a singular noun.

> I noticed <u>less</u> background noise in the computer lab.
>> <u>less</u>—adjective—means a smaller degree or amount

Use *less than*, not *fewer than*, before nouns that express sums of money, percentages, periods of time, distances, or measurements.

> I bought my bookcase for <u>less than</u> $25.
>> <u>less than</u>—used with a sum of money

Real and *Really*

Real is an adjective meaning genuine or authentic. It modifies a noun or pronoun.

> It is a <u>real</u> diamond.
>> <u>real</u>—adjective—modifies the noun *diamond*—means *genuine*

> The <u>real</u> reason I was late is my alarm did not go off.
>> <u>real</u>—adjective—modifies the noun *reason*—means *genuine*

Really is an adverb that means genuinely, actually, or extremely. It modifies a verb, an adjective, or another adverb.

> You <u>really</u> shared some beneficial insights with the group.
>> <u>really</u>—adverb—modifies the verb *shared*—means *actually*

> Burt gave a <u>really</u> good presentation at the meeting.
>> <u>really</u>—adverb—modifies the adjective *good*—means *extremely*

To, Too, and *Two*

To is most often a preposition that is followed by a noun or pronoun in the objective case. (See pages 198 and 213 for a review of prepositional phrases.) Another use of *to* is in an infinitive (the main form of a verb, usually preceded by *to*). (See pages 214–215 for an explanation of infinitive phrases.)

> She said hello <u>to</u> us.
>> <u>to</u>—preposition—begins a prepositional phrase (*to us*)

> He showed me how <u>to</u> run a scan.
>> <u>to</u>—part of the infinitive *to run*—begins an infinitive phrase (*to run a scan*)

Too is an adverb. It means also, besides very, or excessively.

> Yeongri is taking vacation that week, <u>too</u>.
>> <u>too</u>—adverb—modifies the verb *is taking*—means *also*

This class is <u>too</u> hard!

    <u>too</u>—adverb—modifies the adjective *hard*—means *excessively*

Two is a number and is usually an adjective that tells how many.

The <u>two</u> medical records technicians learned the diagnostic codes.

    <u>two</u>—adjective—number

Then and *Than*

Then is usually an adverb and means at that time. It answers the question *when* of the verb.

We studied and <u>then</u> took the test.

    <u>then</u>—adverb meaning at that time—answers the question *when* of the verb *took*

Devinder completed his training in April; <u>then</u> he started his job search.

    <u>then</u>—adverb meaning at that time—answers the question *when* of the verb *started*

Than is a conjunction. It makes or shows a comparison of two or more people, places, things, concepts, qualities, or activities.

Johanna speaks faster <u>than</u> Teresa.

    <u>than</u>—conjunction—shows a comparison of two people, Johanna and Teresa

Ed is a better swimmer <u>than</u> his brother.

    <u>than</u>—conjunction—shows a comparison of two people, Ed and his brother

Different from is always used in comparing different things. Never use *different than*.

Ultrasound technologies are <u>different from</u> radiation technologies.

    <u>different from</u>—used in comparing different things—never *different than*

TRY IT!

Directions Underline the correct word choice in parentheses. Check your answers on page 322 or with your instructor before continuing with your assignment.

1. I was (to, too, two) late (to, too, two) qualify for the early-bird registration rate.

2. Gerry bought a pint of ice cream and (then, than) ate it all.

3. They will be back in (fewer, less) (then, than) 30 minutes.

4. The new software is very (different from, different than, different then) the old version.

APPLICATION   **Complete Application 123, page 289, at this time.**

Between and Among

Between is used when referring to two people, places, things, concepts, qualities, or activities.

> I sat <u>between</u> Chantal and Lauryn.
>> <u>between</u>—refers to two people, Chantal and Lauryn

> We could choose <u>between</u> ushering and selling tickets.
>> <u>between</u>—refers to two activities, ushering and selling tickets

Among is used when referring to more than two people, places, things, concepts, qualities, or activities.

> The students had to decide <u>among</u> themselves who would be the spokesperson.
>> <u>among</u>—referring to more than two people

> <u>Among</u> the nurses, there is a great deal of confidence and enthusiasm.
>> <u>Among</u>—referring to more than two people

Like and As

The preposition *like* is followed by a noun or pronoun in the objective case. It means similar to or resembling.

> Lucien sounds <u>like</u> him.
>> <u>like</u>—preposition—has an object, *him*

> His handwriting is <u>like</u> old script.
>> <u>like</u>—preposition—has an object, *script*

The conjunction *as* introduces a clause. *As if* can be used as a conjunction to join clauses.

> <u>As</u> he studies, he listens to background music.
>> <u>As</u>—conjunction—introduces the clause *As he studies*

> Kylie acts <u>as if</u> she has already won the election.
>> <u>as if</u>—conjunction—introduces the clause *as if she has already won the election*

Lose and Loose

Lose is a verb that means to misplace.

> Do not <u>lose</u> your keys.
> > <u>lose</u>—verb

> With the budget cuts, we will <u>lose</u> a part-time clerk.
> > <u>lose</u>—verb

Loose is most often an adjective that modifies a noun or pronoun. It means free or not restrained.

> Leslie discovered a <u>loose</u> connection to the CPU.
> > <u>loose</u>—adjective—modifies the noun *connection*

> I found some <u>loose</u> change at the bottom of my purse.
> > <u>loose</u>—adjective—modifies the noun *change*

Affect and Effect

The verb *affect* means to influence or to change.

> The hurricane will <u>affect</u> the price of gas.
> > <u>affect</u>—verb—means to influence or to change

> Inflation <u>affects</u> our purchasing power.
> > <u>affects</u>—verb—means to influence or to change

Effect is used as a noun to mean a result. As a verb, it means to bring about or to cause to happen.

> Computers have had a great <u>effect</u> on my work.
> > <u>effect</u>—noun—means a result

> The two sides worked for days to <u>effect</u> a settlement.
> > <u>effect</u>—verb—means to bring about

TRY IT!

Directions Underline the correct word choice in parentheses. Check your answers on page 322 or with your instructor before continuing with your assignment.

1. My brothers and I discussed the problem (between, <u>among</u>) ourselves.

2. She sounds (like, <u>as if</u>) she just woke up.

3. What were the (affects, effects) of the slump in housing prices?

4. With the downturn in the economy, I hope I don't (<u>lose</u>, loose) my job.

APPLICATION ▶ **Complete Application 124, page 290, at this time.**

121 | Who's–Whose, It's–Its, There–Their–They're, Your–You're

Directions Underline the correct word choice in parentheses. Score one point for each correct answer.

Your Score

1. (Who's, Whose) contacting speakers for career day next month?   1. _____

2. (It's, Its) purpose is to make students aware of the many career choices that are available.   2. _____

3. (It's, Its) a good idea to have someone speak on new careers in information technology.   3. _____

4. My friend, (who's, whose) job is to recruit for the wireless industry, could speak.   4. _____

5. (It's, Its) employees must be flexible because the industry is constantly changing.   5. _____

6. I wonder (who's, whose) technology will represent a new way of communicating in five years.   6. _____

7. (It's, Its) a well-known fact that many young people do much of their communicating by text messaging.   7. _____

8. Hillary, (who's, whose) math skills are very good, had multiple job offers in computer information management.   8. _____

9. (It's, Its) always wise to evaluate your personal interests and skills before choosing a career.   9. _____

10. The San Diego Workforce Partnership publishes (it's, its) occupational outlook report annually.   10. _____

11. (It's, Its) wage information was gathered from employers who participated in a study.   11. _____

12. (Who's, Whose) willing to substitute training for experience when filling positions for computer software engineers?   12. _____

_____

13. (There, Their, They're) is much diversity in our 50 states.   13. _____

14. (Your, You're) correct: the fiftieth state to enter the Union was Hawaii.   14. _____

15. (Your, You're) family's favorite vacation spot is Hawaii, isn't it?   15. _____

16. (There, Their, They're) are eight major islands and numerous smaller islands in Hawaii.   16. _____

17. (There, Their, They're) is Haleakala Crater, the largest extinct volcanic crater in the world.   17. _____

18. (Your, You're) surfing lesson is scheduled for 10 a.m. Wednesday at Waimea Bay.   18. _____

19. I heard (your, you're) taking classes at the University of Hawaii.   19. _____

20. (There, Their, They're) planning to tour the USS *Arizona* Memorial and the Battleship *Missouri* Memorial when they go to Pearl Harbor.   20. _____

21. A tour of Pearl Harbor can be one of the most moving experiences of (your, you're) trip.   21. _____

22. Many parents take (there, their, they're) children to the Polynesian Cultural Center.   22. _____

23. (There, Their, They're) are no racial or ethnic majorities in Hawaii.   23. _____

24. (There, Their, They're) guide said that Hawaii is the only state to have been a kingdom.   24. _____

25. If (your, you're) interested in local history, you should visit Iolani Palace, the only official state residence of royalty in the United States.   25. _____

Your Total Score _____/25

If your score was 19 or less, review pages 279–280 before continuing.

122 | *Good–Well, In–Into, Almost–Most, Beside–Besides*

Directions Underline the correct word choice in parentheses. Score one point for each correct answer.

Your Score

1. (Almost, Most) any person can tell you the value of participating in the election process.   1. _____

2. The presidential debate was the (almost, most) engaging I had seen.   2. _____

3. The challenger did as (good, well) as the incumbent.   3. _____

4. The candidate's daughter went (in, into) the Marines Corps.   4. _____

5. It was with great anticipation that we walked (in, into) the convention center.   5. _____

6. (Beside, Besides) participating in a focus group, I was also interviewed by the local television station.   6. _____

7. Our state's delegation sat (beside, besides) the Florida delegation.   7. _____

8. The candidate was escorted (in, into) the convention center by the governor of Ohio.   8. _____

9. We (almost, most) lost our voices while cheering for our candidate.   9. _____

10. The press coverage of the convention was (good, well).   10. _____

11. The woman (beside, besides) me always volunteers to help get voters to the polls.   11. _____

12. Are you feeling (good, well) enough to work at the polls today?   12. _____

13. (Beside, Besides), I'm going door-to-door for her campaign.   13. _____

14. If you expect to be absent from the precinct (in, into) which you are a registered voter, request an absentee ballot.   14. _____

15. Be sure your absentee ballot is (in, into) the mail early.   15. _____

16. How (good, well) do you understand the issues in this election?   16. _____

17. It is (good, well) to study each candidate's position on issues of interest to you.   17. _____

18. What is the (almost, most) important issue to you?   18. _____

19. (Almost, Most) everyone I know says the economy is the number-one issue.   19. _____

20. This candidate has a good voting record; (beside, besides), he has much more experience.   20. _____

21. Her platform sounds (good, well), but I will need to read more about it.   21. _____

22. I am (almost, most) ready to cast my ballot.   22. _____

23. My polling place is at the church (beside, besides) the fire station on Elm Street.   23. _____

24. I saw a long line of people (in, into) the polling place waiting to vote.   24. _____

25. With (almost, most) all precincts reporting, my candidate holds a strong lead.   25. _____

Your Total Score _____/25
If your score was 19 or less, review pages 280–282 before continuing.

123 | *Fewer–Less, Real–Really, To–Too–Two, Then–Than*

Directions Underline the correct word choice in parentheses. Score one point for each correct answer.

Your Score

1. For my birthday, Oliver and I went (to, too, two) Chicago for a three-day mini-vacation.

1. _____

2. There were no (fewer, less) (then, than) a dozen plays for us (to, too, two) choose from.

2. _____

3. Visitors can buy a CityPass that grants admission (to, too, two) five Chicago attractions for (fewer, less) (then, than) $60.

3. _____

4. I quickly came (to, too, two) the conclusion that it is (to, too, two) cold (to, too, two) take long walks in Chicago in December.

4. _____

5. At the Museum of Science and Industry, we saw a (real, really) interesting exhibit about the capture of a U-505 submarine during World War II.

5. _____

6. There are exhibits featuring World War II warplanes, a Stuka dive-bomber, and a Supermarine Spitfire, (to, too, two).

6. _____

7. (Then, Than) Oliver told me that on his first visit (to, too, two) the museum, his favorite exhibit was a walk-through model of the human heart.

7. _____

8. We noticed (fewer, less) people waiting in line at the *Apollo 8* exhibit (then, than) at the Christmas Around the World display.

8. _____

9. Chicago's cultural communities are (real, really) involved in the Christmas Around the World exhibit, which started in 1942.

9. _____

10. Many comic greats give credit (to, too, two) Second City Chicago for launching their careers.

10. _____

11. Second City Chicago has (to, too, two) resident stages.

11. _____

12. The training center has touring troupes that perform all over the country, (to, too, two).

12. _____

13. The (to, too, two) of us visited the Skydeck at the Sears Tower.

13. _____

14. We had a (real, really) good view of the city, and we could see four different states.

14. _____

15. The main entrance (to, too, two) the Art Institute of Chicago is flanked by (to, too, two) large bronze lions.

15. _____

16. (To, Too, Two) wander through the Impressionist paintings was (real, really) enjoyable.

16. _____

17. I liked Camille Pissarro's *Woman and Child at the Well* better (then, than) Claude Monet's *The Artist's House at Argenteuil*.

17. _____

18. However, I admired Pierre Auguste Renoir's painting *Near the Lake*, (to, too, two).

18. _____

19. At The Field Museum, Sue was more impressive (then, than) I could ever have imagined.

19. _____

20. The most complete *Tyrannosaurus rex* fossil ever discovered, Sue is 13 feet high, 42 feet long, and more (then, than) 67,000,000 years old.

20. _____

21. What makes Chicago (different from, different than, different then) other Midwest cities?

21. _____

Your Total Score _____/31
If your score was 23 or less, review pages 283–284 before continuing.

124 | *Between–Among, Like–As, Lose–Loose, Affect–Effect*

Directions Underline the correct word choice in parentheses. Score one point for each correct answer.

Your Score

1. If I miss a week of class, will that (affect, effect) my grade?   1. _____

2. Students who do not participate in class discussions will (lose, loose) 10 percent of their course points.   2. _____

3. We will see more study groups form (like, as) the course work gets more difficult.   3. _____

4. (Between, Among) the three of us, only Evangelia knows the answer.   4. _____

5. I hurried (like, as) a sprinter, racing to my class.   5. _____

6. The choice (between, among) having an in-class final and having a take-home final is an easy one for me.   6. _____

7. The (lose, loose) connection on my computer caused the monitor to flicker on and off while I was doing my homework.   7. _____

8. To study (like, as) Sam does probably earns you straight A's.   8. _____

9. A group of students, faculty, and administrators worked for several months to (affect, effect) the changes in the honor code disciplinary system.   9. _____

10. If you (lose, loose) your handout, you can print another copy from the class website.   10. _____

11. What is the difference (between, among) a molecule and an atom?   11. _____

12. Can you tell me what the (affect, effect) of radiation is on the human body?   12. _____

_____

_____

13. The candidate has a strong lead (between, among) young voters.   13. _____

14. What will be the (affect, effect) of raising the minimum wage for small business owners?   14. _____

15. He speaks passionately about social and fiscal responsibility, (like, as) his predecessor did.   15. _____

16. The candidate's policies have clearly been (affected, effected) by the new polls.   16. _____

17. We must not (lose, loose) sight of the goal of a balanced budget.   17. _____

18. How the legislature votes on the bill will (affect, effect) funding for higher education.   18. _____

19. I like the commercial about a boy searching for (lose, loose) change in the sofa to start a college fund; it is quite powerful.   19. _____

20. (Between, Among) the four candidates running for the vacant city council seat, who do you think will win?   20. _____

21. In her speech this morning, the mayor sounded (like, as) her opponent.   21. _____

22. If, as a state legislator, you had to choose (between, among) raising the sales tax and cutting social services, which would you choose?   22. _____

23. When I asked my dad about this election, he replied with his favorite expression: "Well, I think there are a few (lose, loose) ends to tie up yet."   23. _____

24. Do you think Garry will (lose, loose) the election?   24. _____

25. It sounds (like, as if) the candidate has made some inroads in key states.   25. _____

Your Total Score _____/25

If your score was 19 or less, review pages 285–286 before continuing.

Speech Duds

Use	Don't Use
almost everybody	most everybody
an hour	a hour
anyway	anyways
anywhere	anywheres
aren't you	ain't you
better	more better
brought	brung
can hardly	can't hardly
could hardly	couldn't hardly
could have	could of
couldn't have cared less	could have cared less
drowned	drownded
feel bad	feel badly
grew up	growed up
have a	have got a
have gone	have went
he doesn't	he don't
inside the	inside of the
kind of	kind of a
like for	like
long way	long ways
might have	might of
near to	near
not nearly	nowhere near
off the	off of the
opposite	opposite to
should have	should of
sort of	sort of a

Use	Don't Use
this (tie, dress)	this here (tie, dress)
this kind	these kind
those (shoes)	them (shoes)
try to	try and
very good	awfully good
was hardly	wasn't hardly
were you	was you
where	where . . . at, where . . . to
with regard to	with regards to
would have	would of

WRITE NOW!

Clichés

A cliché is an expression used for conveying an idea or a message quickly. It is, however, considered trite because it has been used so often, and its effectiveness has been lessened by overuse and excessive familiarity. Avoid clichés in your writing. Some examples of clichés are *from the horse's mouth, toe the line, spill the beans, come full circle, from A to Z, dressed to kill,* and *the straw that broke the camel's back.*

Sentence with cliché: I thought our sales projections were <u>too good to be true</u>.
Revised sentence: I thought our sales projections were too optimistic.

TRY IT!

Directions Underline the correct word choice in parentheses. Check your answers on page 322 or with your instructor before continuing with your assignment.

1. (<u>Try to</u>, Try and) bring your lab project with you.

2. What (<u>kind of</u>, kind of a) car are you buying?

3. Could we set up a meeting (<u>with regard to</u>, with regards to) the new contract?

4. The drive to the city takes (a hour, <u>an hour</u>).

 **APPLICATION** **Complete Applications 125–129, pages 293–295 and 297–298, at this time.**

125 | Speech Duds

Directions Underline the correct word choice in parentheses. Score one point for each correct answer.

Your Score

1. What (kind of, kind of a) book on natural resource conservation should I read?   1. _____

2. (Try and, Try to) find a scientifically supported book about it.   2. _____

3. The books on conservation are (near, near to) the back wall.   3. _____

4. Mrs. Buvasi thought the library (should have, should of) had more books on the topic.   4. _____

5. (Anyway, Anyways), a local group donated three books to the collection.   5. _____

6. They (might have, might of) realized that water, soil, forests, and wildlife are major considerations.   6. _____

7. We spent (a hour, an hour) in class talking about biomes.   7. _____

8. It was interesting to learn that I (grew up, growed up) in a temperate deciduous forest biome.   8. _____

9. Each biome has features that don't exist (anywhere, anywheres) else on Earth.   9. _____

10. The forest ranger (brought, brung) deciduous tree samples for us to see.   10. _____

11. (Not nearly, Nowhere near) enough people are willing to take the necessary steps to conserve our forests and woodlands.   11. _____

12. (Aren't you, Ain't you) glad to learn the state forestry department has a replanting program?   12. _____

13. (Almost everybody, Most everybody) can start their conservation efforts by recycling, driving less, and carpooling when possible.   13. _____

14. Check furniture and wood products to see if they (have a, have got a) Forest Stewardship Council label; that indicates the trees were grown in a well-managed forest.   14. _____

15. To help prevent erosion when hiking, do not go (off the, off of the) trails.   15. _____

16. Don't (feel bad, feel badly) about not knowing that natural resources are a vital part of life.   16. _____

17. What (sort of, sort of a) film presentation did the forest ranger show?   17. _____

18. (This, This here) reference book on wildlife conservation is fascinating.   18. _____

19. I would (like, like for) you to have it next.   19. _____

20. Jiao (would have, would of) known that animals use the forest for cover from predators.   20. _____

21. The ranger's pictures were (inside the, inside of the) cabin.   21. _____

22. The mountain closest to us is still a (long way, long ways) from here.   22. _____

23. The Lewis family (can hardly, can't hardly) wait for their annual visit to the redwoods.   23. _____

24. Are (them, those) saws ever used?   24. _____

25. I (was hardly, wasn't hardly) aware of the conservation project that our school is conducting.   25. _____

Your Total Score _____/25

If your score was 19 or less, review Section 33, pages 291–292, before continuing.

126 | Speech Duds

Directions Underline the correct word choice in parentheses. Score one point for each correct answer.

Your Score

1. (Were you, Was you) ever at an authentic Cinco de Mayo celebration?   1. _____

2. My friends should (have gone, have went) to Mexico City last year.   2. _____

3. It's a (long way, long ways) to Guadalajara from Chicago.   3. _____

4. Kazio bought me (this, this here) handcrafted silver bracelet, which was made in Mexico.   4. _____

5. Luisa (might have, might of) given me her tortilla recipe before she moved.   5. _____

6. Though we studied Spanish, we (can hardly, can't hardly) follow their conversation.   6. _____

7. He (grew up, growed up) along the southern border of the United States.   7. _____

8. He (doesn't, don't) know the rich cultural history of Mexico.   8. _____

9. (Where is my hotel, Where is my hotel at) from the Plaza Garibaldi?   9. _____

10. What (kind of, kind of a) country is Mexico?   10. _____

11. I (feel bad, feel badly) because I missed the celebration.   11. _____

12. Laura Hanks bought beautiful pottery (inside the, inside of the) old store.   12. _____

13. She (brought, brung) home a ceramic vase for her niece.   13. _____

14. Why don't we (try to, try and) find a handwoven rug there?   14. _____

15. Let's look at the shop (opposite, opposite to) the market.   15. _____

16. Alma and Helga (should have, should of) visited the Palacio de Bellas Artes.   16. _____

17. Mexico is a wealthy country (with regard to, with regards to) its natural resources.   17. _____

18. Camille almost (drowned, drownded) when she got caught in a riptide at La Bonfil beach in Acapulco.   18. _____

19. There is (not nearly, nowhere near) enough time to see everything.   19. _____

20. (Anyway, Anyways), we saw a movie at the film festival in Morelia.   20. _____

21. We also saw (an awfully good, a very good) film at the Cineteca National last night.   21. _____

22. We (couldn't have cared less, could have cared less) about getting some sleep.   22. _____

23. (Them, Those) guitars we noticed in the store were expensive.   23. _____

24. We are going to see the Ballet de Folklórico de México in Escondido, which is (a hour, an hour) from here.   24. _____

25. The deep-sea fishing in Cabo San Lucas was (better, more better) than in Acapulco.   25. _____

Your Total Score _____/25

If your score was 19 or less, review Section 33, pages 291–292, before continuing.

127 | Unit Review

Directions Underline the correct word choice in parentheses. Score one point for each correct answer.

Your Score

1. Jorie is (real, really) tired this evening. 1. _____

2. (There, Their, They're) are several items that should be put on the agenda. 2. _____

3. The company I work for has (it's, its) own corporate jet. 3. _____

4. The (affect, effect) of the new highway speed limit will be minimal. 4. _____

5. The increased tuition rates may (affect, effect) enrollment at our school for the fall. 5. _____

6. Sydney looks very much (like, as) her sister, Susie. 6. _____

7. Maureen and I (can hardly, can't hardly) wait until our family reunion at Lake Okoboji. 7. _____

8. What (kind of, kind of a) salad is that? 8. _____

9. Lataero wants to sit (beside, besides) Corey at the basketball game. 9. _____

10. What Olondo had earned in his summer job was (not nearly, nowhere near) enough (to, too, two) buy a new computer. 10. _____

11. (Beside, Besides) Zenhichi and Becky, who will be running at the Drake Relays? 11. _____

12. (Who's, Whose) doing (your, you're) taxes this year? 12. _____

13. (It's, Its) (to, too, two) late (to, too, two) request a specific roommate for the fall term. 13. _____

14. (There, Their, They're) remodeling project went over budget. 14. _____

15. In many homes, child care is divided equally (between, among) (to, too, two) parents. 15. _____

16. Lane performed her solo (good, well). 16. _____

17. Vivienne came rushing (in, into) the house when it started (to, too, two) rain. 17. _____

18. My nephew was excited about his first (lose, loose) tooth. 18. _____

19. They sometimes make decisions more quickly (then, than) they should. 19. _____

20. (Your, You're) listing your past employers, (aren't, ain't) you? 20. _____

21. The deli is (opposite to, opposite) the gas station. 21. _____

22. (Almost, Most) all our family members will be at the reunion. 22. _____

23. Genni (should have, should of) realized that the fine for talking on a cell phone when you are driving is $300. 23. _____

24. We should order (fewer, less) lunches for our next meeting. 24. _____

25. (There, Their, They're) waiting for us at the entrance of the movie theater. 25. _____

Your Total Score _____/32

Digital Vision/Getty Images

Many organizations, large and small, use websites to market their products and services. A company website must meet the needs of both the organization and potential customers who will be using it to learn about and purchase products and services.

Web designers create web pages that contain information in the form of text and graphics. They must have a strong background in graphic design and a clear understanding of how web pages apply to and fit in with the marketing goals of an organization. Designers must be proficient with a web page scripting language such as extensible hypertext markup language, as well as with web development software and graphic applications and techniques. They must be aware of the standards and etiquette of the Web and of technical issues, such as browser and platform compatibility, download time, and graphics versus text pages.

Communication skills and certain personal skills are also extremely important. Web designers must be good listeners and should be able to communicate effectively with clients, both verbally and in writing. They also need good time management skills so they can deliver a product within a specified time line.

With the expansion of business conducted on the Internet (business to business and business to consumer), the need for qualified web designers is increasing. As the technology becomes more sophisticated and complex, these positions will demand higher levels of skill and expertise, and salaries should continue to rise.

Directions Underline the correct word choice in parentheses. Score one point for each correct answer.

Your Score

1. Before seeking a loan for (there, their, they're) web design company, Mae and Jaccar developed a business and marketing plan.

1. _____

2. The bank evaluated the plan based on (it's, its) potential for success.

2. _____

3. Mae went (in, into) her home office, which she is setting up today.

3. _____

4. He (might have, might of) taken a course on web optimization so his websites would rank high when searches are made.

4. _____

5. Designers and developers can choose (between, among) several software packages (to, too, two) use in constructing websites.

5. _____

6. My friend Cullen says (fewer, less) people are hiring someone (to, too, two) design and develop websites; they are taking courses and creating the sites themselves.

6. _____

Your Total Score _____/8

128 | Writing Improvement

A | **Directions** Rewrite each sentence, expressing what the underlined cliché means.

Example   Herman <u>spilled the beans</u>. ***Herman divulged something that was confidential.***

1. The financing fell through, and we are <u>up a creek without a paddle</u>. _____

   _____

2. Ms. Tellis inadvertently <u>opened a can of worms</u> by talking about the neighbors. _____

   _____

3. The company accountant says we are <u>in the red</u>. _____

   _____

4. His solution was <u>like setting square pegs in round holes</u>. _____

   _____

5. The reports of identity theft may be just <u>the tip of the iceberg</u>. _____

   _____

6. You can't <u>burn the candle at both ends</u>. _____

   _____

7. <u>Stop beating about the bush</u> and tell me the problem. _____

   _____

8. The new job was <u>right up my alley</u>. _____

   _____

9. Jan Nelson is always <u>passing the buck</u> to another employee. _____

   _____

10. His comment on diversity was <u>off the wall</u>. _____

   _____

B | **Directions** Write three popular clichés. Tell what you think they mean.

1. _____

   _____

2. _____

   _____

3. _____

   _____

APPLICATION   **Give your completed application to your instructor for evaluation.**

129 | Comprehensive Review

Directions Underline the correct word choice in parentheses, double-underline any letters that need to be capitalized, and add the necessary punctuation marks. Score one point for each correctly underlined word choice, correctly underlined letter, and correct punctuation mark.

Your Score

1. the number of people applying for u s citizenship (has, have) increased significantly in recent years   1. _____

2. nicolás and (she, her) want to become citizens   2. _____

3. he (doesn't, don't) know the requirements   3. _____

4. to become a naturalized citizen a person must be able to read write and speak english   4. _____

5. other requirements include a basic understanding of u s history and government as well as (5, five) (year's, years') continuous residence in the united states   5. _____

6. in october 2008 the u s citizenship and immigration services uscis (began, begun) using a new version of the citizenship test   6. _____

7. more (then, than) (6,000, six thousand) people were involved in testing the new test   7. _____

8. to pass the civics portion of the exam the applicant must answer (6, six) of (10, ten) questions correctly   8. _____

9. candidates are not given choices for answers in the testing interview but they can access the uscis website to see (100, one hundred) sample questions in advance   9. _____

10. she (lay, laid) the civics flash cards from the website on the counter   10. _____

11. what is the bill of rights   11. _____

12. when was the constitution written and what are (it's, its) first words   12. _____

13. patrick henry said give me liberty or give me death   13. _____

14. the united states bought louisiana from france in 1803   14. _____

15. applicants may be asked about what happened on september (11, 11th) 2001   15. _____

16. the (3, three) branches of the federal government are the judicial executive and legislative   16. _____

17. if both the president and the vice president are unable to serve who becomes president   17. _____

18. what is susan b anthony known for   18. _____

19. the (13, thirteen) stripes on the flag represent the (13, thirteen) original colonies.   19. _____

20. the statue of liberty which is located on ellis island in new york is a symbol of freedom to many people   20. _____

21. thomas jefferson was the main author of the declaration of independence   21. _____

22. which president was in office during the civil war   22. _____

23. how many supreme court justices are (their, there, they're) and by (who, whom) are they nominated   23. _____

24. presidential elections are held every (4, four) years in november   24. _____

25. in order to vote you must be a citizen and at least (18, eighteen) years old   25. _____

Your Total Score ____/149

PROOF IT!

Directions Proofread the postcard. Mark any changes that are needed using the proofreaders' marks on page 317. Turn in this page to your instructor.

Dear student

I hope you have enjoy this course, and have developed your english skills at the same time. The skills you have learned will help you get the job you want and advancing in you career.

Before you interview for a job you may want to review your answers to the interview questions in some of the applications in this book.

"The first impression you make is a lasting impression". Use your english skills to make that first impression a positive one with you're colleagues instructors, and prospective employers.

Keep your shoulder to the wheel!

Karen Williams

Posttest

Directions Underline the correct word choice in parentheses.

1. (There, Their, They're) are many lending options available to home buyers.

2. Lars Fahlberg, (who's, whose) business specializes in loan modifications, is very busy.

3. The house Hugh bought is (real, really) old and in need of repair.

4. She (might have, might of) decided to refinance her mortgage.

5. Jaclyn studied for her real estate license and (then, than) took the exam.

6. (Your, You're) home inspector will identify any potential problems.

7. (There, Their, They're) real estate agent will help them negotiate the price.

8. My agent says (it's, its) a buyers' market.

9. (Fewer, Less) homes are in escrow (then, than) at this time last year.

10. (Who's, Whose) the listing agent for the house you are touring?

11. (There, Their, They're) asking the sellers to pay the closing costs.

12. When Sharla and Al walked (in, into) the house on Beech Street, they knew it was the right one.

13. The counteroffers were negotiated (between, among) the seller and the prospective buyer.

14. (Almost, Most) everyone has a dream to own a house.

15. What (kind of, kind of a) loan are you considering?

Appendix A: Spelling

To spell correctly is an important part of the communication process. When you allow misspelled words to sneak into your writing, such words stand out. You should do everything possible to avoid misspellings, for they can be a source of embarrassment to you, the writer, and can be misleading or confusing to the reader.

Historically, the English language has been heavily influenced by other languages. Principally, these languages were those brought to the British Isles by invaders over many hundreds of years.

Over a long period of time, numerous attempts were made to standardize or otherwise make sense of the spelling of English words, but these met with little success. Dr. Samuel Johnson's dictionary, published in 1755, became a true spelling guide for the British.

After the Revolutionary War, Noah Webster published a famous spelling book and dictionaries that simplified British spelling and included many new American words. Webster's spelling changes resulted in such words as *color* and *develop* (American) replacing *colour* and *develope* (British).

Even with changes like these, the spelling of English words is not always logical. Sounds are spelled in many different ways, and though some words sound alike, they frequently are not spelled the same (*ate* and *eight*, *their* and *there*). There is not always a uniform relationship between spelling and pronunciation. Another obstacle is that many English words contain letters that are silent and are not pronounced aloud (*debt* and *receipt*).

However, useful spelling rules do exist. If studied and mastered, the following rules will help you become a good speller and writer.

Rule 1: Make a distinction between *ie* and *ei*.

Memorize this rhyme:

> Use *i* before *e*
> Except after *c*
> Or when sounded like *a*
> As in *neighbor* or *weigh*.

i before *e*	*ei* after *c*	*ei* when sounded like *a*
convenient	conceive	freight
believe	receive	reign
review	deceit	neighborhood

There are a good number of exceptions to this rule. Here are some examples:

deficiency	forfeit	neither	seize
foreign	height	science	species

Rule 2: Drop the final *e* when a suffix (word ending) beginning with a vowel is added, but keep the final *e* before a suffix beginning with a consonant.

a. Drop the final *e* before a suffix beginning with a vowel:

sale + able = salable

relocate + ion = relocation

advertise + ing = advertising

There are exceptions to this rule, like these:

dye + ing = dyeing (distinguished from *dying*)

notice + able = noticeable (keeps the *c* sound soft before *a* or *o*)

b. Keep the final *e* before a suffix beginning with a consonant:

encourage + ment = encouragement

use + ful = useful

care + less = careless

complete + ly = completely

The final *e* is sometimes dropped before the suffixes *ly* and *ment*:

true + ly = truly

argue + ment = argument

There are a few other exceptions, such as *awful*, *ninth*, and *wisdom*.

Rule 3: A final *y* preceded by a consonant is usually changed to an *i* when a suffix is added, except before a suffix beginning with *i*.

try + es = tries	timely + ness = timeliness
busy + er = busier	easy + ly = easily

As with most spelling rules, there are a few exceptions, like these:

memory + ize = memorize	shy + ly = shyly
dry + ness = dryness	

Rule 4: Double the final single consonant before adding a suffix that begins with a vowel when a single vowel precedes the consonant and (for words with more than one syllable) the consonant ends an accented syllable.

remit + ed = remitted   control + able = controllable

trim + er = trimmer   swim + ing = swimming

allot + ed = allotted   omit + ing = omitting

This rule has a number of exceptions. Here are two:

gas + eous = gaseous   words with the final consonant *w*, *x*, or *y*

When the accent shifts to the first syllable when a suffix beginning with a vowel is added, the final consonant is not doubled.

refer + ence = reference

Rule 5: Make nouns plural by adding *s* or *es*.

a. Add *s* when the noun ends in a sound that can be smoothly united with an *s*.

text = texts   afternoon = afternoons

job = jobs   computer = computers

Exceptions are some nouns ending in *o* preceded by a consonant, such as these:

potato = potatoes   veto = vetoes

b. Add *es* when the noun ends in a sound that cannot be smoothly united with an *s*.

lunch = lunches   watch = watches

speech = speeches   tax = taxes

c. Change *y* to *i* and add *es* when the noun ends in a *y* preceded by a consonant.

worry = worries   pony = ponies

lady = ladies   company = companies

d. Add *s* when the noun ends in a *y* preceded by a vowel.

boy = boys   valley = valleys

day = days   play = plays

See pages 37–40 for a review of forming the plural of nouns, including irregular plurals and other exceptions.

Rules That Work

How do you know when to use *able* or *ible*? When a related word can be formed ending in *ation*, then *able* is usually the correct suffix.

irritation   irritable   duration   durable

When a word can be formed ending in *ion* or *ive*, then *ible* is usually correct.

permission   permissive   permissible

repression   repressive   repressible

134 | *ie* and *ei* Words

A | **Directions** Underline the misspelled word in each set, and write the correct spelling in the blank at the right. Score one point for each correct identification and one point for each correct spelling. For assistance, refer to Spelling Rule 1 on page 301.

Answers

1. percieve, reign, review, shield

1. _____

2. thief, fronteir, shriek, vein

2. _____

3. sleigh, field, deceive, frieght

3. _____

4. anxiety, deficeint, siege, die

4. _____

5. sieve, their, deceit, sceintific

5. _____

6. obedient, niether, clientele, piece

6. _____

7. hieght, achievement, niece, weight

7. _____

8. releive, efficient, mischief, ceiling

8. _____

9. grievous, eighth, hygiene, foriegn

9. _____

10. brief, biege, diesel, rein

10. _____

B | **Directions** Determine which word in each pair is spelled correctly. Write the letter of the word in the blank at the right. Score one point for each correct answer. For assistance, refer to Spelling Rule 1 on page 301.

Answers

a. conceive   b. concieve   1. _____

a. believe   b. beleive   2. _____

a. inconvenience   b. inconveneince   3. _____

a. reciept   b. receipt   4. _____

a. patience   b. pateince   5. _____

a. oreintation   b. orientation   6. _____

a. repreive   b. reprieve   7. _____

a. expereince   b. experience   8. _____

a. neighbor   b. nieghbor   9. _____

a. quiet   b. queit   10. _____

a. seize   b. sieze   11. _____

a. proprietary   b. propreitary   12. _____

a. hierarchy   b. heirarchy   13. _____

a. leneint   b. lenient   14. _____

a. yield   b. yeild   15. _____

Your Total Score _____ /35

135 | The Final *e*

A | **Directions** Correctly spell each word with the suffix added. Score one point for each correct answer. For assistance, refer to Spelling Rule 2 on page 301.

Answers

1. write + ing   1. _____

2. true + ly   2. _____

3. accommodate + ion   3. _____

4. lone + ly   4. _____

5. hope + ing   5. _____

6. manage + ment   6. _____

7. extreme + ly   7. _____

8. dye + ing   8. _____

9. dose + age   9. _____

10. issue + ing   10. _____

11. notice + able   11. _____

12. sincere + ity   12. _____

13. excite + ment   13. _____

14. come + ing   14. _____

15. fortune + ate   15. _____

B | **Directions** Determine which word is spelled correctly. Write the letter of the word in the blank at the right. Score one point for each correct answer. For assistance, refer to Spelling Rule 2 on page 301.

Answers

a. desireable	b. desirable	1. _____
a. tasteless	b. tastless	2. _____
a. achieveing	b. achieving	3. _____
a. copeing	b. coping	4. _____
a. continuous	b. continueous	5. _____
a. reimbursment	b. reimbursement	6. _____
a. devoteing	b. devoting	7. _____
a. encouragement	b. encouragment	8. _____
a. argument	b. arguement	9. _____
a. solly	b. solely	10. _____

Your Total Score _____ /25

136 | The Final *y*

A | **Directions** Correctly spell each word with the suffix added. Score one point for each correct answer. For assistance, refer to Spelling Rule 3 on page 301.

Answers

1. beauty + ful   1. _____
2. annoy + ance   2. _____
3. funny + er   3. _____
4. lonely + ness   4. _____
5. worry + ing   5. _____
6. liberty + es   6. _____
7. reply + ed   7. _____
8. merry + er   8. _____
9. identify + es   9. _____
10. certify + able   10. _____
11. worthy + ness   11. _____
12. happy + ly   12. _____
13. dry + ed   13. _____
14. reapply + es   14. _____
15. shy + ly   15. _____

B | **Directions** Determine which word is spelled correctly. Write the letter of the word in the blank at the right. Score one point for each correct answer. For assistance, refer to Spelling Rule 3 on page 301.

Answers

a. modifying   b. modifing   1. _____
a. librarys   b. libraries   2. _____
a. defys   b. defies   3. _____
a. readyness   b. readiness   4. _____
a. notifying   b. notifing   5. _____
a. delays   b. delaies   6. _____
a. accompanying   b. accompaning   7. _____
a. securitys   b. securities   8. _____
a. denys   b. denies   9. _____
a. easyer   b. easier   10. _____

Your Total Score _____ /25

137 | Doubling the Final Single Consonant

A | **Directions** Correctly spell each word with the suffix added. Score one point for each correct answer. For assistance, refer to Spelling Rule 4 on page 302.

Answers

1. question + able

2. recur + ence

3. run + ing

4. defer + ed

5. allot + ment

6. regret + able

7. admit + ance

8. win + ing

9. submit + ed

10. begin + er

11. stun + ed

12. commit + ment

13. plan + ing

14. enjoy + able

15. open + ing

1. _____

2. _____

3. _____

4. _____

5. _____

6. _____

7. _____

8. _____

9. _____

10. _____

11. _____

12. _____

13. _____

14. _____

15. _____

B | **Directions** Determine which word is spelled correctly. Write the letter of the correctly spelled word in the blank at the right. Score one point for each correct answer. For assistance, refer to Spelling Rule 4 on page 302.

Answers

a. limitted	b. limited	1. _____
a. jogger	b. joger	2. _____
a. conferring	b. confering	3. _____
a. referal	b. referral	4. _____
a. gaseous	b. gasseous	5. _____
a. quized	b. quizzed	6. _____
a. taxxed	b. taxed	7. _____
a. acquital	b. acquittal	8. _____
a. shopping	b. shoping	9. _____
a. wrapped	b. wraped	10. _____

Your Total Score _____ /25

138 | Making Nouns Plural

A | **Directions** Write the plural form of each noun. Score one point for each correct answer. For assistance, refer to Spelling Rule 5 on page 302.

Answers

1. category
2. swatch
3. employee
4. quality
5. excess
6. present
7. potato
8. fax
9. dignitary
10. video
11. sale
12. wish
13. survey
14. class
15. ratio

1. _____
2. _____
3. _____
4. _____
5. _____
6. _____
7. _____
8. _____
9. _____
10. _____
11. _____
12. _____
13. _____
14. _____
15. _____

B | **Directions** Determine which word is spelled correctly. Write the letter of the correctly spelled word in the blank at the right. Score one point for each correct answer. For assistance, refer to Spelling Rule 5 on page 302.

Answers

a. flaws	b. flawes	1. _____
a. relaies	b. relays	2. _____
a. tries	b. trys	3. _____
a. investments	b. investmentes	4. _____
a. vetos	b. vetoes	5. _____
a. attorneys	b. attornies	6. _____
a. territorys	b. territories	7. _____
a. touchs	b. touches	8. _____
a. joys	b. joies	9. _____
a. supplys	b. supplies	10. _____

Your Total Score _____ /25

139 | Commonly Misspelled Words

Directions Here are 120 words that are frequently misspelled. Study them carefully, and be prepared to write them from memory.

absence	eligibility	library	quite
accommodate	embarrass	license	recommendation
accumulate	emphasize	likable	reminiscent
acknowledgment	emphatically	maintenance	sacrifice
acquisition	endeavor	miniature	schedule
advantageous	enthusiasm	mortgage	seize
advisable	equipped	necessary	separate
all right	exceed	neither	similar
already	explanation	neutral	simultaneous
altogether	extension	noticeable	stationary (immobile)
appreciate	facsimile	occasionally	stationery (writing material)
argument	familiar	occurred	subtle
calendar	fascinating	occurrence	succeed
campaign	gratuity	omission	surprise
category	guarantee	pamphlet	surveys
chargeable	harass	perceive	technique
committee	hindrance	perform	thorough
concede	illegal	persistent	through
conscientious	inaugurate	personnel	transferring
consensus	incidentally	persuade	tremendous
consequently	inconvenient	possession	unanimous
criticism	indispensable	precede	unnecessary
describe	initiative	principal (main or person)	unusual
desirable	interfere	principle (rule)	usable
deterioration	interpret	privilege	valuable
develop	irrelevant	proceed	verify
dilemma	judgment	prominent	voluntarily
disastrous	knowledgeable	questionnaire	volunteer
dissatisfied	laboratory	quiet	warranty
efficient	liaison	quit	wholly

140 | Commonly Misspelled Words

Directions Underline the correctly spelled word in each pair, and write the correct spelling in the blank at the right. Score one point for each correct answer. Use a dictionary for help, if necessary.

Answers

1. maintainence, maintenance

2. unnecessary, unecessary

3. changable, changeable

4. liason, liaison

5. lisense, license

6. precede, preceed

7. definately, definitely

8. recommendation, recomendation

9. compatable, compatible

10. permenent, permanent

11. convenience, conveneince

12. advantageous, advantagous

13. embarrass, embarass

14. congratulate, congradulate

15. apparent, apparant

16. realise, realize

17. indispensible, indispensable

18. compeled, compelled

19. courtious, courteous

20. reimbursement, reimbursment

21. benefited, benefitted

22. questionaire, questionnaire

23. permissible, permissable

24. portfolios, portfolioes

25. accidently, accidentally

1. _____

2. _____

3. _____

4. _____

5. _____

6. _____

7. _____

8. _____

9. _____

10. _____

11. _____

12. _____

13. _____

14. _____

15. _____

16. _____

17. _____

18. _____

19. _____

20. _____

21. _____

22. _____

23. _____

24. _____

25. _____

Your Total Score _____ /25

141 | Commonly Misspelled Words

Directions Underline the incorrectly spelled word in each set, and write the correct spelling in the blank at the right. If there are no errors, write *C* for *correct*. Score one point for each misspelled word identified, one point for each correct spelling, and one point for each identification that all words are spelled correctly (*C*). Use a dictionary for help, if necessary.

Answers

1. (a) finishs (b) thorough (c) respectively (d) forfeit   1. _____

2. (a) greatful (b) exceed (c) compelling (d) enough   2. _____

3. (a) soldier (b) criticizm (c) performed (d) distinction   3. _____

4. (a) apparrently (b) subtle (c) accumulate (d) privileged   4. _____

5. (a) altogether (b) possession (c) miniature (d) incidently   5. _____

6. (a) merited (b) endowment (c) allowance (d) redundant   6. _____

7. (a) negotiation (b) franchising (c) previously (d) seperation   7. _____

8. (a) shining (b) distributer (c) chosen (d) originally   8. _____

9. (a) manufacturing (b) psychology (c) grievance (d) dominent   9. _____

10. (a) magazine (b) responsibilities (c) manageable (d) disatisfied   10. _____

11. (a) ridiculously (b) surveys (c) lunches (d) occured   11. _____

12. (a) valuable (b) desperate (c) calender (d) phase   12. _____

13. (a) consensus (b) ascending (c) acceptance (d) transmittal   13. _____

14. (a) sophmore (b) answering (c) referred (d) forty   14. _____

15. (a) accumulation (b) hinderance (c) piece (d) guard   15. _____

16. (a) saturation (b) exaggerate (c) punctual (d) weather   16. _____

17. (a) unacceptible (b) auxiliary (c) separate (d) simplified   17. _____

18. (a) preformance (b) absence (c) approaches (d) proficient   18. _____

19. (a) volunteer (b) memorised (c) opposite (d) endeavor   19. _____

20. (a) difficulties (b) dictionery (c) reign (d) relieving   20. _____

21. (a) equiped (b) parameters (c) neither (d) lapse   21. _____

22. (a) succede (b) carrying (c) equally (d) holidays   22. _____

23. (a) accommodate (b) oppression (c) advisible (d) management   23. _____

24. (a) disastrous (b) reservoir (c) exaggeration (d) passtime   24. _____

25. (a) inspiring (b) reminiscent (c) manuever (d) pursuing   25. _____

Your Total Score _____ /47

Name _____ Date _____ Score _____

142 | Definitions

Directions Select the word that is closest in meaning to the numbered word. Write the letter of the word in the blank at the right. Score one point for each correct answer. Use a dictionary for help, if necessary.

Answers

1. relevant	(a) pertinent (b) harmonious (c) timely (d) orderly (e) healthy	1. _____
2. provisional	(a) honest (b) temporary (c) influential (d) deceptive (e) unknowing	2. _____
3. objective	(a) opposition (b) challenge (c) protest (d) gadget (e) goal	3. _____
4. proficient	(a) adaptable (b) efficient (c) impressive (d) adept (e) resourceful	4. _____
5. rectify	(a) reduce (b) add (c) correct (d) satisfy (e) strengthen	5. _____
6. convey	(a) pretend (b) judge (c) communicate (d) build (e) pardon	6. _____
7. conscientious	(a) political (b) logical (c) careful (d) sound (e) scandalous	7. _____
8. substantial	(a) trivial (b) large (c) dark (d) substitute (e) permissive	8. _____
9. feasible	(a) possible (b) dispensable (c) scarce (d) attractive (e) vulnerable	9. _____
10. ethical	(a) orderly (b) moral (c) emotional (d) derogatory (e) congenial	10. _____
11. forecast	(a) mold (b) fortune (c) predict (d) review (e) further	11. _____
12. appraise	(a) inform (b) estimate (c) verify (d) laud (e) near	12. _____
13. evolve	(a) finish (b) halt (c) abate (d) swerve (e) develop	13. _____
14. realistic	(a) lifelike (b) put-on (c) varied (d) fragile (e) rigid	14. _____
15. perceptive	(a) negligent (b) insightful (c) punctual (d) despondent (e) paid	15. _____
16. advocate	(a) refer (b) petition (c) dignify (d) promote (e) preside	16. _____
17. persistent	(a) patient (b) changeable (c) wobbling (d) relentless (e) undeveloped	17. _____
18. potential	(a) strong (b) weak (c) light (d) frivolous (e) possible	18. _____
19. comply	(a) conform (b) enable (c) memorize (d) enter (e) glance	19. _____
20. accessible	(a) mobile (b) territorial (c) constructive (d) able (e) approachable	20. _____

Your Total Score _____ /20

143 | Definitions

Directions Select the word that is closest in meaning to the numbered word. Write the letter of the word in the blank at the right. Score one point for each correct answer. Use a dictionary for help, if necessary.

Answers

1. mediate   (a) listen (b) agree (c) arbitrate (d) argue (e) communicate   1. _____

2. rely   (a) ignore (b) agree (c) distrust (d) alter (e) depend   2. _____

3. typical   (a) many (b) characteristic (c) exceptional (d) special (e) motley   3. _____

4. innovative   (a) productive (b) assertive (c) inquisitive (d) creative (e) effective   4. _____

5. optional   (a) demanded (b) elective (c) necessary (d) imperative (e) required   5. _____

6. specific   (a) organized (b) random (c) average (d) usual (e) explicit   6. _____

7. significant   (a) easy (b) important (c) truthful (d) special (e) original   7. _____

8. frugal   (a) thrifty (b) free (c) extravagant (d) rhythmic (e) brotherly   8. _____

9. representative   (a) contrasting (b) typical (c) exact (d) conceivable (e) selective   9. _____

10. appropriate   (a) limited (b) estimate (c) suitable (d) prompt (e) automatic   10. _____

11. trend   (a) lapse (b) tendency (c) run (d) restraint (e) mood   11. _____

12. prohibit   (a) forbid (b) agree (c) decline (d) reject (e) consent   12. _____

13. restitution   (a) reimbursement (b) calculation (c) review (d) contract (e) agreement   13. _____

14. retain   (a) refer (b) point (c) relate (d) oppose (e) keep   14. _____

15. permissible   (a) hesitant (b) fascinating (c) available (d) incorruptible (e) allowable   15. _____

16. comprehend   (a) link (b) confess (c) understand (d) oppose (e) distract   16. _____

17. delegate   (a) reason (b) assign (c) gratify (d) retain (e) restrict   17. _____

18. alleviate   (a) worsen (b) control (c) relieve (d) hurt (e) break   18. _____

19. skeptical   (a) doubtful (b) awkward (c) kindly (d) orderly (e) changeable   19. _____

20. conformity   (a) pride (b) control (c) agreement (d) body (e) rebellion   20. _____

21. prevalent   (a) changing (b) lower (c) dominant (d) improved (e) cozy   21. _____

22. obvious   (a) casual (b) hidden (c) complete (d) evident (e) empowered   22. _____

23. legitimate   (a) illegal (b) financial (c) spirited (d) generous (e) valid   23. _____

24. unity   (a) confusion (b) agreement (c) continuity (d) illusion (e) direction   24. _____

25. exaggeration   (a) understatement (b) depression (c) scrutiny (d) scant (e) embellishment   25. _____

Your Total Score _____ /25

144 | Antonyms

Directions Select the **antonym** (word that means the opposite) for each numbered word. Write the letter of the word in the blank at the right. Score one point for each correct answer. Use a dictionary for help, if necessary.

Answers

1. ratify	(a) confirm (b) approve (c) reject (d) choose (e) emphasize	1. _____
2. impede	(a) instruct (b) defy (c) condense (d) assist (e) block	2. _____
3. conditional	(a) tentative (b) sure (c) oily (d) abundant (e) lengthy	3. _____
4. integrate	(a) relate (b) combine (c) accentuate (d) separate (e) bypass	4. _____
5. succinct	(a) wordy (b) concise (c) bold (d) silent (e) taut	5. _____
6. essential	(a) fundamental (b) prior (c) dispensable (d) enabling (e) progressive	6. _____
7. apprehensive	(a) aware (b) realistic (c) confident (d) cognizant (e) shaky	7. _____
8. competent	(a) adept (b) qualified (c) untrue (d) inept (e) understandable	8. _____
9. constructive	(a) comforting (b) realistic (c) positive (d) building (e) negative	9. _____
10. equitable	(a) equal (b) unfair (c) parry (d) dubious (e) difference	10. _____
11. encompass	(a) contain (b) include (c) exclude (d) direction (e) dilute	11. _____
12. stress	(a) emphasize (b) accent (c) circulate (d) ignore (e) attempt	12. _____
13. terminate	(a) initiate (b) close (c) indicate (d) evade (e) vary	13. _____
14. disclose	(a) quit (b) hide (c) expose (d) disagree (e) reveal	14. _____
15. rational	(a) unreasonable (b) unreachable (c) sensible (d) careful (e) imperfect	15. _____
16. malicious	(a) hateful (b) cunning (c) nasty (d) petty (e) kind	16. _____
17. explicit	(a) precise (b) specific (c) cold (d) unclear (e) outspoken	17. _____
18. probable	(a) scary (b) inevitable (c) likely (d) impossible (e) certain	18. _____
19. ethical	(a) high-principled (b) conforming (c) standardized (d) qualified (e) immoral	19. _____
20. relinquish	(a) quit (b) cede (c) keep (d) detest (e) cherish	20. _____

Your Total Score _____ /20

145 | Homonyms

Directions Homonyms are words that sound the same and sometimes have the same spelling, but differ in meaning. *To, too,* and *two* are homonyms; so are *colon* (part of the large intestine) and *colon* (mark of punctuation). Homonyms can cause problems in spelling and understanding. Underline the correct homonym in parentheses. Score one point for each correct answer. Use a dictionary for help, if necessary.

Your Score

1. We will (canvas, canvass) the neighborhood before setting up a neighborhood watch patrol.   1. _____

2. Janelle (may be, maybe) able to get a copy of the Web design software before (it's, its) release to the public.   2. _____

3. Our guiding (principal, principle) is that the customer is always right.   3. _____

4. I (knew, new) that Jenessa was leaving for a (knew, new) job at Curtis Inc. before she told her supervisor.   4. _____

5. On which (cite, sight, site) will the professional building be constructed?   5. _____

6. If (your, you're) computer is running slow, clean out the (cache, cash).   6. _____

7. I invested my (capital, capitol) in a mutual fund.   7. _____

8. (Cease, Seize) the moment!   8. _____

9. We will (role, roll) out our school promotion in July.   9. _____

10. Lillianne decided to (buy, by) a tablet PC for college.   10. _____

11. On Thursdays, Lynda (councils, counsels) seniors on interviewing skills.   11. _____

12. When you are writing a research paper, it is necessary to (cite, sight, site) the sources you used.   12. _____

13. The product line of the company we recently acquired (complements, compliments) our existing product line.   13. _____

14. I have my clothes (all ready, already) to put in the suitcase.   14. _____

15. The content of Niki's presentation was compelling; however, her delivery was (weak, week).   15. _____

16. Have you (passed, past) your real estate license exam yet?   16. _____

17. Her (patience, patients) was wearing thin by the end of her shift.   17. _____

18. When you (right, write) a business letter, use the proper format.   18. _____

19. Davood's team (one, won) the debate in the final minutes.   19. _____

20. Are you going to Chicago, (to, too, two)?   20. _____

Your Total Score _____/23

146 | Synonyms

A | **Directions** Select the **synonym** (word that has about the same meaning) for each italicized word. Write the letter of the word in the blank at the right. Score one point for each correct answer. Use a dictionary for help, if necessary.

Answers

1. An *objective* decision is (a) vague (b) prejudicial (c) unbiased (d) adequate.   1. _____

2. A *reasonable* solution is (a) easy (b) sensible (c) questionable (d) obvious.   2. _____

3. An *indiscriminate* use is (a) minimal (b) appropriate (c) random (d) complementary.   3. _____

4. An *inquisitive* mind is (a) contemplative (b) curious (c) logical (d) analytical.   4. _____

5. An *intentional* omission is (a) negative (b) deliberate (c) obligatory (d) exceptional.   5. _____

6. An *excessive* expenditure is (a) extravagant (b) cash (c) planned (d) budgeted.   6. _____

7. A *tense* situation is (a) comfortable (b) stress-free (c) practical (d) strained.   7. _____

8. An *inevitable* outcome is (a) sudden (b) embarrassing (c) unavoidable (d) distinctive.   8. _____

9. An *inflammatory* remark is (a) soothing (b) unrehearsed (c) inflexible (d) arousing.   9. _____

10. A *diverse* population is (a) identical (b) different (c) experienced (d) stubborn.   10. _____

B | **Directions** Follow the same procedure. Notice how all the italicized words begin with the letters *im*. Look at the words carefully before you make your choice.

1. An *immeasurable* amount is (a) quantifiable (b) foreign (c) limitless (d) set.   1. _____

2. An *imminent* danger is (a) delayed (b) approaching (c) great (d) fleeting.   2. _____

3. An *implied* warranty is (a) understood (b) desired (c) extravagant (d) evident.   3. _____

4. An *imprudent* action is (a) practical (b) quick (c) reckless (d) discreet.   4. _____

5. An *impartial* statement is (a) prejudiced (b) incomplete (c) truthful (d) fair.   5. _____

6. An *impeccable* reputation is (a) faultless (b) unusual (c) unethical (d) established.   6. _____

7. An *imperfect* product is (a) defective (b) unique (c) faultless (d) handmade.   7. _____

8. An *immobile* fixture is (a) inferior (b) portable (c) obscure (d) fixed.   8. _____

9. An *imposing* building is (a) old (b) ordinary (c) contemporary (d) impressive.   9. _____

10. An *impersonal* letter is (a) emotional (b) neutral (c) angry (d) friendly.   10. _____

Your Total Score _____ /20

147 | Synonyms and Antonyms

Directions Select the **synonym** (word that has about the same meaning) and **antonym** (word that means the opposite) for each italicized word. Write the letters of the synonym and antonym in the blanks at the right. Use a dictionary for help, if necessary. Score one point for each correct answer.

	Synonym	Antonym
Example *Scandalous* behavior is (a) scientific (b) proper (c) shameful (d) sarcastic.	_c_	_b_

1. A *cautious* approach is (a) impetuous (b) trivial (c) careful (d) slow.
1. _____   _____

2. An *interim* position is (a) travel (b) new (c) permanent (d) temporary.
2. _____   _____

3. A *diligent* worker is (a) hardworking (b) tardy (c) careless (d) tiny.
3. _____   _____

4. An *exemplary* employee is (a) outstanding (b) puzzled (c) sad (d) bad.
4. _____   _____

5. A *casual* dress code is (a) stated (b) relaxed (c) revised (d) formal.
5. _____   _____

6. An *amicable* resolution is (a) candid (b) hostile (c) lengthy (d) friendly.
6. _____   _____

7. A *meager* salary is (a) generous (b) unionized (c) paltry (d) unplanned.
7. _____   _____

8. An *obnoxious* customer is (a) pleasant (b) tactful (c) unconcerned (d) offensive.
8. _____   _____

9. A *disastrous* day is (a) catastrophic (b) lucky (c) unbelievable (d) gloomy.
9. _____   _____

10. A *problematic* situation is (a) easy (b) challenging (c) dangerous (d) positive.
10. _____   _____

11. A *prominent* feature is (a) inconspicuous (b) noticeable (c) large (d) unique.
11. _____   _____

12. An *apparent* omission is (a) hidden (b) obvious (c) faulty (d) confusing.
12. _____   _____

13. A *receptive* audience is (a) militant (b) open (c) submissive (d) close-minded.
13. _____   _____

14. A *prosperous* business is (a) thriving (b) failing (c) neglected (d) expensive.
14. _____   _____

15. An *ambiguous* statement is (a) definitive (b) contrary (c) upbeat (d) vague.
15. _____   _____

16. An *immaterial* piece of evidence is (a) significant (b) restricted (c) unimportant (d) lengthy.
16. _____   _____

17. A *fundamental* principle is (a) basic (b) revised (c) advanced (d) new.
17. _____   _____

18. A *precarious* position is (a) lovely (b) insecure (c) ugly (d) stable.
18. _____   _____

19. An *enraged* client is (a) angry (b) confused (c) informed (d) calm.
19. _____   _____

20. An *aggressive* marketing plan is (a) bold (b) creative (c) passive (d) conceptual.
20. _____   _____

Your Total Score _____ /40

Appendix C: Proofreaders' Marks

Mark	Meaning	Mark	Meaning
≡	Capitalize	☐	Move to left
/	Lowercase	☐	Move to right
∧	Insert	↺	Move as indicated
|#	Insert space	(DS)	Double-space
⊙	Insert period	(SS)	Single-space
∧	Insert comma	∽	Transpose
∀ ∀	Insert quotation marks	—	Italic
∨	Insert apostrophe	∿∿∿	Bold
? ∧	Insert other marks	(SP)	Spell out
ℒ	Delete	¶	Paragraph
◡	Close up space	(stet)	Leave as originally written
ℒ	Delete and close up space		

Proofreading on the Computer

1. Spell check the document.

2. Read the document on screen. Proofread a paragraph or block of information at a time to be sure the text makes sense. Make any needed corrections.

3. Print the document and proofread it again. Correct any errors.

Proofreading Against an Original

1. Place the documents side by side.

2. Get two file cards, envelopes, or similar items.

3. Holding one in each hand, move through the documents, comparing them line by line.

Answers to Try It Exercises

Unit 1

Try It, page 3

1. <u>Lindsay</u>, <u>scored</u>
2. <u>Lawrence and Ken</u>, <u>worked</u>
3. <u>Dispatchers</u>, <u>answer</u>
4. <u>Ricky</u>, <u>took</u>
5. <u>Carmen</u>, <u>questioned</u>
6. <u>investigation</u>, <u>involved</u>

Try It, page 4

	D	Int	E	Imp
1.	✓			
2.		✓		
3.			✓	or ✓
4.				✓
5.				✓

Try It, page 12

1. <u>We</u>, <u>planned</u>, <u>party</u>, <u>Jennifer</u>
2. <u>Gillian</u>, <u>gave</u>, <u>us</u>, <u>lesson</u>
3. <u>David</u>, <u>paired</u>, <u>course</u>, <u>wine</u>
4. <u>They</u>, <u>decorated</u>, <u>table</u>, <u>confetti</u>, <u>flowers</u>
5. <u>She</u>, <u>Tom</u>, <u>wrapped</u>, <u>leftovers</u>, <u>foil</u>

Try It, page 16

1. <u>Many</u>, <u>agreed</u>, <u>the</u>, <u>final</u>, <u>the</u>
2. <u>The</u>, <u>natural</u>, <u>quickly</u>, <u>recovered</u>, <u>the</u>, <u>knee</u>
3. <u>A</u>, <u>knowledgeable</u>, <u>often</u>, <u>makes</u>, <u>wise</u>
4. <u>created</u>, <u>a</u>, <u>visually</u>, <u>appealing</u>
5. <u>The</u>, <u>the</u>, <u>losing</u>, <u>rarely</u>, <u>made</u>, <u>a</u>, <u>right</u>
6. <u>performed</u>, <u>poorly</u>, <u>the</u>, <u>entrance</u>
7. <u>nearly</u>, <u>missed</u>, <u>the</u>, <u>last</u>
8. <u>played</u>, <u>there</u>, <u>last</u>

Try It, page 20

1. <u>Hooray!</u>
2. <u>and</u>, <u>at</u>, <u>or</u>, <u>at</u>

3. <u>Wait!</u> <u>with</u>, <u>and</u>
4. <u>When</u>, <u>at</u>, <u>in</u>
5. <u>Shh!</u> <u>to</u>, <u>on</u>

Unit 2

Try It, page 34

1. <u>Girl Scout Troop 6134</u>, <u>trip</u>, <u>company</u>
2. <u>family</u>, <u>countries</u>
3. <u>troop</u>, <u>belongings</u>, <u>campsite</u>
   Common nouns: 7, Proper nouns: 1,
   Collective nouns: 4

Try It, page 37

1. wishes
2. monitors
3. passwords
4. faxes
5. batches
6. departments

Try It, page 38

1. heroes
2. shelves
3. holidays
4. proofs
5. photos
6. vetoes
7. selves
8. entries
9. territories

Try It, page 39

1. earnings
2. feet
3. men
4. children
5. goods

Try It, page 40

1. CEOs
2. boards of directors
3. accts.
4. run-throughs
5. 1980s
6. clipboards

Try It, page 45

A

1. instructor's classroom   instructors' classrooms
2. week's movie   weeks' movies
3. nanny's action   nannies' actions

B

1. driver's
2. representatives'
3. employers'

Unit 3

Try It, page 59
1. They
2. he
3. she
4. I
5. It

Try It, page 61
1. her, DO
2. them, DO
3. us, IO
4. him, OP
5. us, OP
6. me, IO

Try It, page 63
1. Her
2. their
3. Your
4. her
5. His
6. Hers

Try It, page 71
1. Both, S
2. Several, A
3. Many, A
4. None, S
5. everyone, O

Try It, page 76
1. whose
2. that
3. whom
4. who
5. whoever
6. what

Try It, page 77
1. Whose
2. Which
3. Whom
4. Who
5. Which
6. What

Try It, page 78
1. who
2. whom
3. whoever
4. whomever

Unit 4

Try It, page 91
1. gives, S
2. welcomes, S
3. Volunteer, C
4. received, Q
5. attended, S

Try It, page 93
1. was, born
2. have, been, inspired
3. Did, die
4. were, known
5. is, considered
6. are, read
7. has, grossed
8. should, give
9. Would, explain
10. do, like
11. must, rent

Try It, page 94
1. raspy, PA
2. pianist, PN
3. he, PP

Try It, page 101
1. is
2. are
3. were
4. is
5. was
6. are

Try It, page 102
1. has
2. are
3. have
4. were
5. have

Try It, page 106
1. have
2. are
3. was
4. are
5. is

Try It, page 108
1. have
2. is
3. has
4. is
5. are

Unit 5

Try It, page 121
1. C
2. tries
3. doesn't
4. C
5. C
6. watches
7. C
8. C

Try It, page 123
1. played
2. Were
3. opened
4. had
5. copied
6. shipped
7. approved
8. regretted

Try It, page 124

1. Shall
2. Will
3. Shall
4. will

Try It, page 127

1. remembered
2. has contributed
3. had
4. has published
5. have worked
6. arranged

Try It, page 128

1. had composed
2. will have tested
3. had collected
4. will have calculated

Try It, page 134

1. saw
2. had broken
3. did

Unit 6

Try It, page 148

1. lay
2. laid
3. lies
4. laid
5. lay
6. lain
7. lay
8. laid

Try It, page 150

1. set
2. sit
3. set
4. sit
5. sat
6. sit
7. set
8. sat

Try It, page 155

1. May
2. could
3. will, teach
4. let
5. lend
6. would

Try It, page 156

1. take
2. rises
3. led
4. accept
5. bring

Unit 7

Try It, page 170

1. Several, the, thoughtful
2. My, antique, a, recent
3. Manufacturing, eight
4. simple, practical, digital

Try It, page 171

1. a, a, Swedish, the
2. an, the
3. a, Supreme Court
4. The, an, European

Try It, page 172

1. This, my
2. All, your
3. Which
4. Our, those

Try It, page 174

1. Hybrid, gasoline-powered
2. fastest-selling
3. Car, increased, fuel-efficient
4. up-to-date, inventory

Try It, page 179

1. yesterday
2. very
3. usually
4. Finally, completely
5. immediately

Try It, page 184

1. longest
2. busy
3. higher
4. better
5. most
6. least
7. stronger
8. most (or least) thoughtfully

Unit 8

Try It, page 198

1. at the restaurant, adv
2. within the hour, adv
3. into the courtroom, adv
4. for the fall term, adj
5. with the band, adv
6. in the black convertible, adj
7. from my dorm, adj
8. through an online vendor, adv

Try It, page 202

1. and, coordinating
2. not only, but also, correlative
3. Although, subordinating

Unit 9

Try It, page 214

1. through the state park, adv
2. before four o'clock, adv
3. on my computer, adj
4. in the conference room, adj
5. with the leather briefcase, adj

Try It, page 215

1. to run a marathon, adj
2. to relax, adv
3. to finish early, n
4. to discuss the strategy, adj
5. to be heard, adv
6. To ride my horse, n
7. to meet the new regional manager, adv
8. to declare your major, n
9. to tell us, adj
10. to visit Florence and Venice, n
11. to reset Abe's broken wrist, adj
12. to make my wedding cake, n

Try It, page 216

1. <u>Running in the rain</u>, <u>Liam</u>
2. <u>LaWanda</u>, <u>seeing the lightning</u>
3. <u>woman</u>, <u>driving the red convertible</u>
4. <u>articles</u>, <u>supporting her viewpoint</u>
5. <u>president</u>, <u>greeting each guest</u>
6. <u>Speaking quietly but persuasively</u>, <u>he</u>
7. <u>Given the conditions</u>, <u>equipment</u>
8. <u>candidate</u>, <u>demanding a recount</u>

Try It, page 221

1. so that we can contact you, adv
2. that the negotiations would take some time, n
3. As soon as Elise is ready, adv
4. than the others do, adv
5. who took part in the workshop, adj
6. How well we perform our tasks, n
7. where John Hancock, Samuel Adams, and Paul Revere are buried, adj
8. what he had accomplished, n

Unit 10

Try It, page 234

A

1. Next summer, we will visit my sister**.**
2. Wow**!**
3. When are you leaving**?**

B

1. G**.** C**.** Cameron, CLU
2. Ms**.** Maeve Gansenburg
3. gigabyte
4. for your information

Try It, page 246

1. You can protect your credit in several ways**;** for instance**,** you can order a copy of your credit report.

2. Federal law **(**the Fair Credit Reporting Act**)** allows you to request one free copy of your credit report every 12 months from each of the major consumer reporting companies.
3. Some websites pretend to offer a free report—but trick people into buying products or supplying personal information.
4. Look for items like the following**:** mistaken reports of late payments, accounts that aren't yours, accounts you closed, and accounts you never use.
5. If you find an error, **(1)** explain the error in writing to the consumer reporting company and **(2)** notify the creditor, also in writing, that you are disputing an item.
6. Asher verifies his report once a year**;** he also checks it before applying for a loan.

Try It, page 248

1. Margaret**'**s car was vandalized last night.
2. **"**You should look for a house in Dover,**"** Ranga suggested.
3. Three-fourths of the units have already been sold.

Unit 11

Try It, page 263

1. 9th
2. 100
3. 24, 10, 4
4. Three, $59.99
5. 7 p.m., Fourth, 12th

Try It, page 266

1. <u>S</u>elena purchased a <u>S</u>ony stereo system at <u>B</u>est <u>B</u>uy.
2. <u>O</u>n <u>T</u>hanksgiving, <u>I</u> always watch a football game with my brothers.
3. <u>D</u>r. <u>I</u>llyana <u>M</u>axon, chief of surgery, spoke with <u>S</u>enator <u>W</u>ilton about universal health care.
4. <u>M</u>argaret <u>T</u>hatcher was the first female prime minister of <u>G</u>reat <u>B</u>ritain.
5. <u>R</u>eto will receive his bachelor of science degree from the <u>U</u>niversity of <u>F</u>lorida in <u>J</u>une.
6. The <u>A</u>ustin <u>Gazette</u> published an editorial by <u>L</u>aurie <u>H</u>ouston, president of the local chapter of the <u>F</u>uture <u>B</u>usiness <u>L</u>eaders of <u>A</u>merica.
7. <u>A</u>merica <u>G</u>arian, <u>D.D.S.</u>, has opened an office in downtown <u>M</u>edford.
8. <u>O</u>ur first assignment in <u>A</u>merican <u>L</u>iterature 101 was to read <u>The Grapes of Wrath</u> by <u>J</u>ohn <u>S</u>teinbeck.

9. <u>S</u>he lives on the <u>W</u>est <u>C</u>oast—northeast of <u>S</u>an <u>D</u>iego, in <u>S</u>antee.
10. <u>C</u>hapter 16 is entitled "<u>T</u>he <u>P</u>ond in <u>W</u>inter."

Unit 12

Try It, page 281
1. you're
2. Who's
3. its
4. Their

Try It, page 282
1. good
2. beside
3. Almost
4. into

Try It, page 284
1. too, to
2. then
3. less, than
4. different from

Try It, page 286
1. among
2. as if
3. effects
4. lose

Try It, page 292
1. Try to
2. kind of
3. with regard to
4. an hour